PRESERV LOCOMOTIVES
OF BRITISH RAILWAYS

C000040437

SEVENTEENTH EDITION

Robert Pritchard & Peter Hall

Published by Platform 5 Publishing Ltd,
52 Broadfield Road, Sheffield, S8 0XJ, England.

Printed in England by The Lavenham Press Ltd, Lavenham, Suffolk.

ISBN 978 1 909431 29 4

▲ GWR 4073 Class 4-6-0 5043 "EARL OF MOUNT EDGCUMBE" heads a return Llandudno–Tyseley "Seaside Flyer" near Deganwy on 23 May 2015.
Ian Pilkington

CONTENTS

Front Cover Photograph: SR Class U 2-6-0 31806 climbs to Green End on the North Yorkshire Moors Railway with a Grosmont–Pickering train on 27 September 2015. **Robert Falconer**

Back Cover Photograph (top): Superbly restored prototype HST power car 41001 passes Longueville Junction trailing the 09.30 Peterborough–Wansford at the Nene Valley Railway diesel gala on 10 April 2016. **Nigel Gibbs**

Back Cover Photograph (bottom): The Class 202 "Hastings" DEMU, led by DMBSO 60118 "Tunbridge Wells" passes East Goscote, between Melton Mowbray and Leicester, with the 06.37 Hastings-Hotchley Hill (Great Central Ruddington) "Leicestershire Bell" railtour on 19 September 2015. **Aubrey Evans**

FOREWORD TO THE SEVENTEENTH EDITION

Welcome to the 17th edition of the Platform 5 guide to Preserved standard and broad gauge locomotives of British Railways.

The two years that have elapsed since publication of the previous edition have seen many movements of locomotives between locations. A small number of diesel locomotives have been preserved since publication of the last edition but several others, mainly Class 37s, have been acquired from preservation for use on the main line. A full appraisal of all New Build construction projects has been undertaken, with some locomotives that are now well progressed included in sections 1.8 and 1.9 of this book. All Narrow Gauge steam locomotives have been removed as they are now covered by the Platform 5 publication "Narrow Gauge Steam Locomotives of Great Britain & Ireland".

As in previous editions, it should be noted that for some diesel and electric locomotives that are currently considered to be "preserved", this status is not irreversible. Several locomotives that have appeared in previous editions of this book are no longer included here, some having returned to commercial operation and others having been used as a source of spares before being scrapped.

It is our aim that all surviving former BR diesel and electric locomotives will be listed either in this book if considered to be "Preserved" or in the annual Platform 5 "Locomotives Pocket Book" or "British Railways Locomotives & Coaching Stock" bound volume. A small number of locomotives may be found in both books if they are truly preserved locomotives but also have acceptance for use on the main line, for example Deltic D9000 ROYAL SCOTS GREY or 86259 "Les Ross".

Finally, one of the most common queries we receive concerns former BR diesel locomotives that are not listed in this book. Please be aware that some former industrial locomotives that do not fall within the scope of this book, carry "fake" numbers and are not actually ex-BR. Such locomotives can be found in publications that deal with former industrial locomotives. As a general rule, if a "preserved" locomotive carrying a BR number cannot be found in this book, it is likely to be an impostor!

ACKNOWLEDGEMENTS & CONTACT DETAILS

Thanks are given to all those individuals and railways who have knowingly and unknowingly assisted in the updating of this book. In particular the authors would like to thank readers who have contacted us with amendments and comments relating to the sixteenth edition of this book. As the authors are not infallible, they would welcome notification of any corrections or updates to this book of which readers have first-hand knowledge.

Please send comments or amendments to Robert Pritchard at the Platform 5 address on the title page or by e-mail to updates@platform5.com (telephone 0114 255 2625).

The book is updated to information received by June 2016.

Robert Pritchard & Peter Hall.

UPDATES

Updates to this book are published in Platform 5's monthly magazine, **Today's Railways UK**, which is the only magazine to carry official Platform 5 stock changes. **Today's Railways UK** is available from good newsagents or on a direct subscription (see the inside front cover of this book).

INTRODUCTION

This book contains details of preserved standard (4' 8½") and broad (7' 0¼") gauge locomotives and multiple unit vehicles which have been in the ownership of, built to the designs of, or operated under the jurisdiction of, the British Railways Board, its constituents or its descendants, in revenue earning service or on the "main line". Locomotives solely used in workshops and depots are excluded as are those solely built for export. Only vehicles no longer in the ownership of the descendants of the British Railways Board or the commercial railway companies are included.

Also included are War Department "Austerity" design steam locomotives and those steam locomotives built for the USATC which are currently resident in Great Britain. Many of these did see use on Great Britain's main line railways, particularly during World War II.

GENERAL NOTES

This book has been divided into several main categories namely steam locomotives, diesel locomotives, electric locomotives, gas turbine vehicles and multiple unit vehicles. Further details applicable to each category are given in the introductory paragraph of each section.

Notes regarding technical details of the various locomotives and multiple units can be found in the introductory paragraphs for each section. A few details are, however, consistent for each section, these being:

NUMBERS

All numbers carried at various times by locomotives are shown, except in the case of temporary identity changes for filming and similar events and numbers carried by locomotives when in industrial use unless they are still carried. Details are also given of the current identity if it had not previously been carried. For each section, numbers are given in chronological order wherever possible, or other logical order if more appropriate. Where a logical order is used, please refer to the introductory paragraphs of each section for further details.

NAMES AND CLASS NAMES

Names bestowed after preservation are shown in inverted commas and are only shown if still carried. Official names and class names are shown without inverted commas and these are shown irrespective of whether they are still carried.

If more than one official name has been carried then the most recent is shown with those previously carried given as a footnote. If however an earlier official name is carried then this is shown and details of other official names carried are given as a footnote.

LOCATIONS

The location where the locomotive or multiple unit is normally to be found is given. Fuller details of locations in Great Britain including OS grid references are provided in Appendix I: "List of Locations". It is not uncommon for locomotives and multiple units to visit other locations for operation, display or mechanical attention. Where such visits are of a long-term nature, the locomotive or multiple unit is shown as being at its host site.

A select number of steam locomotives are permitted to work steam specials on the national railway network. Such locomotives invariably spend long periods away from their home bases undertaking such duties.

(N) denotes a locomotive or multiple unit vehicle that forms part of the National Collection; a group of historically important items that have been saved as a representation of the nation's railway heritage. The National Collection is maintained under the direction of the National Railway Museum and most items are usually to be found at the museum's York headquarters or at the Shildon outpost. National Collection items can sometimes be found in use or on display at other locations.

GAUGE

All locomotives and multiple units are standard gauge (4' 8½") unless stated otherwise.

BUILD DETAILS

For each locomotive the builder, works number (if any) and year of build are given. Private builder codes can be found in Appendix V.

1. STEAM LOCOMOTIVES

GENERAL

Almost from the birth of the railways until the 1960s, steam was the principal form of propulsion, its rapid decline in the 1960s being the impulse for much of the preservation movement. Steam locomotives are arranged generally in numerical order of the British Railways number, except that very old locomotives which did not receive numbers in the series pertaining at nationalisation in 1948 are listed at the end of each pre-nationalisation company section.

WHEEL ARRANGEMENT

The Whyte notation is used for steam locomotives and diesel shunting locomotives with coupled driving wheels. The number of leading wheels are given, followed by the number of driving wheels and then the trailing wheels. Suffixes are used to denote tank locomotives as follows: T – side tank, PT – pannier tank, ST – saddle tank, WT – well tank. For example 2-6-2T.

DIMENSIONS

These are given in imperial units for steam locomotives as follows:

Boiler pressure	In pounds force per square inch (lbf/sq in).
Cylinders	Cylinder dimensions. The diameter is given first followed by the stroke. (I) indicates two inside cylinders, (O) two outside cylinders, (V) two vertical cylinders, (3) three cylinders (two outside and one inside) and (4) four cylinders (two outside and two inside).
Wheel diameters	These are given from front to back, ie leading, driving, trailing.
Weights	These are given in full working order.

TRACTIVE EFFORT

This is given at 85% boiler pressure to the nearest 10 lbf for steam locomotives. Phillipsons formula has been used to calculate these as follows:

$$TE = \frac{0.85d^2snp}{2w}$$

where
TE = tractive effort in pounds force;
d = cylinder diameter (inches);
s = piston stroke (inches);
n = number of cylinders;
p = maximum boiler pressure (lb/sq in);
w = new driving wheel diameter (inches).

BRAKES

Steam locomotives are assumed to have train vacuum brakes unless otherwise stated.

VALVE GEAR

Unless stated otherwise valve gear on steam locomotives is assumed to be inside the locomotive, except Walschaerts and Caprotti gears which are assumed to be outside. Exceptions are LMS-design 5MT 4-6-0 44767 with outside Stephenson valve gear, LNER (ex-GER) N7 0-6-2T No. 69621 with inside cylinders and Walschaerts valve gear, and various 4-cylinder GWR 4-6-0s with inside Walschaerts valve gear and rocking shafts for the outside cylinders.

1.1. GREAT WESTERN RAILWAY AND ABSORBED COMPANIES' STEAM LOCOMOTIVES

GENERAL

The GWR was the only one of the Big Four companies which existed at the time of the grouping, when a number of other smaller companies were absorbed. These were virtually all in Wales and included the Cambrian Railways, Cardiff Railway, Rhymney Railway and Taff Vale Railway. Prior to 1923 the GWR had also absorbed smaller concerns at various dates.

NUMBERING & CLASSIFICATION SYSTEM

The locomotives of the absorbed companies were given the lower numbers and GWR classes the higher numbers. Instead of arranging classes in blocks, the GWR adopted a system whereby the second digit remained constant within a class, eg the 0-6-2Ts numbered 5600–99 continued with 6600–99. Sometimes earlier numbers were filled in, eg 5101–99 continued with 4100–99. Classes were always denoted by the number of the first member of the class to be built, which was not always the lowest number in the series. GWR locomotives were not renumbered by BR on nationalisation.

The listing here is presented in locomotive number order rather than class number, except that locomotives of the same class are listed together. Locomotives with no GWR number are listed at the end, whilst the surviving broad gauge locomotive is listed at the beginning.

POWER CLASSIFICATION & ROUTE RESTRICTION SYSTEM

The GWR adopted a power classification letter code system which ranged from A to E in ascending order of power. Certain small locomotives which were below group A were said to be unclassified and the "Kings" were classed as "special", being higher than "E". BR power classifications are also shown in brackets in this section.

The power classification letter was shown on the cabside on a coloured spot showing the route restriction. In ascending order of restriction these were as follows: Yellow, Blue, Red, Double Red. Where no restriction is specified, locomotives were unrestricted.

▶ An example of a Great Western route restriction spot (the double red spot) on the National Collection's 6000 Class 4-6-0 6000 "KING GEORGE V". **Robert Pritchard**

1.1.1. BROAD GAUGE LOCOMOTIVE

The fledgling Great Western Railway was laid to a gauge of 7' 0¼" gauge, as directed by engineer Isambard Kingdom Brunel. A number of other companies in the South-West and South Wales also adopted this gauge. However in 1846 the Parliament's Gauge Commission recommended that 4' 8½" gauge be used as standard in the future and by 1892 all broad gauge lines had been converted to standard gauge.

SOUTH DEVON RAILWAY   0-4-0WT

Built: 1868. Vertical boilered locomotive.
Wheel Diameter: 3' 0".   **Cylinders**: 9" x 12" (V).

GWR	SDR		
2180	151 TINY	South Devon Railway (N)	Sara 1868

1.1.2. STANDARD GAUGE LOCOMOTIVES

No. 12   4wT

Built: 1926. Sentinel vertical-boilered geared locomotive. Returned to manufacturer after three months service.
Boiler Pressure: 275 lbf/sq in.   **Weight**: 20 tons.
Wheel Diameter: 2' 6".   **Cylinders**: 6" x 9" (I).
Valve Gear: Rotary cam.   **Tractive Effort**: 7200 lbf.

GWR	Present		
12	49	"No. 2 ISEBROOK"	Buckinghamshire Railway Centre	S 6515/1926

TAFF VALE RAILWAY CLASS O2   0-6-2T

Built: 1899 by Neilson, Reid. Sold by GWR 1926. 9 built.
Boiler Pressure: 160 lbf/sq in.   **Weight**: 61.5 tons.
Wheel Diameters: 4' 6½", 3' 1".   **Cylinders**: 17½" x 26" (I).
Valve Gear: Stephenson. Slide valves.   **Tractive Effort**: 19870 lbf.
Power Classification: B.   **Restriction**: Blue.

GWR	TVR		
426	85	Keighley & Worth Valley Railway	NR 5408/1899

TAFF VALE RAILWAY CLASS O1   0-6-2T

Built: 1894–97. Survivor sold by GWR 1927. 14 built.
Boiler Pressure: 150 lbf/sq in.   **Weight**: 56.4 tons.
Wheel Diameters: 4' 6½", 3' 8¾".   **Cylinders**: 17½" x 26" (I).
Valve Gear: Stephenson. Slide valves.   **Tractive Effort**: 18630 lbf.
Power Classification: A.   **Restriction**: Yellow.

GWR	TVR		
450	28	Gwili Railway (N)	Cardiff West Yard 306/1897

▲ Taff Vale Railway Class O2 0-6-2T 85 at Keighley on 28 February 2016. **Paul Abell**

▼ 2800 Class 2-8-0 2807 of 1905 (one of the oldest locomotives still in regular use) takes on water at Toddington on the Gloucestershire Warwickshire Railway on 6 April 2016. **Robert Pritchard**

PORT TALBOT RAILWAY 0-6-0ST

Built: 1900/01. Survivor sold by GWR 1934. 6 built.
Boiler Pressure: 160 lbf/sq in.
Wheel Diameter: 4' 0½".
Valve Gear: Stephenson. Slide valves.
Power Classification: A.

Weight: 44 tons.
Cylinders: 16" x 24" (I).
Tractive Effort: 17 230 lbf.
Restriction: Yellow.

GWR	PTR		
813	26	Severn Valley Railway	HC 555/1901

POWLESLAND & MASON 0-4-0ST

Built: 1903–06. Survivor sold by GWR 1928 for industrial use.
Boiler Pressure: 140 lbf/sq in.
Wheel Diameter: 3' 6".
Valve Gear: Stephenson. Slide valves.

Weight: 24.85 tons.
Cylinders: 14" x 20" (O).
Tractive Effort: 11 110 lbf.

GWR	P&M		
921	6	Leicestershire County Museum store, Snibston	BE 314/1906

CARDIFF RAILWAY 0-4-0ST

Built: 1898. Rebuilt Tyndall Street Works 1916.
Boiler Pressure: 160 lbf/sq in.
Wheel Diameter: 3' 2½".
Valve Gear: Hawthorn-Kitson.

Weight: 25.5 tons.
Cylinders: 14" x 21" (O).
Tractive Effort: 14 540 lbf.

GWR	CARR		
1338	5	Didcot Railway Centre	K 3799/1898

ALEXANDRA DOCKS & RAILWAY COMPANY 0-4-0ST

Built: 1897. Rebuilt Swindon 1903. Sold by GWR 1932 for industrial use.
Boiler Pressure: 120 lbf/sq in.
Wheel Diameter: 3' 0".
Valve Gear: Stephenson. Slide valves.

Weight: 22.5 tons.
Cylinders: 14" x 20" (O).
Tractive Effort: 11 110 lbf.

GWR	AD		
1340 TROJAN	TROJAN	Didcot Railway Centre	AE 1386/1897

1361 CLASS 0-6-0ST

Built: 1910. Churchward design for dock shunting. 5 built (1361–65).
Boiler Pressure: 150 lbf/sq in.
Wheel Diameter: 3' 8".
Valve Gear: Allan.
Power Classification: Unclassified (0F).

Weight: 35.2 tons.
Cylinders: 16" x 20" (O).
Tractive Effort: 14 840 lbf.

1363	Didcot Railway Centre	Swindon 2377/1910

1366 CLASS 0-6-0PT

Built: 1934. Collett design for dock shunting. Used to work Weymouth Quay boat trains. 6 built (1366–71).
Boiler Pressure: 165 lbf/sq in.
Wheel Diameter: 3' 8".
Valve Gear: Stephenson. Slide valves.
Power Classification: Unclassified (1F).

Weight: 35.75 tons.
Cylinders: 16" x 20" (O).
Tractive Effort: 16 320 lbf.

1369	South Devon Railway	Swindon 1934

NORTH PEMBROKESHIRE & FISHGUARD RAILWAY   0-6-0ST

Built: 1878. Absorbed by GWR 1898. Sold to Gwendraeth Valley Railway in 1910. Absorbed by GWR again in 1923 but sold in March of that year to Kidwelly Tinplate Company.
Boiler Pressure: 140 lbf/sq in.   **Weight:** 30.95 tons.
Wheel Diameter: 4' 0".   **Cylinders:** 16" x 22" (I).
Valve Gear: Stephenson. Slide valves.   **Tractive Effort:** 13 960 lbf.

GWR	GVR			
1378	2	MARGARET	Scolton Manor Museum	FW 410/1878

1500 CLASS   0-6-0PT

Built: 1949. Hawksworth design. 10 built (1500–09).
Boiler Pressure: 200 lbf/sq in.   **Weight:** 58.2 tons.
Wheel Diameter: 4' 7½".   **Cylinders:** 17½" x 24" (O).
Valve Gear: Walschaerts. Piston valves.   **Tractive Effort:** 22 510 lbf.
Power Classification: C (4F).   **Restriction:** Red.

1501	Severn Valley Railway	Swindon 1949

1600 CLASS   0-6-0PT

Built: 1949–55. Hawksworth design. 70 built (1600–69).
Boiler Pressure: 165 lbf/sq in.   **Weight:** 41.6 tons.
Wheel Diameter: 4' 1½".   **Cylinders:** 16½" x 24" (I).
Valve Gear: Stephenson. Slide valves.   **Tractive Effort:** 18 510 lbf.
Power Classification: A (2F).   **Restriction:** Uncoloured.

1638	Kent & East Sussex Railway	Swindon 1951

2301 CLASS   DEAN GOODS   0-6-0

Built: 1883–99. Dean design. 280 built (2301–2580).
Boiler Pressure: 180 lbf/sq in superheated.   **Weight–Loco:** 37 tons.
Wheel Diameter: 5' 2".   **–Tender:** 36.75 tons.
Cylinders: 17½" x 24" (I).   **Valve Gear:** Stephenson. Slide valves.
Tractive Effort: 18 140 lbf.   **Restriction:** Uncoloured.
Power Classification: A (2MT).

2516	Steam – Museum of the Great Western Railway (N)	Swindon 1557/1897

2800 CLASS   2-8-0

Built: 1903–19. Churchward design for heavy freight. 84 built (2800–83).
Boiler Pressure: 225 lbf/sq in superheated.   **Weight–Loco:** 75.5 tons.
Wheel Diameters: 3' 2", 4' 7½".   **–Tender:** 43.15 tons.
Cylinders: 18½" x 30" (O).   **Valve Gear:** Stephenson. Piston valves.
Tractive Effort: 35 380 lbf.   **Restriction:** Blue.
Power Classification: E (8F).

2807	Gloucestershire Warwickshire Railway	Swindon 2102/1905
2818	National Railway Museum, Shildon (N)	Swindon 2122/1905
2857	Severn Valley Railway	Swindon 2763/1918
2859	Llangollen Railway	Swindon 2765/1918
2873	South Devon Railway	Swindon 2779/1918
2874	Gloucestershire Warwickshire Railway	Swindon 2780/1918

2884 CLASS   2-8-0

Built: 1938–42. Collett development of 2800 Class with side window cabs. 81 built (2884–99, 3800–64).
Boiler Pressure: 225 lbf/sq in superheated.
Wheel Diameters: 3' 2", 4' 7½".
Cylinders: 18½" x 30" (O).
Tractive Effort: 35 380 lbf.
Power Classification: E (8F).
Weight–Loco: 76.25 tons.
    –Tender: 43.15 tons.
Valve Gear: Stephenson. Piston valves.
Restriction: Blue.

2885	Tyseley Locomotive Works	Swindon 1938
3802	Llangollen Railway	Swindon 1938
3803	South Devon Railway	Swindon 1939
3814	North Yorkshire Moors Railway	Swindon 1940
3822	Didcot Railway Centre	Swindon 1940
3845	Honeybourne Airfield Industrial Estate	Swindon 1942
3850	Gloucestershire Warwickshire Railway	Swindon 1942
3855	East Lancashire Railway	Swindon 1942
3862	Northampton & Lamport Railway	Swindon 1942

2251 CLASS   0-6-0

Built: 1930–48. Collett design. 120 built (2251–99, 2200–50, 3200–19).
Boiler Pressure: 200 lbf/sq in superheated.
Wheel Diameter: 5' 2".
Cylinders: 17½" x 24" (I).
Tractive Effort: 20 150 lbf.
Power Classification: B (3MT).
Weight–Loco: 43.4 tons.
    –Tender: 36.75 tons.
Valve Gear: Stephenson. Slide valves.
Restriction: Yellow.

| 3205 | South Devon Railway | Swindon 1946 |

3200 CLASS   "DUKEDOG"   4-4-0

Built: Rebuilt 1936–39 by Collett using the frames of "Bulldogs" and the boilers of "Dukes". 30 built (9000–29).
Boiler Pressure: 180 lbf/sq in
Wheel Diameters: 3' 8", 5' 8".
Cylinders: 18" x 26" (I).
Tractive Effort: 18 950 lbf.
Power Classification: B.
Weight–Loco: 49 tons.
    –Tender: 40 tons.
Valve Gear: Stephenson. Slide valves.
Restriction: Yellow.

| 3217–9017 | Bluebell Railway | Swindon 1938 |

3700 CLASS   CITY   4-4-0

Built: 1903. Churchward design. Reputed to be the first loco to achieve 100 mph hauling a Plymouth–Paddington "Ocean Mails" special in 1904. 20 built (3400–09/3433–42).
Boiler Pressure: 200 lbf/sq in superheated.
Wheel Diameters: 3' 2", 6' 8½".
Cylinders: 18" x 26" (I).
Tractive Effort: 17 800 lbf.
Weight–Loco: 55.3 tons.
    –Tender: 36.75 tons.
Valve Gear: Stephenson. Piston valves.

BR	GWR		
3440	3717	CITY OF TRURO	Steam – Museum of the Great Western Railway (N)
			Swindon 2000/1903

5700 CLASS   0-6-0PT

Built: 1929–49. Collett design. The standard GWR shunter. 863 built (5700–99, 6700–79, 7700–99, 8700–99, 3700–99, 3600–99, 4600–99, 9600–82, 9700–9799). Six of the preserved examples saw use with London Transport following withdrawal by British Railways.
Boiler Pressure: 200 lbf/sq in.   **Weight:** 47.5 tons (§ 49 tons).
Wheel Diameter: 4' 7½".   **Cylinders:** 17½" x 24" (I).
Valve Gear: Stephenson. Slide valves.   **Tractive Effort:** 22510 lbf.
Power Classification: C (4F).   **Restriction:** Blue (Yellow from 1950).

GWR	LTE		
3650§		Didcot Railway Centre	Swindon 1939
3738§		Didcot Railway Centre	Swindon 1937
4612§		Bodmin & Wenford Railway	Swindon 1942
5764	L95	Severn Valley Railway	Swindon 1929
5775	L89	Keighley & Worth Valley Railway	Swindon 1929
5786	L92	South Devon Railway	Swindon 1930
7714		Severn Valley Railway	KS 4449/1930
7715	L99	Buckinghamshire Railway Centre	KS 4450/1930
7752	L94	Tyseley Locomotive Works	NBL 24040/1930
7754		Llangollen Railway	NBL 24042/1930
7760	L90	Tyseley Locomotive Works	NBL 24048/1930
9600§		Tyseley Locomotive Works	Swindon 1945
9629§		Pontypool & Blaenavon Railway	Swindon 1946
9642§		Rye Farm, Wishaw, Sutton Coldfield	Swindon 1946
9681§		Dean Forest Railway	Swindon 1949
9682§		Southall Depot, London	Swindon 1949

4000 CLASS   STAR   4-6-0

Built: 1906–23. Churchward design for express passenger trains. 73 built (4000–72).
Boiler Pressure: 225 lbf/sq in superheated.   **Weight–Loco:** 75.6 tons.
Wheel Diameters: 3' 2", 6' 8½".   **–Tender:** 40 tons.
Cylinders: 15" x 26" (4).   **Tractive Effort:** 27800 lbf.
Valve Gear: Inside Walschaerts. Rocking levers for outside valves. Piston valves.
Power Classification: D (5P).   **Restriction:** Red.

4003	LODE STAR	National Railway Museum, York (N)	Swindon 2231/1907

4073 CLASS   CASTLE   4-6-0

Built: 1923–50. Collett development of Star. 166 built (4073–99, 5000–5099, 7000–37). In addition one Pacific (111) and five Stars (4000/09/16/32/37) were rebuilt as Castles.
Boiler Pressure: 225 lbf/sq in superheated.   **Weight–Loco:** 79.85 tons.
Wheel Diameters: 3' 2", 6' 8½".   **–Tender:** 46.7 tons.
Cylinders: 16" x 26" (4).   **Tractive Effort:** 31630 lbf.
Valve Gear: Inside Walschaerts. Rocking levers for outside valves. Piston valves.
Power Classification: D (7P).   **Restriction:** Red.

d	Rebuilt with double chimney.		x	Dual (air/vacuum) brakes.

4073	CAERPHILLY CASTLE	Steam – Museum of the Great Western Railway (N)	Swindon 1923
4079	PENDENNIS CASTLE	Didcot Railway Centre	Swindon 1924
5029 x	NUNNEY CASTLE	London & North Western Railway Heritage Company, Crewe	Swindon 1934
5043 d	EARL OF MOUNT EDGCUMBE	Tyseley Locomotive Works	Swindon 1936
5051	EARL BATHURST	Didcot Railway Centre	Swindon 1936
5080	DEFIANT	Buckinghamshire Railway Centre	Swindon 1939
7027	THORNBURY CASTLE	Peak Rail	Swindon 1949
7029 d	CLUN CASTLE	Tyseley Locomotive Works	Swindon 1950

5043 was named BARBURY CASTLE to 09/37.
5051 was named DRYSLLWYN CASTLE to 08/37.
5080 was named OGMORE CASTLE to 01/41.

5101 CLASS   2-6-2T

Built: 1929–49. Collett development of Churchward 3100 class. 180 built (5101–99, 4100–79).
Boiler Pressure: 200 lbf/sq in superheated.   **Weight:** 78.45 tons.
Wheel Diameters: 3′ 2″, 5′ 8″, 3′ 8″.   **Cylinders:** 18″ x 30″ (O).
Valve Gear: Stephenson. Piston valves.   **Tractive Effort:** 24 300 lbf.
Power Classification: D (4MT).   **Restriction:** Yellow.

4110	West Somerset Railway	Swindon 1936
4121	Tyseley Locomotive Works	Swindon 1937
4141	Epping Ongar Railway	Swindon 1946
4144	Didcot Railway Centre	Swindon 1946
4150	Severn Valley Railway	Swindon 1947
4160	West Somerset Railway	Swindon 1948
5164	Barrow Hill Roundhouse	Swindon 1930
5199	Llangollen Railway	Swindon 1934

In addition 5193 has been rebuilt by the West Somerset Railway as 4300 Class 2-6-0 tender locomotive No. 9351. See New Build Steam Locomotives section.

4160 is currently being overhauled at the Llangollen Railway.

▲ 4500 Class 2-6-2T 4566 at Hood Bridge on the South Devon Railway with the 12.30 Buckfastleigh–Totness Littlehempston on 21 February 2015.   **David Hunt**

4200 CLASS — 2-8-0T

Built: 1910–23. Churchward design. 105 built (4201–99, 4200, 5200–04).
Boiler Pressure: 200 lbf/sq in superheated. **Weight:** 81.6 tons.
Wheel Diameters: 3′ 2″, 4′ 7½″. **Cylinders:** 18½″ x 30″ (O).
Valve Gear: Stephenson. Piston valves. **Tractive Effort:** 31 450 lbf.
Power Classification: E (7F). **Restriction:** Red.

4247		Bodmin & Wenford Railway	Swindon 2637/1916
4248		Steam – Museum of the Great Western Railway (N)	Swindon 2638/1916
4253		Kent & East Sussex Railway	Swindon 2643/1917
4270		Gloucestershire Warwickshire Railway	Swindon 2850/1919
4277	"HERCULES"	Dartmouth Steam Railway	Swindon 2857/1920

4500 CLASS — 2-6-2T

Built: 1906–24. Churchward design. (§ Built 1927–29. Collett development with larger tanks). 175 built (4500–99, 5500–74).
Boiler Pressure: 200 lbf/sq in superheated. **Weight:** 57.9 tons (§ 61 tons).
Wheel Diameters: 3′ 2″, 4′ 7½″, 3′ 2″. **Cylinders:** 17″ x 24″ (O).
Valve Gear: Stephenson. Piston valves. **Tractive Effort:** 21 250 lbf.
Power Classification: C (4MT). **Restriction:** Yellow.

4555		Dartmouth Steam Railway	Swindon 1924
4561		West Somerset Railway	Swindon 1924
4566		Severn Valley Railway	Swindon 1924
4588§		Tyseley Locomotive Works	Swindon 1927
5521§	L150	Avon Valley Railway	Swindon 1927
5526§		South Devon Railway	Swindon 1928
5532§		Llangollen Railway	Swindon 1928
5538§		Flour Mill Workshop, Bream	Swindon 1928
5539§		Barry Rail Centre	Swindon 1928
5541§		Dean Forest Railway	Swindon 1928
5542§		Gloucestershire Warwickshire Railway	Swindon 1928
5552§		Bodmin & Wenford Railway	Swindon 1928
5553§		Peak Rail	Swindon 1928
5572§		Didcot Railway Centre	Swindon 1929

5521 is on loan from the Flour Mill Workshop, Bream

1400 CLASS — 0-4-2T

Built: 1932–36. Collett design. Push & Pull fitted. Locomotives renumbered in 1946. 75 built (1400–74).
Boiler Pressure: 165 lbf/sq in. **Weight:** 41.3 tons.
Wheel Diameters: 5′ 2″, 3′ 8″. **Cylinders:** 16″ x 24″ (I).
Valve Gear: Stephenson. Slide valves. **Tractive Effort:** 13 900 lbf.
Power Classification: Unclassified (1P).

1932 No.	1946 No.		
4820	1420	South Devon Railway	Swindon 1933
4842	1442	Tiverton Museum	Swindon 1935
4850	1450	Severn Valley Railway	Swindon 1935
4866	1466	Didcot Railway Centre	Swindon 1936

4900 CLASS — HALL — 4-6-0

Built: 1928–43. Collett development of Churchward "Saint" Class. 259 in class. (4900 rebuilt from Saint) 4901–99, 5900–99, 6900–58 built as Halls.
Boiler Pressure: 225 lbf/sq in superheated. **Weight–Loco:** 75 tons.
Wheel Diameters: 3′ 2″, 6′ 0″. **–Tender:** 46.7 tons.
Cylinders: 18½″ x 30″ (O). **Valve Gear:** Stephenson. Piston valves.
Tractive Effort: 27 270 lbf. **Restriction:** Red.
Power Classification: D (5MT).

4920	DUMBLETON HALL	South Devon Railway	Swindon 1929
4930	HAGLEY HALL	Severn Valley Railway	Swindon 1929
4936	KINLET HALL	West Somerset Railway	Swindon 1929
4953	PITCHFORD HALL	Epping Ongar Railway	Swindon 1929
4965	ROOD ASHTON HALL	Tyseley Locomotive Works	Swindon 1930
4979	WOOTTON HALL	Ribble Steam Railway	Swindon 1930
5900	HINDERTON HALL	Didcot Railway Centre	Swindon 1931
5952	COGAN HALL	Llangollen Railway	Swindon 1935
5967	BICKMARSH HALL	Northampton & Lamport Railway	Swindon 1937
5972	OLTON HALL	Warner Brothers Studio Tour, Leavesden	Swindon 1937

4936 is on loan from Tyseley Locomotive Works
4965 previously carried 4983 ALBERT HALL.
5972 runs as "HOGWARTS CASTLE" as used in the "Harry Potter" films.

5205 CLASS   2-8-0T

Built: 1923–25/1940. Collett development of 4200 class. 60 built (5205–64).
Boiler Pressure: 200 lbf/sq in superheated.   **Weight:** 82.1 tons.
Wheel Diameters: 3' 2", 4' 7½".   **Cylinders:** 19" x 30" (O).
Valve Gear: Stephenson. Piston valves.   **Tractive Effort:** 33 170 lbf.
Power Classification: E (8F).   **Restriction:** Red.

5224		Peak Rail	Swindon 1925
5227		Didcot Railway Centre	Swindon 1924
5239	"GOLIATH"	Dartmouth Steam Railway	Swindon 1924

5600 CLASS   0-6-2T

Built: 1924–28. Collett design. 200 built (5600–99, 6600–99).
Boiler Pressure: 200 lbf/sq in superheated.   **Weight:** 68 tons.
Wheel Diameters: 4' 7½", 3' 8".   **Cylinders:** 18" x 26" (I).
Valve Gear: Stephenson. Piston valves.   **Tractive Effort:** 25 800 lbf.
Power Classification: D (5MT).   **Restriction:** Red.

5619	Flour Mill Workshop, Bream	Swindon 1925
5637	East Somerset Railway	Swindon 1925
5643	Embsay & Bolton Abbey Railway	Swindon 1925
5668	Kent & East Sussex Railway	Swindon 1926
6619	Kent & East Sussex Railway	Swindon 1928
6634	Severn Valley Railway	Swindon 1928
6686	Barry Rail Centre	AW 974/1928
6695	Swanage Railway	AW 983/1928
6697	Didcot Railway Centre	AW 985/1928

5643 is on loan from the Ribble Steam Railway based Furness Railway Trust.

6000 CLASS   KING   4-6-0

Built: 1927–30. Collett design. 30 built.
Boiler Pressure: 250 lbf/sq in superheated.   **Weight–Loco:** 89 tons.
Wheel Diameters: 3' 0", 6' 6".   **–Tender:** 46.7 tons.
Cylinders: 16¼" x 28" (4).   **Tractive Effort:** 40 290 lbf.
Valve Gear: Inside Walschaerts. Piston valves. Rocking levers for outside valves.
Power Classification: Special (8P).   **Restriction:** Double Red.

x   Dual (air/vacuum) brakes.

6000	KING GEORGE V	Steam – Museum of the Great Western Railway (N)	Swindon 1927
6023	KING EDWARD II	Didcot Railway Centre	Swindon 1930
6024 x	KING EDWARD I	West Somerset Railway	Swindon 1930

▲ The Dartmouth Steam Railway's 5205 Class 2-8-0T 5239 "GOLIATH" climbs Goodrington Bank with the 12.30 Paignton–Kingswear on 29 December 2014. **David Hunt**

▼ 6000 Class 4-6-0 6000 "KING GEORGE V" on display at the STEAM Museum at Swindon on 3 April 2016. Locomotives 9400 and 3717 can be seen behind. **Brian Garvin**

6100 CLASS   2-6-2T

Built: 1931–35. Collett development of 5100. 70 built (6100–69).
Boiler Pressure: 225 lbf/sq in superheated.   **Weight:** 78.45 tons.
Wheel Diameters: 3′ 2″, 5′ 8″, 3′ 8″.   **Cylinders:** 18″ x 30″ (O).
Valve Gear: Stephenson. Piston valves.   **Tractive Effort:** 27340 lbf.
Power Classification: D (5MT).   **Restriction:** Blue.

6106	Didcot Railway Centre	Swindon 1931

6400 CLASS   0-6-0PT

Built: 1932–37. Collett design. Push & Pull fitted. 40 built (6400–39).
Boiler Pressure: 165 lbf/sq in.   **Weight:** 45.6 tons.
Wheel Diameter: 4′ 7½″.   **Cylinders:** 16½″ x 24″ (I).
Valve Gear: Stephenson. Slide valves.   **Tractive Effort:** 16510 lbf.
Power Classification: A (2P).   **Restriction:** Yellow.

6412		South Devon Railway	Swindon 1934
6430		Llangollen Railway	Swindon 1937
6435	"AJAX"	Bodmin & Wenford Railway	Swindon 1937

6959 CLASS   MODIFIED HALL   4-6-0

Built: 1944–49. Hawksworth development of "Hall". 71 built (6959–99, 7900–29).
Boiler Pressure: 225 lbf/sq in superheated.   **Weight–Loco:** 75.8 tons.
Wheel Diameters: 3′ 2″, 6′ 0″.   **–Tender:** 47.3 tons.
Cylinders: 18½″ x 30″ (O).   **Valve Gear:** Stephenson. Piston valves.
Tractive Effort: 27270 lbf.   **Restriction:** Blue.
Power Classification: D (5MT).

6960	RAVENINGHAM HALL	West Somerset Railway	Swindon 1944
6984	OWSDEN HALL	Swindon & Cricklade Railway	Swindon 1948
6989	WIGHTWICK HALL	Buckinghamshire Railway Centre	Swindon 1948
6990	WITHERSLACK HALL	Great Central Railway	Swindon 1948
6998	BURTON AGNES HALL	Didcot Railway Centre	Swindon 1949
7903	FOREMARKE HALL	Gloucestershire Warwickshire Railway	Swindon 1949

7200 CLASS   2-8-2T

Built: 1934–50. Collett rebuilds of 4200 and 5205 Class 2-8-0Ts. 54 built (7200–53).
Boiler Pressure: 200 lbf/sq in superheated.   **Weight:** 92.6 tons.
Wheel Diameters: 3′ 2″, 4′ 7½″, 3′ 8″.   **Cylinders:** 19″ x 30″ (O).
Valve Gear: Stephenson. Piston valves.   **Tractive Effort:** 33170 lbf.
Power Classification: E (8F).   **Restriction:** Blue.

7200	(rebuilt from 5277)	Buckinghamshire Railway Centre	Swindon 1930 reb. 1934
7202	(rebuilt from 5275)	Didcot Railway Centre	Swindon 1930 reb. 1934
7229	(rebuilt from 5264)	East Lancashire Railway	Swindon 1926 reb. 1935

7800 CLASS   MANOR   4-6-0

Built: 1938–50. Collett design for secondary main lines. 30 built (7800–29).
Boiler Pressure: 225 lbf/sq in superheated.   **Weight–Loco:** 68.9 tons.
Wheel Diameters: 3′ 0″, 5′ 8″.   **–Tender:** 40 tons.
Cylinders: 18″ x 30″ (O).   **Valve Gear:** Stephenson. Piston valves.
Tractive Effort: 27340 lbf.   **Restriction:** Blue.
Power Classification: D (5MT).

7802	BRADLEY MANOR	Severn Valley Railway	Swindon 1938
7808	COOKHAM MANOR	Didcot Railway Centre	Swindon 1938
7812	ERLESTOKE MANOR	Severn Valley Railway	Swindon 1939

▲ 6400 Class 0-6-0PT 6412 hauls the 10.35 Buckfastleigh–Totnes Littlehempston with a single Autocoach on 23 May 2015. **David Hunt**

▼ 4300 Class 2-6-0 5322 is normally based at Didcot Railway Centre, but on 30 March 2014 could be found visiting the West Somerset Railway for a Steam Gala. It is seen approaching Bishops Lydeard with the 09.50 from Minehead. **David Hunt**

7819	HINTON MANOR	Designer Outlet Village, Swindon	Swindon 1939
7820	DINMORE MANOR	Gloucestershire Warwickshire Railway	Swindon 1950
7821	DITCHEAT MANOR	Steam – Museum of the Great Western Railway	Swindon 1950
7822	FOXCOTE MANOR	Llangollen Railway	Swindon 1950
7827	LYDHAM MANOR	Dartmouth Steam Railway	Swindon 1950
7828	ODNEY MANOR	West Somerset Railway	Swindon 1950

7828 is currently running as "NORTON MANOR – 40 COMMANDO".

4300 CLASS — 2-6-0

Built: 1911–32. Churchward design. 342 built (4300–99, 5300–99 (renumbered from 8300–99 between 1944 and 1948), 6300–99, 7300–21, 7322–41 (renumbered from 9300–19 between 1956 and 1959).
Boiler Pressure: 200 lbf/sq in superheated.
Wheel Diameters: 3' 2", 5' 8".
Cylinders: 18½" x 30" (O).
Tractive Effort: 25 670 lbf.
Power Classification: D (4MT).
Weight–Loco: 62 tons.
  –Tender: 40 tons.
Valve Gear: Stephenson. Piston valves.
Restriction: Blue.

| 8322–5322 | Didcot Railway Centre | Swindon 1917 |
| 9303–7325 | Severn Valley Railway | Swindon 1932 |

In addition 5101 Class No. 5193 has been rebuilt by the West Somerset Railway as 4300 Class 2-6-0 tender locomotive No. 9351. See New Build Steam Locomotives section.

9400 CLASS — 0-6-0PT

Built: 1947–56. Hawksworth design. 210 built (9400–99, 8400–99, 3400–09).
Boiler Pressure: 200 lbf/sq in (* superheated). **Weight:** 55.35 tons.
Wheel Diameter: 4' 7½". **Cylinders:** 17½" x 24" (I).
Valve Gear: Stephenson. Slide valves. **Tractive Effort:** 22 510 lbf.
Power Classification: C (4F). **Restriction:** Red.

| 9400* | Steam – Museum of the Great Western Railway (N) | Swindon 1947 |
| 9466 | Buckinghamshire Railway Centre | RSH 7617/1952 |

BURRY PORT & GWENDRAETH VALLEY RAILWAY — 0-6-0ST

Built: 1900. **Weight:** 29 tons.
Wheel Diameter: 3' 6". **Cylinders:** 14" x 20"(O)

This loco was supplied new to the BPGVR and was sold into industrial service in 1914.

| 2 | PONTYBEREM | Pontypool & Blaenavon Railway | AE 1421/1900 |

SANDY & POTTON RAILWAY — 0-4-0WT

Built: 1857. The Sandy & Potton Railway became part of the LNWR and the loco worked on the Cromford & High Peak Railway from 1863–78. The loco was sold to the Wantage Tramway in 1878.
Boiler Pressure: 120 lbf/sq in. **Weight:** 15 tons.
Wheel Diameter: 3' 0". **Cylinders:** 9" x 12" (O).
Tractive Effort: 5510 lbf.

| *SPR* | *LNWR* | *WT* | | |
| SHANNON | 1863 | 5 | Didcot Railway Centre (N) | GE 1857 |

SOUTHERN

1.2. SOUTHERN RAILWAY AND CONSTITUENT COMPANIES' STEAM LOCOMOTIVES

GENERAL

The Southern Railway (SR) was an amalgamation of the London, Brighton & South Coast Railway (LBSCR), the London & South Western Railway (LSWR) and the South Eastern & Chatham Railway (SECR). The last of these was formed in 1898 by the amalgamation of the South Eastern Railway (SER) and London, Chatham & Dover Railway (LCDR).

NUMBERING SYSTEM

In 1924, after the formation of the Southern Railway the previous year, all locomotives (including new builds) were given a prefix letter to denote the works which maintained them as follows:

A   Ashford Works. All former SECR locomotives plus some D1, L1, U1.
B   Brighton Works. All former LBSCR locomotives plus some D1.
E   Eastleigh Works. All former LSWR locomotives plus LN, V, Z.

In 1931 locomotives were renumbered. "E" prefix locomotives merely lost the prefix (except locomotives with a "0" in front of the number to which 3000 was added). "A" prefix locomotives had 1000 added and "B" prefix locomotives had 2000 added, eg B636 became 2636, E0298 became 3298.

In 1941 Bulleid developed a most curious numbering system for his new locomotives. This consisted of two numbers representing the numbers of leading and trailing axles respectively followed by a letter denoting the number of the driving axles. This was followed by the locomotive serial number. The first 4-6-2 Pacific was therefore 21C1, and the first Q1 0-6-0 was C1.

In 1948 British Railways added 30000 to all numbers, but the 3xxx series (formerly 0xxx series) were totally renumbered. The Q1s became 33xxx, the MNs 35xxx and the WCs and BBs 34xxx. Isle of Wight locomotives had their own number series, denoted by a "W" prefix. This indicated Ryde Works maintenance and was carried until the end of steam on the island.

In the section which follows, locomotives are listed generally in order of BR numbers, except that locomotives of the same class are listed together. Four old locomotives which were withdrawn before nationalisation are listed at the end of the section.

CLASSIFICATION SYSTEM

The LBSCR originally classified locomotive classes by a letter which denoted the use of the class. A further development was to add a number, to identify different classes of similar use. A rebuild was signified by an "X" suffix. In its latter years, new classes of different wheel arrangement were given different letters. The SECR gave each class a letter. A number after the letter signified either a new class which was a modification of the original or a rebuild. The SR perpetuated this system. The LSWR had an odd system based on the works order number for the first locomotive of the class to be built. These went A1, B1......Z1, A2......Z2, A3......etc. and did not only apply to locomotives. Locomotives bought from outside contractors were classified by the first number to be delivered, eg "0298 Class".

CLASS 02 ⠀⠀⠀⠀⠀⠀⠀⠀⠀⠀⠀⠀⠀⠀⠀⠀0-4-4T

Built: 1889–91. Adams LSWR design.
Boiler Pressure: 160 lbf/sq in.
Wheel Diameters: 4' 10", 3' 1".
Valve Gear: Stephenson. Slide valves.
BR Power Classification: 1P.

Weight: 48.4 tons.
Cylinders: 17" x 24" (I).
Tractive Effort: 17 235 lbf.

Air braked.

BR	SR	LSWR		
W24	E209–W24	209 CALBOURNE	Isle of Wight Steam Railway	Nine Elms 341/1891

CLASS M7 ⠀⠀⠀⠀⠀⠀⠀⠀⠀⠀⠀⠀⠀⠀⠀0-4-4T

Built: 1897–1911. Drummond LSWR design. 105 built.
Boiler Pressure: 175 lbf/sq in.
Wheel Diameters: 5' 7", 3' 7".
Valve Gear: Stephenson. Slide valves.
BR Power Classification: 2P.

Weight: 60.15 tons.
Cylinders: 18½" x 26" (I).
Tractive Effort: 19 760 lbf.

30053 was Push & Pull fitted and air braked.

BR	SR	LSWR		
30053	E53–53	53	Swanage Railway	Nine Elms 1905
30245	E245–245	245	National Railway Museum, York (N)	Nine Elms 501/1897

CLASS USA TC S100 ⠀⠀⠀⠀⠀⠀⠀⠀⠀⠀0-6-0T

Built: 1942–43 by Vulcan Works, Wilkes-Barre, PA, USA for US Army Transportation Corps. 93 built (a further 289 were built by other builders). 15 were sold to SR in 1947 of which 14 became 61–74.
Boiler Pressure: 210 lbf/sq in.
Wheel Diameter: 4' 6".
Valve Gear: Walschaerts. Piston valves.
BR Power Classification: 3F.

Weight: 46.5 tons.
Cylinders: 16½" x 24" (O).
Tractive Effort: 21 600 lbf.

BR	SR	USATC	Present		
30064	64	1959		Bluebell Railway	VIW 4432/1943
30065	65	1968	MAUNSELL	Kent & East Sussex Railway	VIW 4441/1943
30070	70	1960	WAINWRIGHT	Kent & East Sussex Railway	VIW 4433/1943
30072	72	1973		Keighley & Worth Valley Railway	VIW 4446/1943

30065 was also numbered DS237 and 30070 was also numbered DS238 from 1963.

CLASS B4 ⠀⠀⠀⠀⠀⠀⠀⠀⠀⠀⠀⠀⠀⠀⠀⠀0-4-0T

Built: 1891–1909. Adams LSWR design for dock shunting. 25 built.
Boiler Pressure: 140 lbf/sq in.
Wheel Diameter: 3' 9¾".
Valve Gear: Stephenson. Slide valves.
BR Power Classification: 1F.

Weight: 33.45 tons.
Cylinders: 16" x 22" (O).
Tractive Effort: 14 650 lbf.

BR	SR			
30096	E96–96	NORMANDY	Bluebell Railway	Nine Elms 396/1893
30102	E102–102	GRANVILLE	Bressingham Steam Museum	Nine Elms 406/1893

CLASS T9 — 4-4-0

Built: 1889–1924. Drummond LSWR express passenger design. 66 built.
Boiler Pressure: 175 lbf/sq in superheated.
Wheel Diameters: 3′ 7″, 6′ 7″.
Cylinders: 19″ x 26″ (I).
Tractive Effort: 17 670 lbf.
Weight–Loco: 51.8 tons.
–Tender: 44.85 tons.
Valve Gear: Stephenson. Slide valves.
BR Power Classification: 3P.

BR	SR	LSWR		
30120	E120–120	120	Bodmin & Wenford Railway (N)	Nine Elms 572/1899

CLASS S15 (URIE) — 4-6-0

Built: 1920–21. Urie LSWR design. 20 built (30496–515).
Boiler Pressure: 180 lbf/sq in superheated.
Wheel Diameters: 3′ 7″, 5′ 7″.
Cylinders: 21″ x 28″ (O).
Tractive Effort: 28 200 lbf.
Weight–Loco: 79.8 tons.
–Tender: 57.8 tons.
Valve Gear: Walschaerts. Piston valves.
BR Power Classification: 6F.

BR	SR	LSWR		
30499	E499–499	499	Mid Hants Railway	Eastleigh 1920
30506	E506–506	506	Mid Hants Railway	Eastleigh 1920

CLASS Q — 0-6-0

Built: 1938–39. Maunsell SR design. 20 built (30530–549).
Boiler Pressure: 200 lbf/sq in superheated.
Wheel Diameter: 5′ 1″.
Cylinders: 19″ x 26″ (I).
Tractive Effort: 26 160 lbf.
Weight–Loco: 49.5 tons.
–Tender: 40.5 tons.
Valve Gear: Stephenson. Piston valves.
BR Power Classification: 4F.

BR	SR		
30541	541	Bluebell Railway	Eastleigh 1939

0415 CLASS — 4-4-2T

Built: 1882–85. Adams LSWR design. 72 built.
Boiler Pressure: 160 lbf/sq in.
Wheel Diameters: 3′ 0″, 5′ 7″, 3′ 0″.
Valve Gear: Stephenson. Slide valves.
BR Power Classification: 1P.
Weight: 55.25 tons.
Cylinders: 17½″ x 24″ (O).
Tractive Effort: 14 920 lbf.

BR	SR	LSWR		
30583	E0488–3488	488	Bluebell Railway	N 3209/1885

0298 CLASS — 2-4-0WT

Built: 1863–75. WG Beattie LSWR design. Last used on the Wenfordbridge branch in Cornwall. 85 built. Survivors reboilered in 1921.
Boiler Pressure: 160 lbf/sq in.
Wheel Diameters: 3′ 7¾″, 5′ 7″.
Valve Gear: Allan.
BR Power Classification: 0P.
Weight: 35.75 (§ 36.3) tons.
Cylinders: 16½″ x 22″ (O).
Tractive Effort: 12 160 lbf.

BR	SR	LSWR		
30585§	E0314–3314	0314	Buckinghamshire Railway Centre	BP 1414/1874 reb Elh 1921
30587	E0298–3298	0298	Bodmin & Wenford Railway (N)	BP 1412/1874 reb Elh 1921

▲ Class T9 4-4-0 30120 is paired with Battle of Britain Class 4-6-2 34070 "MANSTON" on the approach to New Barn with a Norden–Swanage service on 19 March 2014. **Robin Stewart-Smith**

▼ In superb autumn light, Class Q 0-6-0 30541 is seen topping Freshfield Bank on the Bluebell Railway with a photo charter on 2 November 2015. **Robert Falconer**

CLASS N15   KING ARTHUR   4-6-0

Built: 1925–27. Maunsell SR development of Urie LSWR design. 54 built (30448–457, 30763–806).
Boiler Pressure: 200 lbf/sq in superheated.   **Weight–Loco:** 80.7 tons.
Wheel Diameters: 3' 7", 6' 7".   **–Tender:** 57.5 tons.
Cylinders: 20½" x 28" (O).   **Valve Gear:** Walschaerts. Piston valves.
Tractive Effort: 25320 lbf.   **BR Power Classification:** 5P.

BR	SR			
30777	777	SIR LAMIEL	Great Central Railway (N)	NBL 23223/1925

CLASS S15 (MAUNSELL)   4-6-0

Built: 1927–36. Maunsell SR development of Urie LSWR design. 25 built (30823–847).
Boiler Pressure: 200 lbf/sq in superheated.   **Weight–Loco:** 80.7 (* 79.25) tons.
Wheel Diameters: 3' 7", 5' 7".   **–Tender:** 56.4 tons.
Cylinders: 20½" x 28" (O).   **Valve Gear:** Walschaerts. Piston valves.
Tractive Effort: 29860 lbf.   **BR Power Classification:** 6F.

BR	SR			
30825	825		North Yorkshire Moors Railway	Eastleigh 1927
30828	828	"HARRY A FRITH"	Mid Hants Railway	Eastleigh 1927
30830	830		North Yorkshire Moors Railway	Eastleigh 1927
30847*	847		Bluebell Railway	Eastleigh 1936

30825 has been restored using a substantial number of components from 30841.

CLASS LN   LORD NELSON   4-6-0

Built: 1926–29. Maunsell SR design. 16 built (30850–65).
Boiler Pressure: 220 lbf/sq in superheated.   **Weight–Loco:** 83.5 tons.
Wheel Diameters: 3' 1", 6' 7".   **–Tender:** 57.95 tons.
Cylinders: 16½" x 26" (4).   **Valve Gear:** Walschaerts. Piston valves.
Tractive Effort: 33510 lbf.   **BR Power Classification:** 7P.

Dual (air/vacuum) brakes.

BR	SR			
30850	E850–850	LORD NELSON	Mid Hants Railway (N)	Eastleigh 1926

CLASS V   SCHOOLS   4-4-0

Built: 1930–35. Maunsell SR design. 40 built (30900–39).
Boiler Pressure: 220 lbf/sq in superheated.   **Weight–Loco:** 67.1 tons.
Wheel Diameters: 3' 1", 6' 7".   **–Tender:** 42.4 tons.
Cylinders: 16½" x 26" (3).   **Valve Gear:** Walschaerts. Piston valves.
Tractive Effort: 25130 lbf.   **BR Power Classification:** 5P.

BR	SR			
30925	925	CHELTENHAM	Mid Hants Railway (N)	Eastleigh 1934
30926	926	REPTON	North Yorkshire Moors Railway	Eastleigh 1934
30928	928	STOWE	Bluebell Railway	Eastleigh 1934

CLASS P   0-6-0T

Built: 1909–10. Wainwright SECR design. 8 built.
Boiler Pressure: 160 lbf/sq in.   **Weight:** 28.5 tons.
Wheel Diameter: 3' 9".   **Cylinders:** 12" x 18" (I).
Valve Gear: Stephenson. Slide valves.   **Tractive Effort:** 7830 lbf.
BR Power Classification: 0F.

BR	SR	SECR			
31027	A 27–1027	27		Bluebell Railway	Ashford 1910
31178	A178–1178	178 "PIONEER II"		Bluebell Railway	Ashford 1910
31323	A323–1323	323		Bluebell Railway	Ashford 1910
31556	556–A556–1556	753–5753		Kent & East Sussex Railway	Ashford 1909

CLASS 01   0-6-0

Built: 1903–15. Wainwright SECR design. 66 built. 59 were rebuilt out of 122 "O" class.
Boiler Pressure: 150 lbf/sq in.   **Weight–Loco:** 41.05 tons.
Wheel Diameter: 5' 1".   **–Tender:** 28.20 tons.
Cylinders: 18" x 26" (I).   **Valve Gear:** Stephenson. Slide valves.
Tractive Effort: 17610 lbf.   **BR Power Classification:** 1F.

BR	SR	SECR		
31065	A65–1065	65	Bluebell Railway	Ashford 1896 reb. 1908

CLASS H   0-4-4T

Built: 1904–15. Wainwright SECR design. 66 built.
Boiler Pressure: 160 lbf/sq in.   **Weight:** 54.4 tons.
Wheel Diameters: 5' 6", 3' 7".   **Cylinders:** 18" x 26" (I).
Valve Gear: Stephenson. Slide valves.   **Tractive Effort:** 17360 lbf.
BR Power Classification: 1P.

Push & Pull fitted. Dual (air/vacuum) brakes.

BR	SR	SECR		
31263	A263–1263	263	Bluebell Railway	Ashford 1905

CLASS C   0-6-0

Built: 1900–08. Wainwright SECR design. 109 built.
Boiler Pressure: 160 lbf/sq in.   **Weight–Loco:** 43.8 tons.
Wheel Diameter: 5' 2".   **–Tender:** 38.25 tons.
Cylinders: 18½" x 26" (I).   **Valve Gear:** Stephenson. Slide valves.
Tractive Effort: 19520 lbf.   **BR Power Classification:** 2F.

BR	SR	SECR		
31592–DS239	A592–1592	592	Bluebell Railway	Longhedge 1902

CLASS U   2-6-0

Built: 1928–31. Maunsell SR design. 50 built (31610–639, 31790–809). 31790–809 were converted from Class K (River Class) 2-6-4Ts.
Boiler Pressure: 200 lbf/sq in superheated.   **Weight–Loco:** 61.9 (* 62.55) tons.
Wheel Diameters: 3' 1", 6' 0".   **–Tender:** 42.4 tons.
Cylinders: 19" x 28" (O).   **Valve Gear:** Walschaerts. Piston valves.
Tractive Effort: 23870 lbf.   **BR Power Classification:** 4MT.

*   Formerly Class K 2-6-4T A806 RIVER TORRIDGE built Ashford 1926.

BR	SR		
31618	A618–1618	Bluebell Railway	Brighton 1928
31625	A625–1625	Swanage Railway	Ashford 1929
31638	A638–1638	Bluebell Railway	Ashford 1931
31806*	A806–1806	Swanage Railway	Brighton 1928

CLASS D   4-4-0

Built: 1901–07. Wainwright SECR design. 51 built.
Boiler Pressure: 175 lbf/sq in.   **Weight–Loco:** 50 tons.
Wheel Diameters: 3' 7", 6' 8".   **–Tender:** 39.1 tons.
Cylinders: 19¼" x 26" (I).   **Valve Gear:** Stephenson. Slide valves.
Tractive Effort: 17910 lbf.   **BR Power Classification:** 1P.

BR	SR	SECR		
31737	A737–1737	737	National Railway Museum, York (N)	Ashford 1901

▲ Class C 0-6-0 592 is seen at London King's Cross on 7 February 2016 during filming for "Fantastic Beasts and Where to Find Them". **Alisdair Anderson**

▼ Class A1X "Terrier" 0-6-0T W11 at Haven Street on the Isle of Wight Steam Railway on 18 May 2014. **Nigel Gibbs**

CLASS N   2-6-0

Built: 1917–34. Maunsell SECR design. Some built by SR. 80 built.
Boiler Pressure: 200 lbf/sq in.   **Weight–Loco:** 59.4 tons.
Wheel Diameters: 3′ 1″, 5′ 6″.   **–Tender:** 39.25 tons.
Cylinders: 19″ x 28″ (O).   **Valve Gear:** Walschaerts. Piston valves.
Tractive Effort: 26 040 lbf.   **BR Power Classification:** 4MT.

BR	*SR*		
31874	A874–1874	Swanage Railway	Woolwich Arsenal 1925

CLASS E4   0-6-2T

Built: 1897–1903. R Billinton LBSCR design. 120 built.
Boiler Pressure: 160 lbf/sq in.   **Weight:** 56.75 tons.
Wheel Diameters: 5′ 0″, 4′ 0″.   **Cylinders:** 18″ x 26″ (I).
Valve Gear: Stephenson. Slide valves.   **Tractive Effort:** 19 090 lbf.
BR Power Classification: 2MT.

BR	*SR*	*LBSCR*			
32473	B473–2473	473	BIRCH GROVE	Bluebell Railway	Brighton 1898

CLASSES A1 & A1X   "TERRIER"   0-6-0T

Built: 1872–80 as Class A1*. Stroudley LBSCR design. Most rebuilt to A1X from 1911. 50 built.
Boiler Pressure: 150 lbf/sq in.   **Weight:** 28.25 tons.
Wheel Diameter: 4′ 0″.   **Cylinders:** 14″ († 13″, * 12″) x 20″ (I).
Valve Gear: Stephenson. Slide valves.   **Tractive Effort:** 10 410 lbf († 8890 lbf, * 7650 lbf).
BR Power Classification: 0P.

a   Air brakes   x   Dual (air/vacuum) brakes.

BR	*SR*	*LBSCR*			
32636 x†	B636–2636	72	FENCHURCH	Bluebell Railway	Brighton 1872
32640 a	W11–2640	40	NEWPORT	Isle of Wight Steam Railway	Brighton 1878
32646 a	W2–W8	46–646	FRESHWATER	Isle of Wight Steam Railway	Brighton 1876
32650 x*	B650–W9	50–650	WHITECHAPEL	Spa Valley Railway	Brighton 1876
DS680a*	A751–680S	54–654	WADDON	Canadian Railroad Historical Museum	
					Brighton 1875
32655	B655–2655	55–655	STEPNEY	Bluebell Railway	Brighton 1875
32662 a*	B662–2662	62–662	MARTELLO	Bressingham Steam Museum	
					Brighton 1875
32670		70	POPLAR	Kent & East Sussex Railway	Brighton 1872
32678 x	B678–W4–W14	78–678	KNOWLE	Kent & East Sussex Railway	Brighton 1880
– a	380S	82–682	BOXHILL	National Railway Museum, York (N)	
					Brighton 1880

32640   was also named BRIGHTON and was originally Isle of Wight Central Railway No. 11.
32646   was originally Freshwater Yarmouth and Newport Railway No. 2. It was sold to the LSWR
        and became 734. It has also been named NEWINGTON.
32650   became 515S (departmental) and was named FISHBOURNE when on the Isle of Wight.
        It is now named "SUTTON".
DS680   was sold to the SECR and became its No. 75.
32678   was named BEMBRIDGE when on the Isle of Wight.

CLASS Q1   0-6-0

Built: 1942. Bulleid SR "Austerity" design. Bulleid Firth Brown driving wheels. 40 built (33001–40).
Boiler Pressure: 230 lbf/sq in superheated.   **Weight–Loco:** 51.25 tons.
Wheel Diameter: 5′ 1″.   **–Tender:** 38 tons.
Cylinders: 19″ x 26″ (I).   **Valve Gear:** Stephenson. Slide valves.
Tractive Effort: 30 080 lbf.   **BR Power Classification:** 5F.

BR	*SR*		
33001	C1	National Railway Museum, York (N)	Brighton 1942

CLASSES WC & BB   WEST COUNTRY and BATTLE OF BRITAIN   4-6-2

Built: 1945–51. Bulleid SR design with "air smoothed" casing and Bulleid Firth Brown driving wheels. 110 built (34001–110). All preserved examples built at Brighton except 34101 (Eastleigh).
Boiler Pressure: 250 lbf/sq in superheated.   **Weight–Loco:** 86 (* 91.65) tons.
Wheel Diameters: 3' 1", 6' 2", 3' 1"   **–Tender:** 42.7, 47.9 or 47.75 tons.
Cylinders: 16³/₈" x 24" (3).
Valve Gear: Bulleid chain driven (* Walschaerts. Piston valves).
Tractive Effort: 27 720 lbf.   **BR Power Classification:** 7P.

*   Rebuilt at Eastleigh by Jarvis 1957–61 including the removal of the air-smoothed casing.
x   Dual (air/vacuum) brakes.

BR	SR			
34007	21C107	WADEBRIDGE	Mid Hants Railway	1945
34010*	21C110	SIDMOUTH	Swanage Railway	1945 reb 1959
34016*	21C116	BODMIN	West Coast Railway Company, Carnforth	1945 reb 1958
34023	21C123	BLACKMORE VALE	Bluebell Railway	1946
34027* x	21C127	TAW VALLEY	Severn Valley Railway	1946 reb 1957
34028*	21C128	EDDYSTONE	Swanage Railway	1946 reb 1958
34039*	21C139	BOSCASTLE	Great Central Railway	1946 reb 1959
34046* x	21C146	BRAUNTON	London & North Western Railway Heritage Company, Crewe	1946 reb 1959
34051	21C151	WINSTON CHURCHILL	National Railway Museum, Shildon (N)	1946
34053*	21C153	SIR KEITH PARK	Severn Valley Railway	1947 reb 1958
34058*	21C158	SIR FREDERICK PILE	Mid Hants Railway	1947 reb 1960
34059*	21C159	SIR ARCHIBALD SINCLAIR	Bluebell Railway	1947 reb 1960
34067 x	21C167	TANGMERE	West Coast Railway Company, Carnforth	1947
34070	21C170	MANSTON	Swanage Railway	1947
34072		257 SQUADRON	Swanage Railway	1948
34073		249 SQUADRON	West Coast Railway Company, Carnforth	1948
34081		92 SQUADRON	Nene Valley Railway	1948
34092		CITY OF WELLS	Keighley & Worth Valley Railway	1949
34101*		HARTLAND	North Yorkshire Moors Railway	1950 reb 1960
34105		SWANAGE	Mid Hants Railway	1950

34023 was named BLACKMOOR VALE to 04/50.
34092 was named WELLS to 03/50.

CLASS MN   MERCHANT NAVY   4-6-2

Built: 1941–49. Bulleid SR design with air smoothed casing and similar features to "WC" and "BB". All rebuilt 1956–59 by Jarvis to more conventional appearance. 30 built (35001–30). All locomotives were built and rebuilt at Eastleigh.
Boiler Pressure: 250 lbf/sq in superheated.   **Weight–Loco:** 97.9 tons.
Wheel Diameters: 3' 1", 6' 2", 3' 7".   **–Tender:** 47.8 tons.
Cylinders: 18" x 24" (3).   **Valve Gear:** Walschaerts. Piston valves.
Tractive Effort: 33 490 lbf.   **BR Power Classification:** 8P.

x   Dual (air/vacuum) brakes.   §   Sectioned.

BR	SR			
35005	21C5	CANADIAN PACIFIC	Arlington Fleet Services, Eastleigh Works	1941 reb 1959
35006	21C6	PENINSULAR & ORIENTAL S.N. Co.	Gloucestershire Warwickshire Railway	1941 reb 1959
35009	21C9	SHAW SAVILL	East Lancashire Railway	1942 reb 1957
35010	21C10	BLUE STAR	Colne Valley Railway	1942 reb 1957
35011	21C11	GENERAL STEAM NAVIGATION	Hope Farm, Sellindge	1944 reb 1959
35018	21C18	BRITISH INDIA LINE	West Coast Railway Company, Carnforth	1945 reb 1956
35022		HOLLAND-AMERICA LINE	London & North Western Railway Heritage Company, Crewe	1948 reb 1956
35025		BROCKLEBANK LINE	Hope Farm, Sellindge	1948 reb 1956
35027		PORT LINE	London & North Western Railway Heritage Company, Crewe	1948 reb 1957

▲ Unrebuilt West Country 4-6-2 34092 "WELLS" at Ewood Bridge on the East Lancashire Railway with a train for Rawtenstall on 8 August 2015. **Robert Falconer**

▼ Rebuilt Merchant Navy 4-6-2 35028 "CLAN LINE" passes Great Cheverell on the Berks & Hants route between Pewsey and Westbury with the London Victoria–Bristol VSOE on 14 May 2014. **Glen Batten**

| 35028 x | CLAN LINE | Stewarts Lane Depot, London | 1948 reb 1959 |
| 35029 § | ELLERMAN LINES | National Railway Museum, York (N) | 1949 reb 1959 |

35028 is currently under overhaul at London & North Western Railway Heritage Company, Crewe.

CLASS E1   0-6-0T

Built: 1874–83. Stroudley LBSCR design. 80 built.
Boiler Pressure: 160 lbf/sq in.
Wheel Diameter: 4' 6".
Valve Gear: Stephenson. Slide valves.
Weight: 44.15 tons.
Cylinders: 17" x 24" (I).
Tractive Effort: 17 470 lbf.

BR	SR	LBSCR			
–	B110	110	BURGUNDY	Isle of Wight Steam Railway	Brighton 1877

CLASS B1   "GLADSTONE"   0-4-2

Built: 1882–91. Stroudley LBSCR design. 49 built.
Boiler Pressure: 150 lbf/sq in.
Wheel Diameters: 6' 6", 4' 6".
Cylinders: 18¼" x 26" (I).
Tractive Effort: 14 160 lbf.
Weight–Loco: 38.7 tons.
–Tender: 29.35 tons.
Valve Gear: Stephenson. Slide valves.

Air brakes.

SR	LBSCR			
B618	214–618	GLADSTONE	National Railway Museum, York (N)	Brighton 1882

CLASS T3   4-4-0

Built: 1882–93. Adams LSWR design. 20 built.
Boiler Pressure: 175 lbf/sq in.
Wheel Diameters: 3' 7", 6' 7".
Cylinders: 19" x 26" (O).
Tractive Effort: 17 670 lbf.
Weight–Loco: 48.55 tons.
–Tender: 33.2 tons.
Valve Gear: Stephenson. Slide valves.

SR	LSWR		
E563–563	563	King's Cross Theatre, London (N)	Nine Elms 380/1893

On loan from the National Railway Museum, Shildon.

CANTERBURY & WHITSTABLE RAILWAY   0-4-0

Built: 1830. Robert Stephenson & Company design.
Boiler Pressure: 40 lbf/sq in.
Wheel Diameter: 4' 0".
Cylinders: 10½" x 18" (O).
Weight–Loco: 6.25 tons
–Tender:
Tractive Effort: 2680 lbf.

INVICTA	Museum of Canterbury	RS 24/1830

1.3. LONDON MIDLAND & SCOTTISH RAILWAY & CONSTITUENT COMPANIES' STEAM LOCOMOTIVES

GENERAL

The LMS was formed in 1923 by the amalgamation of the Midland Railway (MR), London & North Western Railway (LNWR), Caledonian Railway (CR), Glasgow & South Western Railway (GSWR) and Highland Railway (HR), plus a few smaller railways. Prior to this the North London Railway (NLR) and the Lancashire & Yorkshire Railway (L&Y) had been absorbed by the LNWR and the London, Tilbury & Southend Railway (LTSR) had been absorbed by the Midland Railway.

NUMBERING SYSTEM

Originally number series were allocated to divisions as follows:

1– 4999	Midland Division (Midland and North Staffordshire Railway).
5000– 9999	Western Division "A" (LNWR).
10000–13999	Western Division "B" (L&Y).
14000–17999	Northern Division (Scottish Railways).

From 1934 onwards, all LMS standard locomotives and new builds were numbered in the range from 1–9999, and any locomotives which would have had their numbers duplicated had 20000 added to their original number.

At nationalisation 40000 was added to all LMS numbers except that locomotives which were renumbered in the 2xxxx series were further renumbered generally in the 58xxx series. In the following section locomotives are listed in order of BR number or in the position of the BR number they would have carried if they had lasted into BR days, except for very old locomotives which are listed at the end of the section.

CLASSIFICATION SYSTEM

LMS locomotives did not generally have unique class designations but were referred to by their power classification which varied from 0 to 8 followed by the letters "P" for a passenger locomotive and "F" for a freight locomotive. BR adopted the LMS system and used the description "MT" to denote mixed traffic locomotives. The power classifications are generally shown in the class headings.

MIDLAND 115 CLASS (1P)   "SPINNER"   4-2-2

Built: 1896–99. Johnson design. 15 built (670–684).
Boiler Pressure: 170 lbf/sq in.
Wheel Diameters: 3' 10", 7' 9", 4' 4½".
Cylinders: 19" x 26" (I).
Tractive Effort: 15 280 lbf.

Weight–Loco: 43.95 tons.
–Tender: 21.55 tons.
Valve Gear: Stephenson. Slide valves.

LMS	MR		
673	118–673	National Railway Museum, York (N)	Derby 1897

CLASS 4P   COMPOUND   4-4-0

Built: 1902–03. Johnson Midland design, rebuilt by Deeley 1914–19 to a similar design to the Deeley compounds which were built 1905–09. A further similar batch was built by the LMS in 1924–32. 240 built (41000–199, 40900–939).
Boiler Pressure: 200 lbf/sq in superheated.
Wheel Diameters: 3' 6½", 7' 0".
Cylinders: One high pressure. 19" x 26" (I).
            Two low pressure. 21" x 26" (O).
Valve Gear: Stephenson. Slide valves on low pressure cylinders, piston valves on high pressure cylinder.
Tractive Effort: 23 205 lbf.

Weight–Loco: 61.7 tons.
–Tender: 45.9 tons.

BR	LMS	MR		
41000	1000	1000 (2631 pre-1907)	Barrow Hill Roundhouse (N)	Derby 1902 reb 1914

CLASS 2MT   2-6-2T

Built: 1946–52. Ivatt LMS design. 130 built (41200–329).
Boiler Pressure: 200 lbf/sq in superheated.
Wheel Diameters: 3' 0", 5' 0", 3' 0".
Valve Gear: Walschaerts. Piston valves.
Tractive Effort: 18 510 (* 17 410) lbf.

Weight: 65.2 (* 63.25) tons.
Cylinders: 16½" (* 16") x 24" (O).

41241*	Keighley & Worth Valley Railway	Crewe 1949
41298	Isle of Wight Steam Railway	Crewe 1951
41312	Mid Hants Railway	Crewe 1952
41313	East Somerset Railway	Crewe 1952

41313 is on loan from the Isle of Wight Steam Railway

CLASS 1F   0-6-0T

Built: 1878–99. Johnson Midland design. Rebuilt with Belpaire boiler 1926. 240 built (1660–1899).
Boiler Pressure: 150 lbf/sq in.
Wheel Diameter: 4' 7".
Valve Gear: Stephenson. Slide valves.

Weight: 45.45 tons.
Cylinders: 17" x 24" (I).
Tractive Effort: 16 080 lbf.

BR	LMS	MR		
41708	1708	1708	1418	Barrow Hill Roundhouse	Derby 1880

LTSR 79 CLASS (3P)   4-4-2T

Built: 1909. Whitelegg LTSR design. 4 built.
Boiler Pressure: 170 lbf/sq in.
Wheel Diameters: 3', 6", 6' 6", 3' 6".
Valve Gear: Stephenson. Slide valves.

Weight: 69.35 tons.
Cylinders: 19" x 26" (O).
Tractive Effort: 17 390 lbf.

BR	LMS	MR	LTSR			
41966	2148	2177	80	THUNDERSLEY	Bressingham Steam Museum (N)	RS 3367/1909

▲ Class 4P Compound 4-4-0 1000, part of the National Collection, on display at Barrow Hill Roundhouse on 27 February 2016. **Alisdair Anderson**

▼ Class 5MT "Crab" 2-6-0 13000 at the National Railway Museum, York on 5 September 2015. **Robert Pritchard**

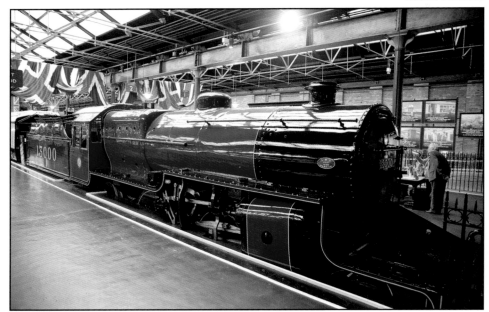

CLASS 4MT   2-6-4T

Built: 1945–51. Fairburn modification of Stanier design (built 1936–43). This in turn was a development of a Fowler design built 1927–34. 383 built (Stanier & Fairburn) (42050–299/425–494/537–699).
Boiler Pressure: 200 lbf/sq in superheated.
Wheel Diameters: 3' 3½", 5' 9", 3' 3½".
Valve Gear: Walschaerts. Piston valves.
Weight: 85.25 tons.
Cylinders: 19¾" x 26" (O).
Tractive Effort: 24670 lbf.

| 42073 | Lakeside & Haverthwaite Railway | Brighton 1950 |
| 42085 | Lakeside & Haverthwaite Railway | Brighton 1951 |

CLASS 4MT   2-6-4T

Built: 1934. Stanier LMS 3-cylinder design for LTSR line. 37 built (42500–536).
Boiler Pressure: 200 lbf/sq in superheated.
Wheel Diameters: 3' 3½", 5' 9", 3' 3½".
Valve Gear: Walschaerts. Piston valves.
Weight: 92.5 tons.
Cylinders: 16" x 26" (3).
Tractive Effort: 24600 lbf.

| *BR* | *LMS* | | |
| 42500 | 2500 | Barrow Hill Roundhouse (N) | Derby 1934 |

CLASS 5MT   "CRAB"   2-6-0

Built: 1926–32. Hughes LMS design. 245 built (42700–944).
Boiler Pressure: 180 lbf/sq in superheated.
Wheel Diameters: 3' 6½", 5' 6".
Cylinders: 21" x 26" (O).
Tractive Effort: 26580 lbf.
Weight—Loco: 66 tons.
       —Tender: 42.2 (* 41.5) tons.
Valve Gear: Walschaerts. Piston valves.

BR	*LMS*		
42700	13000–2700	National Railway Museum, York (N)	Horwich 1926
42765*	13065–2765	East Lancashire Railway	Crewe 5757/1927
42859	13159–2859	*Location unknown*	Crewe 5981/1930

CLASS 5MT   2-6-0

Built: 1933–34. Stanier LMS design. 40 built (42945–984).
Boiler Pressure: 225 lbf/sq in superheated.
Wheel Diameters: 3' 3½", 5' 6".
Cylinders: 18" x 28" (O).
Tractive Effort: 26290 lbf.
Weight—Loco: 69.1 tons.
       —Tender: 42.2 tons.
Valve Gear: Walschaerts. Piston valves.

| *BR* | *LMS* | | |
| 42968 | 13268–2968 | Severn Valley Railway | Crewe 1934 |

CLASS 4MT   2-6-0

Built: 1947–52. Ivatt design. 162 built (43000–161).
Boiler Pressure: 225 lbf/sq in superheated.
Wheel Diameters: 3' 0", 5' 3".
Cylinders: 17½" x 26" (O).
Tractive Effort: 24170 lbf.
Weight—Loco: 59.1 tons.
       —Tender: 40.3 tons.
Valve Gear: Walschaerts. Piston valves.

| 43106 | Severn Valley Railway | Darlington 2148/1951 |

CLASS 4F 0-6-0

Built: 1911–41. Fowler Midland "Big Goods" design. Locomotives from 44027 onwards were LMS design with tenders with solid coal guards (Midland tenders had coal rails). The preserved Midland locomotive was given an LMS tender by BR. 772 built (43835–44606).

Boiler Pressure: 175 lbf/sq in superheated. **Weight–Loco:** 48.75 tons.
Wheel Diameter: 5' 3". **–Tender:** 41.2 tons
Cylinders: 20" x 26" (I). **Valve Gear:** Stephenson. Piston valves.
Tractive Effort: 24560 lbf.

BR	LMS	MR		
43924	3924	3924	Keighley & Worth Valley Railway	Derby 1920
44027	4027		Vale of Berkeley Railway, Sharpness (N)	Derby 1924
44123	4123		Avon Valley Railway	Crewe 5658/1925
44422	4422		West Somerset Railway	Derby 1927

CLASS 5MT "BLACK 5" 4-6-0

Built: 1934–51. Stanier design. 842 built (44658–45499).
Boiler Pressure: 225 lbf/sq in superheated. **Weight–Loco:** 72.1 (* 75.3) tons.
Wheel Diameters: 3' 3½", 6' 0". **–Tender:** 53.65 (* 53.8) tons.
Cylinders: 18½" x 28" (O). **Tractive Effort:** 25450 lbf.
Valve Gear: Walschaerts. Piston valves. 44767 has outside Stephenson with piston valves.

x Dual (air/vacuum) brakes.

BR	LMS			
44767*	4767	"GEORGE STEPHENSON"	Midland Railway-Butterley	Crewe 1947
44806	4806	"KENNETH ALDCROFT"	North Yorkshire Moors Railway	Derby 1944
44871x	4871		East Lancashire Railway	Crewe 1945
44901	4901		Vale of Berkeley Railway, Sharpness	Crewe 1945
44932	4932		West Coast Railway Company, Carnforth	Horwich 1945
45000	5000		National Railway Museum, Shildon (N)	Crewe 216/1935
45025	5025		Strathspey Railway	VF 4570/1934
45110	5110		Severn Valley Railway	VF 4653/1935
45163	5163		Colne Valley Railway	AW 1204/1935
45212	5212		East Lancashire Railway	AW 1253/1935
45231	5231	"THE SHERWOOD FORESTER"	West Coast Railway Company, Carnforth	AW 1286/1936
45293	5293		Colne Valley Railway	AW 1348/1936
45305	5305	"ALDERMAN AE DRAPER"	Great Central Railway	AW 1360/1937
45337	5337		Llangollen Railway	AW 1392/1937
45379	5379		Mid Hants Railway	AW 1434/1937
45407x	5407	"THE LANCASHIRE FUSILIER"	East Lancashire Railway	AW 1462/1937
45428	5428	"ERIC TREACY"	North Yorkshire Moors Railway	AW 1483/1937
45491	5491		Great Central Railway	Derby 1943

CLASS 6P (Formerly 5XP) JUBILEE 4-6-0

Built: 1934–36. Stanier taper boiler development of Patriot class. 191 built (45552–742).
Boiler Pressure: 225 lbf/sq in superheated. **Weight–Loco:** 79.55 tons.
Wheel Diameters: 3' 3½", 6' 9". **–Tender:** 53.65 tons.
Cylinders: 17" x 26" (3). **Valve Gear:** Walschaerts. Piston valves.
Tractive Effort: 26610 lbf.

* Fitted with double chimney.

BR	LMS			
45593	5593	KOLHAPUR	Tyseley Locomotive Works	NBL 24151/1934
45596*	5596	BAHAMAS	Tyseley Locomotive Works	NBL 24154/1935
45690	5690	LEANDER	West Coast Railway Company, Carnforth	Crewe 288/1936
45699	5699	GALATEA	West Coast Railway Company, Carnforth	Crewe 297/1936

45596 is visiting Tyseley Locomotive Works from the Keighley & Worth Valley Railway for overhaul.

▲ Class 4F 0-6-0 44422 pilots Class 7F 2-8-0 53808 on the approach to Bishops Lydeard, West Somerset Railway, with the 08.25 from Minehead on 5 March 2016. **David Hunt**

▼ Class 5MT "Black 5" 4-6-0 45231 "THE SHERWOOD FORESTER" passes Lostock Hall Junction with the Lancaster–Carlisle "Fellsman" on 12 August 2015. **Fred Kerr**

CLASS 7P (Formerly 6P)   ROYAL SCOT   4-6-0

Built: 1927–30. Fowler parallel design. All rebuilt 1943–55 with taper boilers and curved smoke deflectors. 71 built (46100–170).

Boiler Pressure: 250 lbf/sq in superheated.
Wheel Diameters: 3′ 3½″, 6′ 9″.
Cylinders: 18″ x 26″ (3).
Tractive Effort: 33150 lbf.

Weight–Loco: 83 tons.
–Tender: 54.65 tons.
Valve Gear: Walschaerts. Piston valves.

BR	LMS			
46100	6100	ROYAL SCOT	London & North Western Railway Heritage Company, Crewe	Derby 1930 reb Crewe 1950
46115	6115	SCOTS GUARDSMAN	West Coast Railway Company, Carnforth	NBL 23610/1927 reb Crewe 1947

6100 was built as 6152 THE KING'S DRAGOON GUARDSMAN. This loco swapped identities permanently with 6100 ROYAL SCOT in 1933 for a tour of the USA.

CLASS 8P (Formerly 7P)   PRINCESS ROYAL   4-6-2

Built: 1933–35. Stanier design. 13 built (46200–212).

Boiler Pressure: 250 lbf/sq in superheated.
Wheel Diameters: 3′ 0″, 6′ 6″, 3′ 9″.
Cylinders: 16¼″ x 28″ (4).
Tractive Effort: 40290 lbf.

Weight–Loco: 105.5 tons.
–Tender: 54.65 tons.
Valve Gear: Walschaerts. Piston valves.

x   Dual (air/vacuum) brakes.

BR	LMS			
46201 x	6201	PRINCESS ELIZABETH	Tyseley Locomotive Works	Crewe 107/1933
46203	6203	PRINCESS MARGARET ROSE	Midland Railway-Butterley	Crewe 253/1935

CLASS 8P (Formerly 7P)   PRINCESS CORONATION   4-6-2

Built: 1937–48. Stanier design. 24 of this class were built streamlined but had the casing removed later. Certain locomotives were built with single chimneys, but all finished up with double chimneys. The tenders were fitted with steam driven coal-pushers. 38 built (46220–257).

Boiler Pressure: 250 lbf/sq in superheated.
Wheel Diameters: 3′ 0″, 6′ 9″, 3′ 9″.
Cylinders: 16½″ x 28″ (4).
Tractive Effort: 40000 lbf.

Weight–Loco: 105.25 tons.
–Tender: 56.35 tons.
Valve Gear: Walschaerts. Piston valves.

[1]   Built streamlined and with single chimney. Double chimney fitted 1943. Destreamlined 1947–2009.
[2]   Never streamlined and built with single chimney. Double chimney fitted 1941. Dual (air/vacuum) brakes.
[3]   Built streamlined and with double chimney. Destreamlined 1946.

BR	LMS			
46229[1]	6229	DUCHESS OF HAMILTON	National Railway Museum, York (N)	Crewe 1938
46233[2]	6233	DUCHESS OF SUTHERLAND	Midland Railway-Butterley	Crewe 1938
46235[3]	6235	CITY OF BIRMINGHAM	Thinktank: Birmingham Science Museum	Crewe 1939

6229 was numbered 6220 whilst in the USA between 1938 and 1943.

CLASS 2MT   2-6-0

Built: 1946–53. Ivatt design. 128 built (46400–527).
Boiler Pressure: 200 lbf/sq in superheated.   **Weight–Loco:** 47.1 (* 48.45) tons.
Wheel Diameters: 3' 0", 5' 0".   **–Tender:** 37.15 tons.
Cylinders: 16" (* 16½") x 24" (O).   **Valve Gear:** Walschaerts. Piston valves.
Tractive Effort: 17 410 (* 18 510) lbf.

46428		East Lancashire Railway	Crewe 1948
46441		Ribble Steam Railway	Crewe 1950
46443		Severn Valley Railway	Crewe 1950
46447		East Somerset Railway	Crewe 1950
46464		Caledonian Railway	Crewe 1950
46512*	"E.V. COOPER ENGINEER"	Strathspey Railway	Swindon 1952
46521*		Great Central Railway	Swindon 1953

CLASS 3F   "JINTY"   0-6-0T

Built: 1924–31. Fowler LMS development of Midland design. 422 built (47260–47681).
Boiler Pressure: 160 lbf/sq in.   **Weight:** 49.5 tons.
Wheel Diameter: 4' 7".   **Cylinders:** 18" x 26" (I).
Valve Gear: Stephenson. Slide valves.   **Tractive Effort:** 20 830 lbf.

BR	LMS		
47279	7119–7279	Keighley & Worth Valley Railway	VF 3736/1924
47298	7138–7298	Riley & Son (Electromec), Heywood	HE 1463/1924
47324	16407–7324	East Lancashire Railway	NBL 23403/1926
47327	16410–7327	Midland Railway-Butterley	NBL 23406/1926
47357	16440–7357	Midland Railway-Butterley	NBL 23436/1926
47383	16466–7383	Severn Valley Railway	VF 3954/1926
47406	16489–7406	Great Central Railway	VF 3977/1926
47445	16528–7445	Midland Railway-Butterley	HE 1529/1927
47493	16576–7493	Spa Valley Railway	VF 4195/1928
47564	16647–7564	Midland Railway-Butterley	HE 1580/1928

47564 was latterly used as a stationary boiler numbered–2022.

CLASS 8F   2-8-0

Built: 1934–46. Stanier design. 331 built for LMS (8000–8225, 8301–8399, 8490–8495). A further 521 were built to Ministry of Supply (208) Railway Executive Committee (245) and LNER (68) orders. Many of these operated on Britain's Railways with 228 being shipped overseas during the war. Post-war many were taken into LMS/BR stock including some returned from overseas.
Boiler Pressure: 225 lbf/sq in superheated.   **Weight–Loco:** 72.1 tons.
Wheel Diameters: 3' 3½", 4' 8½".   **–Tender:** 53.65 tons.
Cylinders: 18½" x 28" (O).   **Valve Gear:** Walschaerts. Piston valves.
Tractive Effort: 32 440 lbf.

§   Became Persian Railways 41.109.

BR	LMS	WD		
48151	8151		West Coast Railway Company, Carnforth	Crewe 1942
48173	8173		Churnet Valley Railway	Crewe 1943
48305	8305		Great Central Railway	Crewe 1943
48431	8431		Keighley & Worth Valley Railway	Swindon 1944
48624	8624		Great Central Railway	Ashford 1943
48773	8233	307–70307–500§	Severn Valley Railway	NBL 24607/1940

48518 has been dismantled at the Llangollen Railway and the boiler used for the replica 1014 COUNTY OF GLAMORGAN.

▲ Class 7P 4-6-0 46100 "ROYAL SCOT" works a Crewe–Carlisle "Scot Commemorative" tour north along the Cumbrian Coast line near Bootle on 16 April 2015. **Ian Pilkington**

▼ Class 2MT 2-6-0 46521, ex-works in BR green livery, passes Woodthorpe shortly after departure from Loughborough with the 15.15 to Leicester North on 8 May 2016. **Paul Biggs**

In addition the following two locomotives were built to Ministry of Supply orders and have been repatriated to Great Britain:

* Number allocated but never carried.

Dual (air/vacuum) brakes.

BR	LMS	WD	TCDD		
–	8274*	348	45160	Nottingham Transport Heritage Centre	NBL 24648/1940
–		554	45170	Bo'ness & Kinneil Railway	NBL 24755/1942

LNWR CLASS G2 (7F)   0-8-0

Built: 1921–22. Beames development of earlier Bowen-Cooke LNWR design. 60 built (49395–454). In addition many earlier locos were rebuilt to similar condition.
Boiler Pressure: 175 lbf/sq in superheated.   **Weight–Loco:** 62 tons.
Wheel Diameter: 4' 5½".   **–Tender:** 40.75 tons.
Cylinders: 20½" x 24" (I).   **Valve Gear:** Joy. Piston valves.
Tractive Effort: 28040 lbf.

BR	LMS	LNWR		
49395	9395	485	National Railway Museum, Shildon (N)	Crewe 5662/1921

L&Y CLASS 5 (2P)   2-4-2T

Built: 1889–1909. Aspinall L&Y design. 309 built.
Boiler Pressure: 180 lbf/sq in.   **Weight:** 55.45 tons.
Wheel Diameters: 3' 7⅛", 5' 8", 3' 7⅛".   **Cylinders:** 18" x 26" (I).
Valve Gear: Joy. Slide valves.   **Tractive Effort:** 18990 lbf.

BR	LMS	L&Y		
50621	10621	1008	National Railway Museum, York (N)	Horwich 1/1889

L&Y CLASS 21 (0F)   "PUG"   0-4-0ST

Built: 1891–1910. Aspinall L&Y design. 57 built.
Boiler Pressure: 160 lbf/sq in.   **Weight:** 21.25 tons.
Wheel Diameter: 3' 0¾".   **Cylinders:** 13" x 18" (O).
Valve Gear: Stephenson. Slide valves.   **Tractive Effort:** 11370 lbf.

BR	LMS	L&Y		
51218	11218	68	Keighley & Worth Valley Railway	Horwich 811/1901
	11243	19	Ribble Steam Railway	Horwich 1097/1910

L&Y CLASS 23 (2F)   0-6-0ST

Built: 1891–1900. Aspinall rebuild of Barton Wright L&Y 0-6-0. 230 rebuilt.
Boiler Pressure: 140 lbf/sq in.   **Weight:** 43.85 tons.
Wheel Diameter: 4' 6".   **Cylinders:** 17½" x 26" (I).
Valve Gear: Joy. Slide valves.   **Tractive Effort:** 17590 lbf.

BR	LMS	L&Y		
–	11456	752	Keighley & Worth Valley Railway	BP 1989/1881 reb. Hor. 1896

L&Y CLASS 25 (2F)   0-6-0

Built: 1876–87. Barton Wright L&Y design. 280 built.
Boiler Pressure: 140 lbf/sq in.   **Weight–Loco:** 39.05 tons.
Wheel Diameter: 4' 6".   **–Tender:** 28.5 tons.
Cylinders: 17½" x 26" (I).   **Valve Gear:** Joy. Slide valves.
Tractive Effort: 17590 lbf.

BR	LMS	L&Y		
52044	12044	957	Keighley & Worth Valley Railway	BP 2840/1887

L&Y CLASS 27 (3F)   0-6-0

Built: 1889–1917. Aspinall L&Y design. 448 built.
Boiler Pressure: 180 lbf/sq in.   **Weight–Loco:** 44.3 tons.
Wheel Diameter: 5″ 1″.   **–Tender:** 26.1 tons.
Cylinders: 18″ x 26″ (I).   **Valve Gear:** Joy. Slide valves.
Tractive Effort: 21 170 lbf.

BR	*LMS*	*L&Y*		
52322	12322	1300	Ribble Steam Railway	Horwich 420/1896

CLASS 7F   2-8-0

Built: 1914–25. Fowler design for Somerset & Dorset Joint Railway (Midland and LSWR jointly owned). 11 built (53800–810).
Boiler Pressure: 190 lbf/sq in superheated.   **Weight–Loco:** 64.75 tons.
Wheel Diameters: 3′ 3½″, 4′ 7½″.   **–Tender:** 26.1 tons.
Cylinders: 21″ x 28″ (O).   **Valve Gear:** Walschaerts. Piston valves.
Tractive Effort: 35 950 lbf.

BR	*LMS*	*S&DJR*		
53808	9678–13808	88	West Somerset Railway	RS 3894/1925
53809	9679–13809	89	Midland Railway-Butterley	RS 3895/1925

53808 is on loan from the Somerset & Dorset Railway Trust, Washford.

CALEDONIAN RAILWAY (1P)   4-2-2

Built: 1886. Drummond design. 1 built for the Edinburgh International Exhibition.
Boiler Pressure: 160 lbf/sq in.   **Weight–Loco:** 41.35 tons.
Wheel Diameters: 3′ 6″, 7′ 0″, 4′ 6″.   **–Tender:** 35.4 tons.
Cylinders: 18″ x 26″ (I).   **Valve Gear:** Stephenson. Slide valves.
Tractive Effort: 13 640 lbf.

BR	*LMS*	*CR*		
–	14010	123	Glasgow Riverside Museum	N 3553/1886

CALEDONIAN RAILWAY 439 CLASS (2P)   0-4-4T

Built: 1900–14. McIntosh design. 68 built.
Boiler Pressure: 160 lbf/sq in.   **Weight:** 53.95 tons.
Wheel Diameters: 5′ 9″, 3′ 2″.   **Cylinders:** 18″ x 26″ (I).
Valve Gear: Stephenson. Slide valves. **Tractive Effort:** 16 600 lbf.

Dual (air/vacuum) brakes.

BR	*LMS*	*CR*		
55189	15189	419	Bo'ness & Kinneil Railway	St Rollox 1907

GSWR 322 CLASS (3F)   0-6-0T

Built: 1917. Drummond design. 3 built.
Boiler Pressure: 160 lbf/sq in.   **Weight:** 40 tons.
Wheel Diameter: 4′ 2″.   **Cylinders:** 17″ x 22″ (O).
Valve Gear: Walschaerts. Piston valves. **Tractive Effort:** 17 290 lbf.

BR	*LMS*	*GSWR*		
–	16379	9	Glasgow Riverside Museum	NBL 21521/1917

▲ Class 8F 2-8-0 8274 at Barrow Hill Roundhouse on 23 September 2015. **Fred Kerr**

▼ Highland Railway (4F) 4-6-0 103 and above it GSWR 322 Class (3F) 0-6-0T No. 9 on display at the Glasgow Riverside Museum on 12 September 2015. **Robert Pritchard**

CALEDONIAN RAILWAY 812 CLASS (3F)   0-6-0

Built: 1899–1900. McIntosh design. 96 built (57550–645).
Boiler Pressure: 160 lbf/sq in.
Wheel Diameter: 5' 0".
Cylinders: 18½" x 26" (I).
Tractive Effort: 20 170 lbf.

Weight—Loco: 45.7 tons.
      —Tender: 37.9 tons.
Valve Gear: Stephenson. Slide valves.

Air brakes.

BR	LMS	CR		
57566	17566	828	Strathspey Railway	St Rollox 1899

HIGHLAND RAILWAY (4F)   "JONES GOODS"   4-6-0

Built: 1894. Jones design. 15 built.
Boiler Pressure: 175 lbf/sq in.
Wheel Diameters: 3' 3", 5' 3".
Cylinders: 20" x 26" (O).
Tractive Effort: 24 560 lbf.

Weight—Loco: 56 tons.
      —Tender: 38.35 tons.
Valve Gear: Stephenson. Slide valves.

BR	LMS	HR		
–	17916	103	Glasgow Riverside Museum	SS 4022/1894

NORTH LONDON RAILWAY 75 CLASS (2F)   0-6-0T

Built: 1879–1905. Park design. 30 built.
Boiler Pressure: 160 lbf/sq in.
Wheel Diameter: 4' 4".
Valve Gear: Stephenson. Slide valves.

Weight: 45.55 tons.
Cylinders: 17" x 24" (O).
Tractive Effort: 18 140 lbf.

BR	LMS	LNWR	NLR		
58850	7505–27505	2650	76–116	Bluebell Railway	Bow 181/1881

LNWR COAL TANK (2F)   0-6-2T

Built: 1881–97. Webb design. 300 built.
Boiler Pressure: 150 lbf/sq in.
Wheel Diameters: 4' 5½", 3' 9".
Valve Gear: Stephenson. Slide valves.

Weight: 43.75 tons.
Cylinders: 17" x 24" (I).
Tractive Effort: 16 530 lbf.

BR	LMS	LNWR		
58926	7799	1054	Keighley & Worth Valley Railway	Crewe 2979/1888

MIDLAND 156 CLASS (1P)   2-4-0

Built: 1866–68. Kirtley design. 31 built.
Boiler Pressure: 140 lbf/sq in.
Wheel Diameters: 4' 3", 6' 3".
Cylinders: 18" x 24" (I).
Tractive Effort: 12 340 lbf.

Weight—Loco: 41.25 tons.
      —Tender: 34.85 tons.
Valve Gear: Stephenson. Slide valves.

BR	LMS	MR		
–	2–20002	158–158A–2	Midland Railway-Butterley (N)	Derby 1866

NORTH STAFFS RAILWAY New L CLASS (3F)   0-6-2T

Built: 1903–23. Hookham design. 34 built.
Boiler Pressure: 175 lbf/sq in.
Wheel Diameters: 5' 0", 4' 0".
Valve Gear: Stephenson. Slide valves.

Weight: 64.95 tons.
Cylinders: 18½" x 26" (I).
Tractive Effort: 22 060 lbf.

LMS	NSR		
2271	2	Foxfield Railway	Stoke 1923

Although built in 1923, this loco carried an NSR number, since the NSR was not taken over by the LMS until 1 July 1923.

LNWR PRECEDENT (1P)

2-4-0

Built: 1874–82 (renewed 1887–1901). Webb design. 166 built.
Boiler Pressure: 150 lbf/sq in.
Wheel Diameters: 3' 9", 6' 9".
Cylinders: 17" x 24" (I).
Tractive Effort: 10 920 lbf.

Weight–Loco: 35.6 tons.
–Tender: 25 tons.
Valve Gear: Allan.

LMS	LNWR			
5031	790	HARDWICKE	National Railway Museum, Shildon (N)	Crewe 3286/1892

LNWR

2-2-2

Built: 1847. Trevithick design rebuilt by Ramsbottom in 1858.
Boiler Pressure: 140 lbf/sq in.
Wheel Diameters: 3' 6", 8' 6", 3' 6".
Cylinders: 17¼" x 24" (O).
Tractive Effort: 8330 lbf.

Weight–Loco: 29.9 tons.
–Tender: 25 tons.
Valve Gear: Stephenson. Slide valves.

LNWR			
173–3020	CORNWALL	National Railway Museum, Shildon (N)	Crewe 35/1847

LNWR

0-4-0ST

Built: 1865. Ramsbottom design.
Boiler Pressure: 120 lbf/sq in.
Wheel Diameter: 4' 0".
Tractive Effort: 8330 lbf.

Weight: 22.75 tons.
Cylinders: 14" x 20" (I).

LNWR		
1439–1985–3042	Ribble Steam Railway (N)	Crewe 842/1865

▲ LNWR Precedent (1P) 2-4-0 790 "HARDWICKE" on display at the National Railway Museum, Shildon on 5 September 2015.
Robert Pritchard

GRAND JUNCTION RAILWAY   2-2-2

Built: 1845. Trevithick design.
Boiler Pressure: 120 lbf/sq in.
Wheel Diameters: 3' 6", 6' 0", 3' 6".
Cylinders: 15" x 20" (O).
Tractive Effort: 6375 lbf.

Weight—Loco: 20.4 tons.
—Tender: 16.4 tons. (stored at the Science
Museum Store, Wroughton, Wiltshire).
Valve Gear: Allan.

LNWR	GJR			
49	49–1868	COLUMBINE	Science Museum, London (N)	Crewe 25/1845

FURNESS RAILWAY   0-4-0

Built: 1846.
Boiler Pressure: 110 lbf/sq in.
Wheel Diameter: 4' 9".
Cylinders: 14" x 24" (I).
Tractive Effort: 7720 lbf.

Weight—Loco: 20 tons.
—Tender: 13 tons.
Valve Gear: Stephenson. Slide valves.

3	COPPERNOB	National Railway Museum, York (N)	BCK 1846

FURNESS RAILWAY   0-4-0

Built: 1863 as 0-4-0. Sold in 1870 to Barrow Steelworks and numbered 7. Rebuilt 1915 as
0-4-0ST. Restored to original condition 1999.
Boiler Pressure: 120 lbf/sq in.
Cylinders: 15½" x 24"(I).

Wheel Diameter: 4'10".
Tractive Effort: 10 140 lbf.

20	National Railway Museum, Shildon	SS 1435/1863

On loan from the Ribble Steam Railway based Furness Railway Trust

FURNESS RAILWAY   0-4-0ST

Built: 1865 as 0-4-0. Sold in 1873 to Barrow Steelworks and numbered 17. Rebuilt 1921 as
0-4-0ST.
Boiler Pressure: 120 lbf/sq in.
Cylinders: 15½" x 24"(I).

Wheel Diameter: 4'3".
Tractive Effort: 11 532 lbf.

FR	Present		
25	6	West Coast Railway Company, Carnforth	SS 1585/1865

LIVERPOOL & MANCHESTER RAILWAY   0-2-2

Built: 1829 for the Rainhill trials.
Boiler Pressure: 50 lbf/sq in.
Wheel Diameters: 4' 8½", 2' 6".
Cylinders: 8" x 17" (O).

Weight—Loco: 4.25 tons.
—Tender: 5.2 tons.
Tractive Effort: 820 lbf.

ROCKET	Science Museum, London (N)	RS 1/1829

LIVERPOOL & MANCHESTER RAILWAY   0-4-0

Built: 1829 for the Rainhill trials.
Boiler Pressure: 50 lbf/sq in.
Wheel Diameter: 4' 6".
Cylinders: 7" x 18" (O).

Weight—Loco: 4.25 tons.
—Tender: 5.2 tons.
Tractive Effort: 690 lbf.

SANS PAREIL	National Railway Museum, Shildon (N)	Hack 1829

LIVERPOOL & MANCHESTER RAILWAY

0-4-2

Built: 1838–39. 4 built. The survivor was the star of the film "The Titfield Thunderbolt".
Boiler Pressure: 50 lbf/sq in.
Wheel Diameters: 5' 0", 3' 3".
Cylinders: 14" x 24" (I).
Weight–Loco: 14.45 tons.
–Tender:
Tractive Effort: 3330 lbf.

L&MR	*LNWR*			
57	116	LION	Museum of Liverpool	TKL 1838

MERSEY RAILWAY

0-6-4T

Built: 1885. Withdrawn 1903 on electrification. No. 5 was sold to Shipley colliery in Derbyshire.
Boiler Pressure: 150 lbf/sq in.
Wheel Diameters: 4' 7", 3' 0".
Valve Gear: Stephenson. Slide valves.
Weight: 67.85 tons.
Cylinders: 21" x 26" (I).
Tractive Effort: 26 600 lbf.

1	THE MAJOR	Rail Transport Museum, Thirlmere, NSW, Australia	BP 2601/1885
5	CECIL RAIKES	Museum of Liverpool Store, Bootle	BP 2605/1885

HIGHLAND RAILWAY (DUKE OF SUTHERLAND)

0-4-4T

Built: 1895 for the Duke of Sutherland. Exported to Canada 1965, repatriated to Britain 2011.
Boiler Pressure: 150 lbf/sq in.
Wheel Diameters: 4' 6", 2' 6".
Valve Gear: Stephenson.
Weight: 25 tons.
Cylinders: 13" x 18" (I).
Tractive Effort: 7183 lbf.

–	DUNROBIN	Severn Valley Railway	SS 4085/1895

Visiting the Severn Valley Railway for overhaul from Beamish: The Living Museum of the North.

▲ Furness Railway 0-4-0 No. 20 at Bo'ness during a visit to the Bo'ness & Kinneil Railway for a steam gala on 23 October 2015.
Ian Lothian

1.4. LONDON & NORTH EASTERN RAILWAY AND CONSTITUENT COMPANIES' STEAM LOCOMOTIVES

GENERAL

The LNER was formed in 1923 by the amalgamation of the Great Northern Railway (GNR), North Eastern Railway (NER), Great Eastern Railway (GER), Great Central Railway (GCR), North British Railway (NBR) and Great North of Scotland Railway (GNSR). Prior to this the Hull & Barnsley Railway (H&B) had been absorbed by the NER in 1922.

The newly-built Class A1 Pacific 60163 TORNADO can be found in the New Build Steam Locomotives section on page 72.

NUMBERING SYSTEM

Initially pre-grouping locomotive numbers were retained, but in September 1923 suffix letters started to be applied depending upon the works which repaired the locomotives. In 1924 locomotives were renumbered in blocks as follows: NER locomotives remained unaltered, GNR locomotives had 3000 added, GCR 5000, GNSR 6800, GER 7000 and NBR 9000. New locomotives filled in gaps between existing numbers. By 1943 the numbering of new locomotives had become so haphazard that it was decided to completely renumber locomotives so that locomotives of a particular class were all contained in the same block of numbers. This was carried out in 1946. On nationalisation in 1948, 60000 was added to LNER numbers.

In the following section locomotives are listed in order of BR number or in the position of the BR number they would have carried if they had lasted into BR days, except for very old locomotives which are listed at the end of the section.

CLASSIFICATION SYSTEM

The LNER gave each class a unique code consisting of a letter denoting the wheel arrangement and a number denoting the individual class within the wheel arrangement. Route availability (RA) was denoted by a number, the higher the number the more restricted the route availability.

▲ Recently returned to operational condition is A3 4-6-2 60103 "FLYING SCOTSMAN". On 13 March 2016 the iconic locomotive leaves Goathland for Pickering on the North Yorkshire Moors Railway.
Robert Falconer

▲ Class A4 4-6-2 60007 "SIR NIGEL GRESLEY" heads north between Dawlish Warren and Cockwood with the return "Dartmouth Express" (16.45 Kingswear–Guildford) on 19 April 2014. **Tony Christie**

▼ Class B1 4-6-0 61306 "MAYFLOWER" drifts through Maidstone East with a Salisbury–Canterbury "Cathedrals Express" on 29 August 2015. **Robert Pritchard**

CLASS A4   4-6-2

Built: 1935–38. Gresley streamlined design. "MALLARD" attained the world speed record for a steam locomotive of 126 mph in 1938 and is still unbeaten. 35 built (2509–12, 4462–69/82–4500/4900–03).

Boiler Pressure: 250 lbf/sq in superheated.   **Weight–Loco:** 102.95 tons.
Wheel Diameters: 3' 2", 6' 8", 3' 8".   **–Tender:** 64.15 tons.
Cylinders: 18½" x 26" (3).   **Tractive Effort:** 35450 lbf.
Valve Gear: Walschaerts with derived motion for inside cylinder. Piston valves.
BR Power Classification: 8P.   **RA:** 9.

x   Dual (air/vacuum) brakes.

BR	LNER			
60007x	4498–7	SIR NIGEL GRESLEY	North Yorkshire Moors Railway	Doncaster 1863/1937
60008	4496–8	DWIGHT D. EISENHOWER	National Railroad Museum, Green Bay, Wisconsin, USA	Doncaster 1861/1937
60009x	4488–9	UNION OF SOUTH AFRICA	Thornton Depot, Fife	Doncaster 1853/1937
60010	4489–10	DOMINION OF CANADA	Canadian Railway Museum, Montreal, Canada	Doncaster 1854/1937
60019	4464–19	BITTERN	London & North Western Railway Heritage Company, Crewe	Doncaster 1866/1937
60022	4468–22	MALLARD	National Railway Museum, York (N)	Doncaster 1870/1938

60007 is currently under overhaul at the National Railway Museum, York.
60008 was originally named GOLDEN SHUTTLE and 60010 was originally named WOODCOCK.
60019 sometimes operates with a second tender carrying extra water.

CLASS A3   4-6-2

Built: 1922–35. Gresley design. Built as Class A1 (later reclassified A10 after the Peppercorn A1s were being designed), but rebuilt to A3 in 1947. 79 built. (60035–113). Fitted (1959) with Kylchap blastpipe, double chimney and (1961) German-style smoke deflectors. Restored to single chimney on preservation in 1963, but reverted to double chimney in 1993. The locomotive has also carried the number 4472 in preservation, a number it never carried as an A3, since it was renumbered 103 in 1946.

Boiler Pressure: 220 lbf/sq in superheated.   **Weight–Loco:** 96.25 tons.
Wheel Diameters: 3' 2", 6' 8", 3' 8".   **–Tender:** 62.4 tons.
Cylinders: 19" x 26" (3).   **Tractive Effort:** 32910 lbf.
Valve Gear: Walschaerts with derived motion for inside cylinder. Piston valves.
BR Power Classification: 7P.   **RA:** 9.

Dual (air/vacuum) brakes.

BR	LNER			
60103	1472–4472–502–103	FLYING SCOTSMAN	National Railway Museum, York (N)	Doncaster 1564/1923

CLASS A2   4-6-2

Built: 1947–48. Peppercorn development of Thompson design. 15 built.
Boiler Pressure: 250 lbf/sq in superheated.   **Weight–Loco:** 101 tons.
Wheel Diameters: 3' 2", 6' 2", 3' 8".   **–Tender:** 60.35 tons.
Cylinders: 19" x 26" (3).   **Valve Gear:** Walschaerts. Piston valves.
Tractive Effort: 40430 lbf.   **BR Power Classification:** 8P.
RA: 9.

60532		BLUE PETER	London & North Western Railway Heritage Company, Crewe	Doncaster 2023/1948

CLASS V2   2-6-2

Built: 1936–44. Gresley design for express passenger and freight. 184 built (60800–983).
Boiler Pressure: 220 lbf/sq in superheated.   **Weight–Loco:** 93.1 tons.
Wheel Diameters: 3′ 2″, 6′ 2″, 3′ 8″.   **–Tender:** 52 tons.
Cylinders: 18½″ x 26″ (3).   **Tractive Effort:** 33730 lbf.
Valve Gear: Walschaerts with derived motion for inside cylinder. Piston valves.
BR Power Classification: 6MT.   **RA:** 9.

BR	LNER		
60800	4771–800	GREEN ARROW	National Railway Museum, Shildon (N) Doncaster 1837/1936

CLASS B1   4-6-0

Built: 1942–52. Thompson design. 410 built (61000–409).
Boiler Pressure: 225 lbf/sq in superheated.   **Weight–Loco:** 71.15 tons.
Wheel Diameters: 3′ 2″, 6′ 2″.   **–Tender:** 52 tons.
Cylinders: 20″ x 26″ (O).   **Valve Gear:** Walschaerts. Piston valves.
Tractive Effort: 26880 lbf.   **BR Power Classification:** 5MT.
RA: 5.

BR	LNER	Present		
61264	1264		North Yorkshire Moors Railway	NBL 26165/1947
61306		1306 "MAYFLOWER"	North Norfolk Railway	NBL 26207/1948

The original MAYFLOWER was 61379. 61264 also carried Departmental 29.

CLASS B12   4-6-0

Built: 1911–28. Holden GER design. 81 built (1500–70, 8571–80). GER Class S69.
61572 Rebuilt to B12/3 1933.
Boiler Pressure: 180 lbf/sq in superheated.   **Weight –Loco:** 69.5 tons.
Wheel Diameters: 3′ 3″, 6′ 6″.   **–Tender:** 39.3 tons.
Cylinders: 20″ x 28″ (I).   **Valve Gear:** Stephenson. Piston valves.
Tractive Effort: 21970 lbf.   **BR Power Classification:** 4P.
RA: 5.

Dual (air/vacuum) brakes.

BR	LNER			
61572	8572	1572	North Norfolk Railway	BP 6488/1928

CLASS K4   2-6-0

Built: 1937–38. Gresley design for West Highland line. 6 built (61993–98).
Boiler Pressure: 200 lbf/sq in superheated.   **Weight–Loco:** 68.4 tons.
Wheel Diameters: 3′ 2″, 5′ 2″.   **–Tender:** 44.2 tons.
Cylinders: 18½″ x 26″ (3).   **Tractive Effort:** 36600 lbf.
Valve Gear: Walschaerts with derived motion for inside cylinder. Piston valves.
BR Power Classification: 5P6F.   **RA:** 6.

BR	LNER			
61994	3442–1994	THE GREAT MARQUESS	Thornton Depot, Fife	Darlington 1761/1938

CLASS K1   2-6-0

Built: 1949–50. Peppercorn design. 70 built (62001–070).
Boiler Pressure: 225 lbf/sq in superheated.   **Weight–Loco:** 66 tons.
Wheel Diameters: 3′ 2″, 5′ 2″.   **–Tender:** 52.2 tons.
Cylinders: 20″ x 26″ (O).   **Valve Gear:** Walschaerts. Piston valves.
Tractive Effort: 32080 lbf.   **BR Power Classification:** 6MT.
RA: 6.

BR	Present		
62005	2005	North Yorkshire Moors Railway	NBL 26609/1949

CLASS D40   4-4-0

Built: 1899–1921. Pickersgill GNSR Class F. 21 built.
Boiler Pressure: 165 lbf/sq in superheated.   **Weight –Loco:** 48.65 tons.
Wheel Diameters: 3' 9½", 6' 1".   **–Tender:** 37.4 tons.
Cylinders: 18" x 26" (I).   **Valve Gear:** Stephenson. Slide valves.
Tractive Effort: 16 180 lbf.   **BR Power Classification:** 1P.
RA: 4.

BR	LNER	GNSR			
62277	6849–2277	49	GORDON HIGHLANDER	Bo'ness & Kinneil Railway	NBL 22563/1920

CLASS D34   GLEN   4-4-0

Built: 1913–20. Reid NBR Class K. 32 built.
Boiler Pressure: 165 lbf/sq in superheated.   **Weight–Loco:** 57.2 tons.
Wheel Diameters: 3' 6", 6' 0".   **–Tender:** 46.65 tons.
Cylinders: 20" x 26" (I).   **Valve Gear:** Stephenson. Piston valves.
Tractive Effort: 22 100 lbf.   **BR Power Classification:** 3P.
RA: 6.

BR	LNER	NBR			
62469	9256–2469	256	GLEN DOUGLAS	Glasgow Riverside Museum	Cowlairs 1913

CLASS D11   IMPROVED DIRECTOR   4-4-0

Built: 1919–22. Robinson GCR Class 11F. 11 built (62660–670). 24 similar locos were built by the LNER.
Boiler Pressure: 180 lbf/sq in superheated.   **Weight–Loco:** 61.15 tons.
Wheel Diameters: 3' 6", 6' 9".   **–Tender:** 48.3 tons.
Cylinders: 20" x 26" (I).   **Valve Gear:** Stephenson. Piston valves.
Tractive Effort: 19 640 lbf.   **BR Power Classification:** 3P.
RA: 6.

BR	LNER	GCR			
62660	5506–2660	506	BUTLER HENDERSON	Barrow Hill Roundhouse (N)	Gorton 1919

CLASS D49/1   4-4-0

Built: 1927–29. Gresley design. 36 built (62700–735).
Boiler Pressure: 180 lbf/sq in superheated.   **Weight–Loco:** 66 tons.
Wheel Diameters: 3' 1¼", 6' 8".   **–Tender:** 52 tons.
Cylinders: 17" x 26" (3).   **Tractive Effort:** 21 560 lbf.
Valve Gear: Walschaerts with derived motion for inside cylinder. Piston valves.
BR Power Classification: 4P.   **RA:** 8.

BR	LNER			
62712	246–2712	MORAYSHIRE	Bo'ness & Kinneil Railway	Darlington 1391/1928

CLASS E4   2-4-0

Built: 1891–1902. Holden GER Class T26. 100 built.
Boiler Pressure: 160 lbf/sq in.   **Weight–Loco:** 40.3 tons.
Wheel Diameters: 4' 0", 5' 8".   **–Tender:** 30.65 tons.
Cylinders: 17½" x 24" (I).   **Valve Gear:** Stephenson. Slide valves.
Tractive Effort: 14 700 lbf.   **BR Power Classification:** 1MT.
RA: 2.

Air brakes.

BR	LNER	GER		
62785	7490–7802–2785	490	Bressingham Steam Museum (N)	Stratford 836/1894

▲ Class D40 4-4-0 49 "GORDON HIGHLANDER" on display at the Bo'ness & Kinneil Railway museum on 12 July 2014.　　**Alisdair Anderson**

▼ Class D49/1 4-4-0 62712 "MORAYSHIRE" at Wansford on the Nene Valley Railway on 23 February 2015.　　**Fred Kerr**

CLASS C1   4-4-2

Built: 1902–10. Ivatt GNR Class C1. 94 built.
Boiler Pressure: 170 lbf/sq in.
Wheel Diameters: 3′ 8″, 6′ 8″, 3′ 8″.
Cylinders: 20″ x 24″ (O).
Tractive Effort: 17 340 lbf.
RA: 7.

Weight–Loco: 69.6 tons.
          –Tender: 43.1 tons.
Valve Gear: Stephenson. Slide valves.
BR Power Classification: 2P.

BR	LNER	GNR		
–	3251–2800	251	National Railway Museum, Shildon (N)	Doncaster 991/1902

CLASS Q6   0-8-0

Built: 1913–21. Raven NER Class T2. 120 built (63340–459).
Boiler Pressure: 180 lbf/sq in superheated.
Wheel Diameter: 4′ 7¼″.
Cylinders: 20″ x 26″ (O).
Tractive Effort: 28 800 lbf.
RA: 6.

Weight–Loco: 65.9 tons.
          –Tender: 44.1 tons.
Valve Gear: Stephenson. Piston valves.
BR Power Classification: 6F.

BR	LNER	NER		
63395	2238–3395	2238	North Yorkshire Moors Railway	Darlington 1918

CLASS Q7   0-8-0

Built: 1919–24. Raven NER Class T3. 15 built (63460–474).
Boiler Pressure: 180 lbf/sq in superheated.
Wheel Diameter: 4′ 7¼″.
Cylinders: 18½″ x 26″ (3).
Tractive Effort: 36 960 lbf.
RA: 7.

Weight–Loco: 71.6 tons.
          –Tender: 44.1 tons.
Valve Gear: Stephenson. Piston valves.
BR Power Classification: 8F.

BR	LNER	NER		
63460	901–3460	901	Head of Steam, Darlington Railway Museum (N)	Darlington 1919

CLASS O4   2-8-0

Built: 1911–20. Robinson GCR Class 8K. 129 built. A further 521 were built, being ordered by the Railway Operating Department (ROD). These saw service on British and overseas railways during and after World War I. Some subsequently passed to British railway administrations whilst others were sold abroad.
Boiler Pressure: 180 lbf/sq in superheated.
Wheel Diameters: 3′ 6″, 4′ 8″.
Cylinders: 21″ x 26″ (O).
Tractive Effort: 31 330 lbf.
RA: 6.

Weight–Loco: 73.2 tons.
          –Tender: 48.3 tons.
Valve Gear: Stephenson. Piston valves.
BR Power Classification: 7F.

BR	LNER	GCR		
63601	5102–3509–3601	102	Great Central Railway (N)	Gorton 1911

ROD			
1984	Dorrigo Steam Railway Museum, New South Wales, Australia	NBL 22042/1918
2003	Dorrigo Steam Railway Museum, New South Wales, Australia	Gorton 1918
2004	Richmond Vale Railway Museum, Kurri-Kurri, NSW, Australia	Gorton 1918

CLASS J21   0-6-0

Built: 1886–95. Worsdell NER Class C. 201 built.
Boiler Pressure: 160 lbf/sq in superheated.
Wheel Diameter: 5′ 1¼″.
Cylinders: 19″ x 24″ (I).
Tractive Effort: 19 240 lbf.
RA: 3.
Weight–Loco: 43.75 tons.
–Tender: 36.95 tons.
Valve Gear: Stephenson. Piston valves.
BR Power Classification: 2F.

BR	*LNER*	*NER*		
65033	876–5033	876	National Railway Museum, Shildon	Gateshead 1889

CLASS J36   0-6-0

Built: 1888–1900. Holmes NBR Class C. 168 built.
Boiler Pressure: 165 lbf/sq in.
Wheel Diameter: 5′ 0″.
Cylinders: 18″ x 26″ (I).
Tractive Effort: 20 240 lbf.
RA: 3.
Weight–Loco: 41.95 tons.
–Tender: 33.5 tons.
Valve Gear: Stephenson. Slide valves.
BR Power Classification: 2F.

BR	*LNER*	*NBR*		
65243	9673–5243	673	MAUDE Bo'ness & Kinneil Railway	N 4392/1891

CLASS J15   0-6-0

Built: 1883–1913. Worsdell GER Class Y14. 189 built.
Boiler Pressure: 160 lbf/sq in.
Wheel Diameter: 4′ 11″.
Cylinders: 17½″ x 24″ (I).
Tractive Effort: 16 940 lbf.
RA: 1.
Weight–Loco: 37.1 tons.
–Tender: 30.65 tons.
Valve Gear: Stephenson. Slide valves.
BR Power Classification: 2F.

Dual (air/vacuum) brakes.

BR	*LNER*	*GER*		
65462	7564–5462	564	North Norfolk Railway	Stratford 1912

CLASS J17   0-6-0

Built: 1900–11. Holden GER Class G58. 90 built (65500–589).
Boiler Pressure: 180 lbf/sq in superheated.
Wheel Diameter: 4′ 11″.
Cylinders: 19″ x 26″ (I).
Tractive Effort: 24 340 lbf.
RA: 4.
Weight–Loco: 45.4 tons.
–Tender: 38.25 tons.
Valve Gear: Stephenson. Slide valves.
BR Power Classification: 4F.

Air brakes.

BR	*LNER*	*GER*		
65567	8217–5567	1217	Barrow Hill Roundhouse (N)	Stratford 1905

CLASS J27   0-6-0

Built: 1906–23. Worsdell NER Class P3. 115 built.
Boiler Pressure: 180 lbf/sq in superheated.
Wheel Diameter: 4′ 7¼″.
Cylinders: 18½″ x 26″ (I).
Tractive Effort: 24 640 lbf.
RA: 5.
Weight–Loco: 47 tons.
–Tender: 37.6 tons.
Valve Gear: Stephenson. Piston valves.
BR Power Classification: 4F.

BR	*LNER*		
65894	2392–5894	NELPG, Hopetown, Darlington	Darlington 1923

57

▲ Class E4 2-4-0 490 on display at Bressingham Steam Museum, Norfolk on 8 May 2016.
Brian Garvin

▼ Class J52 0-6-0ST 1247 at the National Railway Museum, York on 5 September 2015.
Robert Pritchard

CLASS Y5 — 0-4-0ST

Built: 1874–1903. Neilson & Company design for GER (Class 209). 8 built. Survivor sold in 1917.
Boiler Pressure: 140 lbf/sq in.
Weight: 21.2 tons.
Wheel Diameter: 3' 7".
Cylinders: 12" x 20" (O).
Valve Gear: Stephenson. Slide valves.
Tractive Effort: 7970 lbf.
RA: 1.

GER		
229	Flour Mill Workshop, Bream	N 2119/1876

CLASS J94. 68077/078 (LNER 8077/078) – see War Department Steam Locomotives.

CLASS Y7 — 0-4-0T

Built: 1888–1923. Worsdell NER Class H. 24 built.
Boiler Pressure: 160 lbf/sq in.
Weight: 22.7 tons.
Wheel Diameter: 4' 0".
Tractive Effort: 11 140 lbf.
Cylinders: 14" x 20" (I).
Valve Gear: Joy. Slide valves.
BR Power Classification: 0F.
RA: 1.

BR	LNER	NER		
68088	985–8088		North Norfolk Railway	Darlington 1205/1923
–	1310	1310	Middleton Railway	Gateshead 38/1891

CLASS Y9 — 0-4-0ST

Built: 1882–99. Drummond NBR Class G. 35 built.
Boiler Pressure: 130 lbf/sq in.
Weight: 27.8 tons.
Wheel Diameter: 3' 8".
Cylinders: 14" x 20" (I).
Valve Gear: Stephenson. Slide valves.
Tractive Effort: 9840 lbf.
BR Power Classification: 0F.
RA: 2.

BR	LNER	NBR		
68095	10094–8095	42–894–1094	Bo'ness & Kinneil Railway	Cowlairs 1887

CLASS Y1 — 4wT

Built: 1925–33. Sentinel geared loco. 24 built.
Boiler Pressure: 275 lbf/sq in superheated.
Weight: 19.8 tons.
Wheel Diameter: 2' 6".
Cylinders: 6¾" x 9" (I).
Valve Gear: Rotary cam. Poppet valves.
BR Power Classification: 0F.
Tractive Effort: 7260 lbf.
RA: 1.

BR	LNER		
68153	59–8153	Middleton Railway	S 8837/1933

Also carried DEPARTMENTAL LOCOMOTIVE No. 54.

CLASS J69 — 0-6-0T

Built: 1890–1904. Holden GER Class S56. 126 locomotives (including many rebuilt from J67).
Boiler Pressure: 180 lbf/sq in.
Weight: 42.45 tons.
Wheel Diameter: 4' 0".
Cylinders: 16½" x 22" (I).
Valve Gear: Stephenson. Slide valves.
Tractive Effort: 19 090 lbf.
BR Power Classification: 2F.
RA: 3.

Air brakes.

BR	LNER	GER		
68633	7087–8633	87	Bressingham Steam Museum (N)	Stratford 1249/1904

CLASS J52   0-6-0ST

Built: 1897–1909. Ivatt GNR Class J13. Many rebuilt from Stirling locomotives (built 1892–97).
Boiler Pressure: 170 lbf/sq in.   **Weight:** 51.7 tons.
Wheel Diameter: 4' 8".   **Cylinders:** 18" x 26" (I).
Valve Gear: Stephenson. Slide valves.   **Tractive Effort:** 21 740 lbf.
BR Power Classification: 3F.   **RA:** 5.

BR	*LNER*	*GNR*		
68846	4247–8846	1247	National Railway Museum, York (N)	SS 4492/1899

CLASS J72   0-6-0T

Built: 1898–1925. Worsdell NER Class E1. Further batch built 1949–51 by BR. 113 built.
Boiler Pressure: 140 lbf/sq in.   **Weight:** 38.6 tons.
Wheel Diameter: 4' 1¼".   **Cylinders:** 17" x 24" (I).
Valve Gear: Stephenson. Slide valves.   **Tractive Effort:** 16 760 lbf.
BR Power Classification: 2F.   **RA:** 5.

69023–Departmental No. 59   Wensleydale Railway   Darlington 2151/1951

On loan from NELPG, Hopetown, Darlington

▲ Class J72 0-6-0T 69023 passes Wensley on the Wensleydale Railway with the 12.50 Leeming Bar–Redmire on 25 March 2016.   **Robert Pritchard**

CLASS N2   0-6-2T

Built: 1920–29. Gresley GNR Class N2. 107 built (69490–596).
Boiler Pressure: 170 lbf/sq in superheated.   **Weight:** 70.25 tons.
Wheel Diameter: 5' 8", 3' 8".   **Cylinders:** 19" x 26" (I).
Valve Gear: Stephenson. Piston valves.   **Tractive Effort:** 19950 lbf.
BR Power Classification: 3MT.   **RA:** 6.

BR	LNER	GNR		
69523	4744–9523	1744	Great Central Railway	NBL 22600/1921

CLASS N7   0-6-2T

Built: 1915–28. Hill GER Class L77. 134 built (69600–733). 69621 rebuilt to N7/4 1946.
Boiler Pressure: 180 lbf/sq in superheated.   **Weight:** 61.8 tons.
Wheel Diameters: 4' 10", 3' 9".   **Cylinders:** 18" x 24" (I).
Valve Gear: Walschaerts (inside). Piston valves.   **Tractive Effort:** 20510 lbf.
RA: 5.   **BR Power Classification:** 3MT.

Dual (air/vacuum) brakes.

BR	LNER	GER			
69621	999E–7999–9621	999	"A.J. HILL"	East Anglian Railway Museum	Stratford 1924

CLASS X1   2-2-4T

Built: 1869 by NER as 2–2–2WT. Rebuilt 1892 to 2-cylinder compound 4–2–2T and rebuilt as 2–2–4T in 1902 and used for pulling inspection saloons. NER Class 66.
Boiler Pressure: 175 lbf/sq in.   **Weight:** 44.95 tons.
Wheel Diameters: 3' 7", 5' 7¾", 3' 1¼".   **Cylinders:** 13" x 24" (hp) + 18½" x 20" (lp) (I).
Valve Gear: Stephenson. Slide valves.   **Tractive Effort:** 6390 lbf.

LNER	NER			
66	1478–66	AEROLITE	National Railway Museum, York (N)	Gateshead 1869

NER 901 CLASS   2-4-0

Built: 1872–82. Fletcher design. 55 built.
Boiler Pressure: 160 lbf/sq in.   **Weight–Loco:** 39.7 tons.
Wheel Diameters: 4' 6", 7' 0".   **–Tender:** 29.9 tons.
Cylinders: 18" x 24" (I).   **Valve Gear:** Stephenson. Slide valves.
Tractive Effort: 12590 lbf.

LNER	NER		
910	910	Stainmore Railway (N)	Gateshead 1875

NER 1001 CLASS   0-6-0

Built: 1864–75. Bouch design for Stockton & Darlington Railway.
Boiler Pressure: 130 lbf/sq in.   **Weight–Loco:** 35 tons.
Wheel Diameter: 5' 0½".   **Cylinders:** 17" x 26" (I).
Valve Gear: Stephenson. Slide valves.   **Tractive Effort:** 13720 lbf.

LNER	NER		
1275	1275	National Railway Museum, York (N)	Glasgow 707/1874

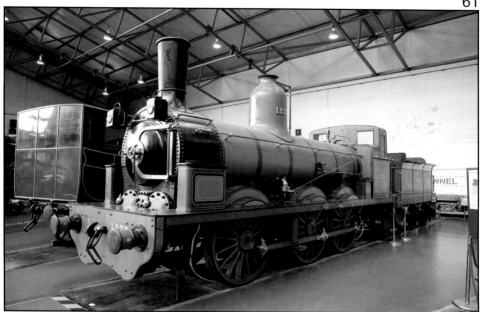

▲ NER 1001 Class 1275 at the National Railway Museum, York on 5 September 2015.
Robert Pritchard

▼ Stockton & Darlington Railway 0-6-0 No. 25 "DERWENT" at Head of Steam, Darlington Railway Museum on 14 August 2014. **John Pritchard**

CLASS E5   2-4-0

Built: 1885. Tennant NER 1463 Class. 20 built.
Boiler Pressure: 160 lbf/sq in.
Wheel Diameters: 4' 6", 7' 0".
Cylinders: 18" x 24" (I).
Tractive Effort: 12 590 lbf.

Weight–Loco: 42.1 tons.
    –Tender: 32.1 tons.
Valve Gear: Stephenson. Slide valves.

LNER	NER		
1463	1463	Head of Steam, Darlington Railway Museum (N)	Darlington 1885

CLASS D17/1   4-4-0

Built: 1893–97. Worsdell NER Class M1 (later Class M). 20 built.
Boiler Pressure: 160 lbf/sq in.
Wheel Diameters: 3' 7¼", 7' 1¼".
Cylinders: 19" x 26" (I).
Tractive Effort: 14 970 lbf.

Weight–Loco: 52 tons.
    –Tender: 41 tons.
Valve Gear: Stephenson. Slide valves.
RA: 6.

LNER	NER		
1621	1621	National Railway Museum, Shildon (N)	Gateshead 1893

CLASS C2   "KLONDYKE"   4-4-2

Built: 1898–1903. HA Ivatt GNR Class C1. 22 built.
Boiler Pressure: 170 lbf/sq in superheated.
Wheel Diameters: 3' 8", 6' 8", 3' 8".
Cylinders: 19" x 24" (O).
Tractive Effort: 15 650 lbf.

Weight–Loco: 62 tons.
    –Tender: 42.1 tons.
Valve Gear: Stephenson. Piston valves.
RA: 4.

LNER	GNR			
3990	990	HENRY OAKLEY	National Railway Museum, York (N)	Doncaster 769/1898

GNR CLASS A2   4-2-2

Built: 1870–93. Stirling design. 47 built. No. 1 is currently matched with a GNR "Stirling" tender (built 1893) that had been paired with GNR 1002. The GNR "Stirling Goods" tender that had been paired with No. 1 is currently stored at the National Railway Museum, Shildon.
Boiler Pressure: 140 lbf/sq in.
Wheel Diameters: 3' 10", 8' 1", 4' 1".
Cylinders: 18" x 28" (O).
Tractive Effort: 11 130 lbf.

Weight–Loco: 38.5 tons.
    –Tender: 30 tons.
Valve Gear: Stephenson. Slide valves.

1	National Railway Museum, York (N)	Doncaster 50/1870

STOCKTON & DARLINGTON RAILWAY   0-4-0

Built: 1825–26. George Stephenson design. 6 built.
Boiler Pressure: 50 lbf/sq in.
Wheel Diameter: 3' 11".
Cylinders: 9½" x 24" (O).

Weight–Loco: 6.5 tons.
    –Tender:
Tractive Effort: 2050 lbf.

1	LOCOMOTION	Head of Steam, Darlington Railway Museum (N)	RS 1/1825

STOCKTON & DARLINGTON RAILWAY   0-6-0

Built: 1845.
Boiler Pressure: 75 lbf/sq in.
Wheel Diameter: 4' 0".
Tractive Effort: 6700 lbf.

Weight–Loco: 6.5 tons.
Cylinders: 14½" x 24" (O).

25	DERWENT	Head of Steam, Darlington Railway Museum (N)	Kitching 1845

1.5. BRITISH RAILWAYS STANDARD STEAM LOCOMOTIVES

GENERAL

From 1951 onwards British Railways produced a series of standard steam locomotives under the jurisdiction of RA Riddles. Examples of most classes have been preserved, the exceptions being the Class 6MT "Clan" Pacifics, the Class 3MT 2-6-0s (77000 series), the Class 3MT 2-6-2Ts (82000 series) and the Class 2MT 2-6-2Ts (84000 series).

NUMBERING SYSTEM

Tender engines were numbered in the 70000 series and tank engines in the 80000 series, the exceptions being the Class 9F 2-10-0s which were numbered in the 92000 series.

CLASSIFICATION SYSTEM

British Railways standard steam locomotives were referred to by power classification like LMS locomotives. All locomotives were classed as "MT" denoting "mixed traffic" except for 71000 and the Class 9F 2-10-0s. The latter, although freight locos, were often used on passenger trains on summer Saturdays.

▲ Class 7MT 4-6-2 70000 "BRITANNIA" approaches Stoneycombe on the climb from Newton Abbot to Daignton with the "Royal Duchy" from Bristol Temple Meads to Par on 6 June 2015.

David Hunt

CLASS 7MT BRITANNIA 4-6-2

Built: 1951–54. 55 built (70000–54).
Boiler Pressure: 250 lbf/sq in superheated.
Wheel Diameters: 3′ 0″, 6′ 2″, 3′ 3½″.
Cylinders: 20″ x 28″ (O).
Tractive Effort: 32 160 lbf.

Weight–Loco: 94 tons.
  –Tender: 49.15 tons.
Valve Gear: Walschaerts. Piston valves.
RA: 7

x   Dual (air/vacuum) brakes.

70000 x	BRITANNIA	London & North Western Railway Heritage Company, Crewe	Crewe 1951
70013	OLIVER CROMWELL	Great Central Railway (N)	Crewe 1951

CLASS 8P 4-6-2

Built: 1954. 1 built.
Boiler Pressure: 250 lbf/sq in superheated.
Wheel Diameters: 3′ 0″, 6′ 2″, 3′ 3½″.
Cylinders: 18″ x 28″ (3).
Tractive Effort: 39 080 lbf.

Weight–Loco: 101.25 tons.
  –Tender: 53.7 tons.
Valve Gear: British Caprotti (outside). Poppet valves.
RA: 8.

Dual (air/vacuum) brakes.

71000	DUKE OF GLOUCESTER	Tyseley Locomotive Works	Crewe 1954

CLASS 5MT 4-6-0

Built: 1951–57. 172 built (73000–171).
Boiler Pressure: 225 lbf/sq in superheated.
Wheel Diameters: 3′ 0″, 6′ 2″.
Cylinders: 19″ x 28″ (O).
Valve Gear: Walschaerts. Piston valves (* outside British Caprotti. Poppet valves).
Tractive Effort: 26 120 lbf.

Weight–Loco: 76 tons.
  –Tender: 49.15 tons.

RA: 5.

x   Dual (air/vacuum) brakes.

73050 x	"CITY OF PETERBOROUGH"	Nene Valley Railway	Derby 1954
73082	CAMELOT	Bluebell Railway	Derby 1955
73096		Southall Depot, London	Derby 1955
73129 *		Midland Railway-Butterley	Derby 1956
73156		Great Central Railway	Doncaster 1956

CLASS 4MT 4-6-0

Built: 1951–57. 80 built (75000–79).
Boiler Pressure: 225 lbf/sq in superheated.
Wheel Diameters: 3′ 0″, 5′ 8″.
Cylinders: 18″ x 28″ (O).
Tractive Effort: 25 520 lbf.

Weight–Loco: 67.9 tons.
  –Tender: 42.15 tons.
Valve Gear: Walschaerts. Piston valves.
RA: 4.

*   Fitted with double chimney.

75014	"BRAVEHEART"	Dartmouth Steam Railway	Swindon 1951
75027		Bluebell Railway	Swindon 1954
75029 *	"THE GREEN KNIGHT"	North Yorkshire Moors Railway	Swindon 1954
75069 *		Severn Valley Railway	Swindon 1955
75078 *		Keighley & Worth Valley Railway	Swindon 1956
75079 *		Mid Hants Railway	Swindon 1956

▲ Class 4MT 2-6-0 76084 is seen on the North Norfolk Railway near Sheringham golf course with the 15.00 Sheringham–Holt on 26 September 2015. **Paul Biggs**

▼ BR Class 4MT 2-6-4T 80104 passes Townsend Bridge near Corfe Castle with the 14.30 Norden–Swanage during the Swanage Railway's Autumn Steam Gala on 16 October 2015. **Stephen Ginn**

CLASS 4MT   2-6-0

Built: 1952–57. 115 built (76000–114).
Boiler Pressure: 225 lbf/sq in superheated.
Wheel Diameters: 3' 0", 5' 3".
Cylinders: 17½" x 26" (O).
Tractive Effort: 24 170 lbf.

Weight–Loco: 59.75 tons.
      –Tender: 42.15 tons.
Valve Gear: Walschaerts. Piston valves.
RA: 4.

x   Dual (air/vacuum) brakes.

76017	Mid Hants Railway	Horwich 1953
76077	Gloucestershire Warwickshire Railway	Horwich 1956
76079x	North Yorkshire Moors Railway	Horwich 1957
76084	North Norfolk Railway	Horwich 1957

CLASS 2MT   2-6-0

Built: 1952–56. 65 built (78000–64). These locomotives were almost identical to the Ivatt LMS
Class 2MT 2-6-0s (46400–46527).
Boiler Pressure: 200 lbf/sq in superheated.
Wheel Diameters: 3' 0", 5' 0".
Cylinders: 16½" x 24" (O).
Tractive Effort: 18 510 lbf.

Weight–Loco: 49.25 tons.
      –Tender: 36.85 tons.
Valve Gear: Walschaerts. Piston valves.
RA: 3.

78018	Great Central Railway	Darlington 1954
78019	Great Central Railway	Darlington 1954
78022	Keighley & Worth Valley Railway	Darlington 1954

CLASS 4MT   2-6-4T

Built: 1951–57. 155 built (80000–154).
Boiler Pressure: 225 lbf/sq in superheated.
Wheel Diameters: 3' 0", 5' 8", 3' 0".
Valve Gear: Walschaerts. Piston valves.
RA: 4.

Weight: 86.65 tons.
Cylinders: 18" x 28" (O).
Tractive Effort: 25 520 lbf.

80002	Keighley & Worth Valley Railway	Derby 1952
80064	Bluebell Railway	Brighton 1953
80072	Llangollen Railway	Brighton 1953
80078	Mangapps Railway Museum	Brighton 1954
80079	Severn Valley Railway	Brighton 1954
80080	East Lancashire Railway	Brighton 1954
80097	East Lancashire Railway	Brighton 1954
80098	Midland Railway-Butterley	Brighton 1954
80100	Bluebell Railway	Brighton 1955
80104	Swanage Railway	Brighton 1955
80105	Bo'ness & Kinneil Railway	Brighton 1955
80135	North Yorkshire Moors Railway	Brighton 1956
80136	North Yorkshire Moors Railway	Brighton 1956
80150	Mid Hants Railway	Brighton 1956
80151	Bluebell Railway	Brighton 1957

80080 is on loan from the Midland Railway-Butterley

CLASS 9F   2-10-0

Built: 1954–60. 251 built (92000–250). 92220 EVENING STAR was the last steam locomotive to be built for British Railways.

Boiler Pressure: 250 lbf/sq in superheated.
Wheel Diameters: 3' 0", 5' 0".
Cylinders: 20" x 28" (O).
Tractive Effort: 39670 lbf.

Weight–Loco: 86.7 tons.
–Tender: 52.5 tons.
Valve Gear: Walschaerts. Piston valves.
RA: 9.

*   Fitted with a single chimney. All other surviving members of the class have double chimneys.

92134 *		East Lancashire Railway	Crewe 1957
92203	"BLACK PRINCE"	North Norfolk Railway	Swindon 1959
92207	"MORNING STAR"	North Dorset Railway Trust, Shillingstone	Swindon 1959
92212		Mid Hants Railway	Swindon 1959
92214	"COCK O' THE NORTH"	Great Central Railway	Swindon 1959
92219		Wensleydale Railway	Swindon 1960
92220	EVENING STAR	National Railway Museum, York (N)	Swindon 1960
92240		Bluebell Railway	Crewe 1958
92245		Barry Rail Centre	Crewe 1958

92207 is undergoing overhaul at Somerset & Dorset Steam, Poole.

▲ Class 9F 2-10-0 92220 "EVENING STAR", the last steam locomotive built for British Railways, is seen on display at the National Railway Museum, York on 22 May 2011.   **Jonathan Webb**

1.6. WAR DEPARTMENT STEAM LOCOMOTIVES

GENERAL

During the Second World War the War Department (WD) of the British Government acquired and used a considerable number of steam locomotives. On the cessation of hostilities many of these locomotives were sold for further service both to industrial users and other railway administrations. The bulk of WD steam locomotives preserved date from this period. By 1952 many of the large wartime fleet of steam locomotives had been disposed of and those remaining were renumbered into a new series. From 1 April 1964 the WD became the Army Department of the Ministry of Defence with consequent renumbering taking place in 1968. The locomotives considered to be main line locomotives built to "Austerity" designs are included here. Also included in this section are the steam locomotives built to WD "Austerity" designs for industrial users.

CLASS WD — AUSTERITY — 2-10-0

Built: 1943–45 by North British. 150 built. Many sold to overseas railways. 25 sold to British Railways in 1948 and numbered 90750–774.

Boiler Pressure: 225 lbf/sq in superheated.
Wheel Diameters: 3' 2", 4' 8½".
Cylinders: 19" x 28" (O).
Tractive Effort: 34210 lbf.

Weight–Loco: 78.3 tons.
–Tender: 55.5 tons
Valve Gear: Walschaerts. Piston valves.
BR Power Classification: 8F.

g   Hellenic Railways (Greece) number.

WD	AD/Overseas			
3651–73651	600	GORDON	Severn Valley Railway	NBL 25437/1943
3652–73652	Lb951 g	"90775"	North Norfolk Railway	NBL 25438/1943
3672–73672	Lb960 g	"DAME VERA LYNN"	North Yorkshire Moors Railway	NBL 25458/1944

CLASS WD — AUSTERITY — 2-8-0

Built: 1943–45 by North British & Vulcan Foundry. 935 built. Many sold to overseas railways. 200 were sold to LNER in 1946. These became LNER Nos. 3000–3199 and BR 90000–100, 90422–520. A further 533 were sold to British Railways in 1948 and numbered 90101–421, 90521–732.

Boiler Pressure: 225 lbf/sq in superheated.
Wheel Diameters: 3' 2", 4' 8½".
Cylinders: 19" x 28" (O).
Tractive Effort: 34210 lbf.

Weight–Loco: 70.25 tons.
–Tender: 55.5 tons.
Valve Gear: Walschaerts. Piston valves.
BR Power Classification: 8F.

This locomotive was purchased from Swedish State Railways (SJ), it previously having seen service with Netherlands Railways (NS). It has been restored to BR condition.

WD	NS	SJ	Present		
79257	4464	1931	90733	Keighley & Worth Valley Railway	VF 5200/1945

CLASS 50550 — 0-6-0ST

Built: 1941–42. Eight locomotives were built to this design, all being intended for Stewarts and Lloyd Minerals. Only one was delivered with three being taken over by WD becoming 65–67. The other four went to other industrial users and two of these survive.

Boiler Pressure: 170 lbf/sq in.
Wheel Diameter: 4' 5".
Valve Gear: Stephenson. Slide valves.

Weight: 48.35 tons.
Cylinders: 18" x 26" (I).
Tractive Effort: 22150 lbf.

WD	Present		
–	Unnumbered	Swindon & Cricklade Railway	HE 2411/1941
–	GUNBY	Swindon & Cricklade Railway	HE 2413/1942
66-70066	S112 SPITFIRE	Embsay & Bolton Abbey Railway	HE 2414/1942

CLASS WD   AUSTERITY   0-6-0ST

Built: 1943–53 for Ministry of Supply and War Department. 391 built. 75 bought by LNER and classified J94. Many others passed to industrial users. The design of this class was derived from the "50550" Class of Hunslet locomotives (see above).

Boiler Pressure: 170 lbf/sq in.
Wheel Diameter: 4' 3".
Valve Gear: Stephenson. Slide valves.
BR Power Classification: 4F.

Weight: 48.25 tons.
Cylinders: 18" x 26" (I).
Tractive Effort: 23870 lbf.
RA: 5.

§   Oil fired.
†   Rebuilt as 0-6-0 tender locomotive.

x   Dual (air/vacuum) brakes.

BR	LNER	WD		
68078	8078	71463	Hope Farm, Sellindge	AB 2212/1946
68077	8077	71466	Spa Valley Railway	AB 2215/1946

WD/AD	Present		
71480	Unnumbered	Tyseley Locomotive Works	RSH 7289/1945
71499	Unnumbered	Bryn Engineering, Blackrod	HC 1776/1944
71505–118 §	BRUSSELS LONGMOOR MILITARY RAILWAY	Keighley & Worth Valley Railway	HC 1782/1945
71515	MECH. NAVVIES LTD.	Pontypool & Blaenavon Railway	RSH 7169/1944
71516	WELSH GUARDSMAN/ GWARCHODWR CYMREIG	Gwili Railway	RSH 7170/1944
71529–165	W.P.R No. 15 "EARL DAVID"	Avon Valley Railway	AB 2183/1945
75006		Nene Valley Railway	HE 2855/1943
75008	SWIFTSURE	East Lancashire Railway	HE 2857/1943
75015	48	Strathspey Railway	HE 2864/1943
75019–168	LORD PHIL	Peak Rail	HE 2868/1943
			rebuilt HE 3883/1963
75030	Unnumbered	Caledonian Railway	HE 2879/1943
75031–101	No. 17	Bo'ness & Kinneil Railway	HE 2880/1943
75041–107†	10 DOUGLAS	Ribble Steam Railway	HE 2890/1943
			rebuilt HE 3882/1962
75050	No. 69 NORMAN 68005	Embsay & Bolton Abbey Railway	RSH 7086/1943
75061	No. 9 CAIRNGORM	Strathspey Railway	RSH 7097/1943
75062	49	Tanfield Railway	RSH 7098/1943
75091	ROBERT	Great Central Railway	HC 1752/1943
75105	WALKDEN	Spa Valley Railway	HE 3155/1944
75113–132	SAPPER	East Lancashire Railway	HE 3163/1944
			rebuilt HE 3885/1964
75118–134	S134 WHELDALE	Embsay & Bolton Abbey Railway	HE 3168/1944
75130	No. 3180 ANTWERP	Hope Farm, Sellindge	HE 3180/1944
75133–138	Unnumbered	Flour Mill Workshop, Bream (N)	HE 3183/1944
75141–139 x	68006	Barrow Hill Roundhouse	HE 3192/1944
			rebuilt HE 3888/1964
75142–140	68012 BLACKIE	Mid Norfolk Railway	HE 3193/1944
			rebuilt HE 3887/1964
75158–144	68012 THE DUKE	Ecclesbourne Valley Railway	WB 2746/1944
75161	Unnumbered	Caledonian Railway	WB 2749/1944
75170	Unnumbered	Cefn Coed Colliery Museum	WB 2758/1944
75171–147	Unnumbered	Caledonian Railway	WB 2759/1944
75178	Unnumbered	Bodmin & Wenford Railway	WB 2766/1945
75186–150	68013	Peak Rail	RSH 7136/1944
			rebuilt HE 3892/1969
75189–152	No. 8	Flour Mill Workshop, Bream	RSH 7139/1944
			rebuilt HE 3880/1962
75254–175		Bo'ness & Kinneil Railway	WB 2777/1945
75256	No. 20 TANFIELD	Tanfield Railway	WB 2779/1945
75282–181	HAULWEN	Gwili Railway	VF 5272/1945
			rebuilt HE 3879/1961
75319	72	Mangapps Railway Museum	VF 5309/1945
190–90		Colne Valley Railway	HE 3790/1952
191–91	No. 23 HOLMAN F. STEPHENS	Kent & East Sussex Railway	HE 3791/1952

192–92	WAGGONER	Isle of Wight Steam Railway	HE 3792/1953
193–93	Unnumbered	Ribble Steam Railway	HE 3793/1953
194–94	CUMBRIA	Ribble Steam Railway	HE 3794/1953
197	No. 25 NORTHIAM	Kent & East Sussex Railway	HE 3797/1953
198–98	ROYAL ENGINEER	Isle of Wight Steam Railway	HE 3798/1953
200	No. 24 ROLVENDEN	Colne Valley Railway	HE 3800/1953

In addition to the 391 locomotives built for the Ministry of Supply and the War Department, a further 93 were built for industrial users, those that survive being:

No. 60	Strathspey Railway	HE 3686/1949
WHISTON	Foxfield Railway	HE 3694/1950
IR	Ribble Steam Railway	HE 3696/1950
11 REPULSE	Lakeside & Haverthwaite Railway	HE 3698/1950
NORMA	Oswestry Railway Centre	HE 3770/1952
8 SIR ROBERT PEEL	Embsay & Bolton Abbey Railway	HE 3776/1952
68030	Churnet Valley Railway	HE 3777/1952
1	Mid Hants Railway	HE 3781/1952
No. 69	Embsay & Bolton Abbey Railway	HE 3785/1953
N.C.B. MONCKTON No.1	Embsay & Bolton Abbey Railway	HE 3788/1953
WILBERT REV.W.AWDRY	Dean Forest Railway	HE 3806/1953
3809	Great Central Railway	HE 3809/1954
GLENDOWER	South Devon Railway	HE 3810/1954
No. 19	Bo'ness & Kinneil Railway	HE 3818/1954
WARRIOR	Dean Forest Railway	HE 3823/1954
68009	Stainmore Railway	HE 3825/1954
Unnumbered	Gwili Railway	HE 3829/1955
No. 5	Bo'ness & Kinneil Railway	HE 3837/1955
WIMBLEBURY	Foxfield Railway	HE 3839/1956
PAMELA 68070	Garw Valley Railway	HE 3840/1956
No. 22	Appleby-Frodingham RPS, Scunthorpe	HE 3846/1956

▲ Class WD Austerity 0-6-0T 71515 "MECH. NAVVIES LTD." is seen in action during a visit to the Tanfield Railway on 19 June 2015. **Alistair Grieve**

JUNO	National Railway Museum, Shildon	HE 3850/1958
CADLEY HILL No. 1	Leicestershire County Museum store, Snibston	HE 3851/1962
28 – 65	Flour Mill Workshop, Bream	HE 3889/1964
66	Buckinghamshire Railway Centre	HE 3890/1964

HE 3781/1952 has been rebuilt in preservation as a side tank.

HE 3846/1956 is on loan from the Nene Valley Railway.

HE 3850/1958 is on loan from the Isle of Wight Steam Railway.

SHROPSHIRE & MONTGOMERY RAILWAY　　　　0-4-2WT

Built: 1893 by Alfred Dodman & Company for William Birkitt. Sold to Shropshire & Montgomery Railway in 1911 when it was rebuilt from 2-2-2WT.
Boiler Pressure: 60 lbf/sq in.　　　　　**Weight:** 5.5 tons.
Wheel Diameters: 2' 3", 2'3".　　　　　**Cylinders:** 4" x 9" (I).

This locomotive together with three others (LNWR coal engines) became BR (WR) stock in 1950 when this line was nationalised. The locomotives were then withdrawn.

| 1 | GAZELLE | Kent & East Sussex Railway | Dodman/1893 |

1.7. UNITED STATES ARMY TRANSPORTATION CORPS STEAM LOCOMOTIVES

GENERAL

During World War II many locomotives were constructed by various American builders for the USATC. Many saw use on Britain's railways, particularly in the period 1943–45. After the war many of these locomotives were sold to overseas railway administrations, but several have now been repatriated to the British Isles. Only those locomotives currently resident in Great Britain are shown here.

CLASS S160　　　　　　　　　　　　　　　　2-8-0

Built: 1942–45 by various American builders. It is estimated that 2120 were built.
Boiler Pressure: 225 lbf/sq in superheated.　　**Weight–Loco:** 73 tons.
Wheel Diameters: 3' 2", 4' 9".　　　　　　　　**–Tender:** 52.1 tons.
Cylinders: 19" x 26" (O).　　　　　　　　　　**Tractive Effort:** 31 490 lbf.
Valve Gear: Walschaerts. Piston valves.

USATC	Overseas Railway		
1631	MAV (Hungarian Railways) 411.388	Nottingham Transport Heritage Centre	AL 70284/1942
2138	MAV (Hungarian Railways) 411.009	Nottingham Transport Heritage Centre	AL 70620/1943
2253	PKP (Polish Railways) Ty203-288	Adam Dalgleish Engineering, Stockton-on-Tees	
			BLW 69496/1943
2364	MAV (Hungarian Railways) 411.337	Nottingham Transport Heritage Centre	BLW 69621/1943
3278	FS (Italian State Railways) 736.073	Tyseley Locomotive Works	AL 71533/1944
5197	Chinese State Railways KD6.463	Churnet Valley Railway	Lima 8856/1945
5820	PKP (Polish Railways) Ty203.474	Keighley & Worth Valley Railway	Lima 8758/1945
6046	MAV (Hungarian Railways) 411.144	Churnet Valley Railway	BLW 72080/1945

3278 passed to Hellenic Railways (Greece) and was numbered 575. Carries name "FRANKLYN D. ROOSEVELT".

5820 is currently running as BR 95820.

See also the Southern Railway section for Class USATC S100 0-6-0Ts.

1.8. NEW BUILD STEAM LOCOMOTIVES

GENERAL

The following is a list of new build projects that have either been completed or are expected to be completed within two years or have at least a boiler and frames in place. Technical details refer to the original locomotives and the new build locomotives may differ from these.

1.8.1. COMPLETED NEW BUILD STEAM LOCOMOTIVES

GWR 4300 CLASS   2-6-0

Original Class Built: 1911–32 (see page 20).
Boiler Pressure: 225 lbf/sq in superheated.
Wheel Diameters: 3′ 2″, 5′ 8″.
Cylinders: 18″ x 30″ (O).
Tractive Effort: 28880 lbf.
Weight–Loco: 63.85 tons.
–Tender: 40 tons.
Valve Gear: Stephenson. Piston valves.

Rebuilt from 5101 Class 2-6-2T No. 5193 by the West Somerset Railway.

9351   West Somerset Railway   Swindon 1934 rebuilt WSR/2006

LNER CLASS A1   4-6-2

Original Class Built: 1948–49. Peppercorn development of Thompson A1/1. None of the class were preserved so this new locomotive has been constructed, working its first services in 2008.
Boiler Pressure: 250 lbf/sq in superheated.
Wheel Diameters: 3′ 2″, 6′ 8″, 3′ 8″.
Cylinders: 19″ x 26″ (3).
Tractive Effort: 37400 lbf.
RA: 9.
Weight–Loco: 104.7 tons.
–Tender: 66.1 tons.
Valve Gear: Walschaerts. Piston valves.
BR Power Classification: 8P.

Dual (air/vacuum) brakes.

60163   TORNADO   Stewarts Lane Depot, London   Darlington Hope Street 2195/2008

1.8.2. NEW BUILD STEAM LOCOMOTIVES UNDER CONSTRUCTION

GWR DESIGN

2900 CLASS   SAINT   4-6-0

Original Class Built: 1902–13. 77 built (2910–55, 2971–90, 2998). The new build locomotive is being rebuilt from GWR 4900 Class 4-6-0 4942 MAINDY HALL.
Boiler Pressure: 225 lbf/sq in superheated.
Wheel Diameters: 3′ 2″, 6′ 8½″.
Cylinders: 18½″ x 30″ (O).
Tractive Effort: 24390 lbf.
Power Classification: D (4P).
Weight–Loco: 72 tons.
–Tender: 43.15 tons.
Valve Gear: Stephenson.
Restriction: Red.

2999   LADY OF LEGEND   Didcot Railway Centre   Under construction

▲ Class S160 2-8-0 6046 (ex MAV 411.144) is seen with a demonstration freight train between Consall and Cheddleton on the Churnet Valley Railway on 12 March 2016. **Robert Falconer**

▼ New build LNER design A1 4-6-2 60163 "TORNADO" crosses Oldbury Viaduct on the Severn Valley Railway with an empty stock train for Kidderminster on 9 October 2015. **Robin Stewart-Smith**

4700 CLASS   2-8-0

Original Class Built: 1919–23. 9 built (4700–08). This new build locomotive will use parts from three other GWR donor locomotives – 2800 Class 2-8-0 2861, 5101 Class 2-6-2T 4115 and 5205 Class 2-8-0T 5227 but with completely new frames. 4115 is the main donor locomotive.
Boiler Pressure: 225 lbf/sq in superheated.
Wheel Diameters: 3′ 2″, 5′ 8″.
Cylinders: 19″ x 30″ (O).
Tractive Effort: 30460 lbf.
Power Classification: D (7F).

Weight–Loco: 82 tons.
–Tender: 46 tons.
Valve Gear: Stephenson. Piston valves.
Restriction: Red.

4709	Llangollen Railway	Under construction

6800 CLASS   GRANGE   4-6-0

Original Class Built: 1936–39. 80 built (6800–79). The new build locomotive is using the boiler from GWR 6959 Class 4-6-0 7927 WILLINGTON HALL.
Boiler Pressure: 225 lbf/sq in superheated.
Wheel Diameters: 3′ 0″, 5′ 8″.
Cylinders: 18½″ x 30″ (O).
Tractive Effort: 28875 lbf.
Power Class: D (5MT).

Weight–Loco: 74 tons.
–Tender: 40 tons.
Valve Gear: Stephenson. Piston valves.
Restriction: Red.

6880	BETTON GRANGE	Llangollen Railway	Under construction

BRITISH RAILWAYS DESIGN

CLASS 3MT   2-6-2T

Original Class built: 1952–55. 45 built (82000–44).
Boiler Pressure: 200 lbf/sq in superheated.
Wheel Diameters: 3′ 0″, 5′ 3″, 3′ 0″.
Valve Gear: Walschaerts. Piston valves.
RA: 4.

Weight: 74.05 tons.
Cylinders: 17½″ x 26″ (O).
Tractive Effort: 21 490 lbf.

82045	Severn Valley Railway	Under construction

CLASS 2MT   2-6-2T

Original Class built: 1953–57. 30 built (84000–29). This new build locomotive is being rebuilt from BR 2MT 2-6-0 78059.
Boiler Pressure: 200 lbf/sq in superheated.
Wheel Diameters: 3′ 0″, 5′ 0″, 3′ 0″.
Valve Gear: Walschaerts. Piston valves.
RA: 1.

Weight: 66.25 tons.
Cylinders: 16½″ x 24″ (O).
Tractive Effort: 18 510 lbf.

84030	Bluebell Railway	Darlington 1956 reb. Bluebell

1.9. REPLICA STEAM LOCOMOTIVES

GENERAL

Details are included of locomotives which would have been included in the foregoing had the original locomotive survived or does survive. Locomotives are listed under the heading of the original Railway/Manufacturer. Only locomotives which work, previously worked or can be made to work are included.

1.9.1 COMPLETED REPLICA STEAM LOCOMOTIVES

STOCKTON & DARLINGTON RAILWAY   0-4-0

Built: 1975.
Boiler Pressure: 50 lbf/sq in.
Wheel Diameter: 3' 11".
Cylinders: 9½" x 24" (O).

Weight–Loco: 6.5 tons.
–Tender:
Tractive Effort: 1960 lbf.

LOCOMOTION   Beamish, The Living Museum of the North   Loco Ent 1/1975

LIVERPOOL & MANCHESTER RAILWAY   0-2-2

Built: 1934/79.
Boiler Pressure: 50 lbf/sq in.
Wheel Diameters: 4' 8½", 2' 6".
Cylinders: 8" x 17" (O).

Weight–Loco: 4.5 tons.
–Tender: 5.2 tons.
Tractive Effort: 820 lbf.

ROCKET   National Railway Museum, York (N)   RS 4089/1934
ROCKET   National Railway Museum, York (N)   Loco Ent 2/1979

LIVERPOOL & MANCHESTER RAILWAY   0-4-0

Built: 1979.
Boiler Pressure: 50 lbf/sq in.
Wheel Diameter: 4' 6".
Cylinders: 7" x 18" (O).

Weight–Loco: 4.5 tons.
–Tender: 5.2 tons.
Tractive Effort: 690 lbf.

SANS PAREIL   National Railway Museum, Shildon   Shildon 1980

LIVERPOOL & MANCHESTER RAILWAY   2-2-0

Built: 1992 (original dated from 1832).
Boiler Pressure: 100 lbf/sq in (original 50 lbf/sq in).
Wheel Diameters: 5'.
Cylinders: 9" x 22" (O).

Weight–Loco: 8 tons.
–Tender: 4 tons.
Tractive Effort:

PLANET   9   Museum of Science & Industry, Manchester   Manchester 1992

BRAITHWAITE & ERICSSON & COMPANY   0-2-2WT

Built: 1929 (using parts from 1829 original)/1980.
Boiler Pressure:
Wheel Diameter:
Cylinders:

Weight–Loco:
–Tender:
Tractive Effort:

NOVELTY   Museum of Science & Industry, Manchester (N)   Science Museum 1929
NOVELTY   Swedish Railway Museum, Gayle, Sweden   Loco Ent 3/1980

▲ Replica Liverpool & Manchester Railway 0-4-0 "SANS PAREIL" at the National Railway Museum, Shildon on 5 September 2015. **Robert Pritchard**

▼ Rarely photographed Braithwaite & Ericsson & Company 0-2-2WT replica "NOVELTY" at the Swedish Railway Museum in Gayle, Sweden on 17 April 2015. **Alisdair Anderson**

GREAT WESTERN RAILWAY 2-2-2

Built: 1925 (using parts from 1837 original).
Boiler Pressure: 90 lbf/sq in.
Wheel Diameters: 4' 0", 7' 0", 4' 0".
Cylinders: 16" x 16" (I).
Gauge: 7' 0¼".
Weight–Loco: 23.35 tons.
   –Tender: 6.5 tons.
Tractive Effort: 3730 lbf.

NORTH STAR   Steam – Museum of the Great Western Railway (N)   Swindon 1925

GREAT WESTERN RAILWAY 2-2-2

Built: 2005.
Boiler Pressure: 50 lbf/sq in.
Wheel Diameters: 4' 0", 7' 0", 4' 0".
Cylinders: 15" x 18" (I).
Gauge: 7' 0¼".
Weight–Loco: 23.35 tons.
   –Tender: 6.5 tons.
Tractive Effort: 2050 lbf.

FIRE FLY   Didcot Railway Centre   Didcot/Bristol 2005

GREAT WESTERN RAILWAY 4-2-2

Built: 1985.
Boiler Pressure:
Wheel Diameters: 4' 6", 8' 0", 4' 6".
Cylinders: 18" x 24" (I).
Gauge: 7' 0¼".
Weight–Loco: 35.5 tons.
   –Tender:
Tractive Effort: 7920 lbf.

IRON DUKE   Didcot Railway Centre (N)   Resco 1985

1.9.2. REPLICA STEAM LOCOMOTIVES UNDER CONSTRUCTION

GWR DESIGN

1000 CLASS   COUNTY   4-6-0

Original Class Built: 1945–47. 30 built (1000–29). The replica locomotive uses the frames from GWR 6959 Class 4-6-0 7927 WILLINGTON HALL and the firebox from Stanier 8F 2-8-0 48518. It is assuming the identity of a former member of the class.
Boiler Pressure: 250 lbf/sq in superheated.
Wheel Diameters: 3' 0", 6'3".
Cylinders: 18½" x 30" (O).
Tractive Effort: 29090 lbf.
BR Power Classification: D (6MT).
Weight–Loco: 76.85 tons.
   –Tender: 49.00 tons.
Valve Gear: Stephenson. Piston valves.
Restriction: Red.

1014   COUNTY OF GLAMORGAN   Didcot Railway Centre   Under construction

▲ The broad gauge Great Western Railway replica of 2-2-2 "FIRE FLY" is seen in action at Didcot Railway Centre on 5 May 2014.   **Ian McLoughlin**

▼ Progress with the frames of GWR design 1000 Class 4-6-0 new build 1014 "COUNTY OF GLAMORGAN" at Didcot Railway Centre on 5 April 2014.   **Alisdair Anderson**

SOUTHERN RAILWAY DESIGN

CLASS H2   4-4-2

Original Class Built: 1911–12. 6 built (32421–426). The replica locomotive uses the boiler from a GNR C1 Atlantic which is similar to the LBSCR class.

Boiler Pressure: 170 lbf/sq in.
Wheel Diameters: ?", 6'7½".
Cylinders: 21" x 26" (O).
Tractive Effort: 20840 lbf.

Weight–Loco: 68.25 tons.
    –Tender: 39.25 tons.
Valve Gear: Stephenson. Piston valves.
BR Power Classification: 3P.

32424	BEACHY HEAD	Bluebell Railway	Under construction

LMS DESIGN

CLASS 6P (formerly 5XP)   PATRIOT   4-6-0

Original Class Built: 1930–34. Fowler design. The first two members of the class were rebuilt from LNWR "Claughtons". 52 built (45500–51). This will be the 53rd locomotive built but will assume the identity of a former member of the class, 45551.

Boiler Pressure: 200 lbf/sq in superheated.
Wheel Diameters: 3' 3", 6'9".
Cylinders: 18" x 26" (3).
Tractive Effort: 26520 lbf.
BR Power Classification: 6P.

Weight–Loco: 80.75 tons.
    –Tender: 42.70 tons.
Valve Gear: Walschaerts. Piston valves.
Restriction: Red.

45551	THE UNKNOWN WARRIOR	Llangollen Railway	Under construction

LNER DESIGN

CLASS G5   0-4-4T

Original Class Built: 1894–1901. Wilson Worsdell North Eastern Railway design for branch line and suburban use. 110 built (67240–349). LNER 7306 was one of two members of the class withdrawn in 1948 and never received its allocated BR number 67306. The original was built at Darlington in 1897 as NER 1759.

Boiler Pressure: 160 lbf/sq in.
Wheel Diameters: 3' 1¼", 5' 1¼".
Valve Gear: Stephenson. Slide valves.
BR Power Classification: 1P.

Weight: 54.20 tons.
Cylinders: 18" x 24" (I).
Tractive Effort: 17200 lbf.
RA: 4.

67306		Class G5 Locomotive Company, Shildon	Under construction

2. DIESEL LOCOMOTIVES

GENERAL

It was not until the mid-1950s that diesel locomotives appeared in great numbers. However, during the 1930s, particularly on the LMS with diesel shunting locomotives, several small building programmes were authorised. A few locomotives survive from this period along with several others built in the immediate post-war period. During World War II a large proportion of LMS locomotives were transferred to the War Department who also authorised the construction of further orders. Many of these were shipped across the English Channel and were subsequently lost in action. It is, however, possible some still remain undiscovered. Notification of these would be gratefully appreciated. Those known to survive are listed in Section 2.1.

From the mid-1950s the re-equipment of the railway network began in earnest and vast numbers of new, mainly diesel locomotives, were constructed by British Railways and private contractors. Those from this period now considered to be preserved can be found in Section 2.3. Some examples from this period are still in service with main line and industrial users; details of these can be found in the Platform 5 "British Railways Pocket Book 1: Locomotives" or the bound volume "British Railways Locomotives & Coaching Stock".

WHEEL ARRANGEMENT

The Whyte notation is used for diesel shunting locomotives with coupled driving wheels (see steam section). For other shunting and main line diesel and electric locomotives, the system whereby the number of powered axles on a bogie or frame is denoted by a letter (A = 1, B = 2, C = 3 etc) and the number of unpowered axles is denoted by a number is used. The letter "o" after a letter indicates that each axle is individually powered and a + sign indicates that the bogies are intercoupled.

DIMENSIONS

SI units are generally used. Imperial units are sometimes given in parentheses.

TRACTIVE EFFORT

Continuous and maximum tractive efforts are generally quoted for vehicles with electric transmission.

BRAKES

Locomotives are assumed to have train vacuum brakes unless otherwise stated.

NUMBERING SYSTEMS

Prior to nationalisation each railway company allocated locomotive numbers in accordance with its own policy. However, after nationalisation in 1948 a common system was devised and internal combustion locomotives were allocated five figure numbers in the series 10000–19999.

Diesel locomotives built prior to nationalisation or to pre-nationalisation designs are arranged generally in order of the 1948 numbers with those withdrawn before 1948 listed at the beginning of each section. In 1957 a new numbering scheme was introduced for locomotives built to British Railways specifications and details of this are given in the introduction to the British Railways section.

2.1. LONDON MIDLAND & SCOTTISH RAILWAY

DIESEL MECHANICAL — 0-4-0

Built: 1934 by English Electric at Preston Works for Drewry Car Company.
Engine: Allan 8RS18 of 119 kW (160 hp) at 1200 rpm (now fitted with a Gardner 6L3 of 114 kW (153 hp)).
Transmission: Mechanical. Wilson four-speed gearbox driving a rear jackshaft.
Maximum Tractive Effort: 50 kN (11 200 lbf). **Weight:** 25.8 tonnes.
Maximum Speed: 12 mph. **Wheel Diameter:** 914 mm.

No train brakes.

LMS	*WD*	*AD*		
7050	224–70224–846	240	National Railway Museum, York (N)	DC 2047/EE/DK 847 1934

DIESEL MECHANICAL — 0-6-0

Built: 1932 by Hunslet Engine Company (taken into stock 1933).
Engine: MAN 112 kW (150 hp) at 900 rpm (now fitted with a Maclaren/Ricardo 98 kW engine).
Transmission: Mechanical. Hunslet constant mesh four-speed gearbox.
Maximum Tractive Effort: **Weight:** 21.7 tonnes.
Maximum Speed: 30 mph. **Wheel Diameter:** 914 mm.

Built without train brakes, but vacuum brakes now fitted.

7401–7051	"JOHN ALCOCK"	Middleton Railway	HE 1697/1933

DIESEL ELECTRIC — 0-6-0

Built: 1935 by English Electric. 11 built, 3 taken over by BR as 12000–002 (LMS 7074/76/79) and scrapped 1956–62. Others sold to WD for use in France.
Engine: English Electric 6K of 261 kW (350 hp) at 675 rpm.
Transmission: Electric. Two axle-hung traction motors with a single reduction drive.
Maximum Tractive Effort: 147 kN (33 000 lbf). **Weight:** 52 tonnes.
Maximum Speed: 30 mph. **Wheel Diameter:** 1232 mm.

No train brakes.

LMS	*WD*		
7069	18	Vale of Berkeley Railway, Sharpness	EE/HL 3841 1935

DIESEL ELECTRIC — 0-6-0

Built: 1939–42 at Derby. 40 built, 30 taken over by BR as 12003–032 (LMS 7080–99, 7110–19) and scrapped 1964–67. Others sold to WD for use in Italy and Egypt. Four were operated by FS – Ne 700.001–004 in Italy.
Engine: English Electric 6KT of 261 kW (350 hp) at 680 rpm.
Transmission: Electric. One traction motor with jackshaft drive.
Maximum Tractive Effort: 147 kN (33 000 lbf). **Weight:** 56 tonnes.
Maximum Speed: 20 mph. **Wheel Diameter:** 1295 mm.

Built without train brakes, but air brakes now fitted.

LMS	*WD*	*FS*	*Present*		
7103	52–70052	Ne 700.001	Unnumbered	Museo Ferroviario Piemontese store, Torino (Turin) Ponte Mosca station, Italy	Derby 1941
7106	55–70055	Ne 700.003		LFI, Arezzo Pescaiola, Italy	Derby 1941

BR CLASS 11   DIESEL ELECTRIC   0-6-0

Built: 1945–52. LMS design. 120 built. The first order for 20 was for the WD, 14 being delivered as 260–268/70269–273, the balance passing to the LMS as 7120–7125 (BR 12033–038). 260–268 were renumbered 70260–268 and 70260–269 were sold to the NS (Netherlands Railways) in 1946.

Engine: English Electric 6KT of 261 kW (350 hp) at 680 rpm.
Transmission: Electric. Two EE 506 axle-hung traction motors.
Maximum Tractive Effort: 156 kN (35 000 lbf).
Continuous Tractive Effort: 49.4 kN (11 100 lbf) at 8.8 mph.
Wheel Diameter: 1372 mm.   **Weight:** 56 tonnes.
Power at Rail: 183 kW (245 hp).   **Maximum Speed:** 20 mph.

No train brakes except 70272, 12099 and 12131 which have since been fitted with vacuum brakes and 12083 which has since been fitted with air brakes.

BR	WD	AD	Present		
–	70269		508§	Netherlands National Railway Museum, Utrecht	Derby 1944
–	70272–878	601	7120	Lakeside & Haverthwaite Railway	Derby 1944
12052			MP228	Caledonian Railway	Derby 1949
12077				Midland Railway-Butterley	Derby 1950
12082			12049	Mid Hants Railway	Derby 1950
12083				Battlefield Railway	Derby 1950
12088	"SHIRLEY"			Aln Valley Railway, Alnwick	Derby 1950
12093			MP229	Caledonian Railway	Derby 1951
12099				Severn Valley Railway	Derby 1952
12131				North Norfolk Railway	Darlington 1952

§ NS number.

2.2. SOUTHERN RAILWAY

BR CLASS 12   DIESEL ELECTRIC   0-6-0

Built: 1949–52. Based on pre-war LMS design. Bulleid Firth Brown wheels. 26 built.
Engine: English Electric 6KT of 350 hp at 680 rpm.
Transmission: Electric. Two EE 506A axle-hung traction motors.
Maximum Tractive Effort: 107 kN (24 000 lbf).
Continuous Tractive Effort: 36 kN (8000 lbf) at 10.2 mph.
Wheel Diameter: 1370 mm.   **Weight:** 45 tonnes.
Power at Rail: 163 kW (218 hp).   **Maximum Speed:** 27 mph.

No train brakes.

15224	Spa Valley Railway	Ashford 1949

2.3. BRITISH RAILWAYS

NUMBERING & CLASSIFICATION SYSTEM

In 1957 British Railways introduced a new numbering system which applied to all diesel locomotives except those built to pre-nationalisation designs. Each locomotive was allocated a number of up to four digits prefixed with a "D". Diesel electric shunters already built numbered in the 13xxx series had the "1" replaced by a "D". Diesel mechanical shunters already built numbered in the 11xxx series were allocated numbers in the D2xxx series.

When all steam locomotives had been withdrawn, the prefix letter was officially eliminated from the number of diesel locomotives, although it continued to be carried on many of them. For this reason, no attempt is made to distinguish between those locomotives which did or did not have the "D" prefix removed. Similarly, in preservation, no distinction is made between locomotives which do or do not carry a "D" prefix at present.

British Railways also introduced a new classification system for diesel & electric locomotives. Each main line diesel locomotive class was designated a "Type", based on engine horsepower. This broadly took the following form:

Type	Engine Horsepower (hp)	Number Range
1	800–1000	D 8000–D 8999
2	1001–1499	D 5000–D 6499
3	1500–1999	D 6500–D 7999
4	2000–2999	D 1 –D 1999
5	3000+	D 9000–D 9499
Shunting	150/300	D 2000–D 2999
Shunting	350/400	D 3000–D 4999
Shunting/trip	650	D 9500–D 9999
AC Electric		E 1000–E 4999
DC Electric		E 5000–E 6999

In 1968 British Railways introduced a two digit numerical class code for diesel & electric locomotives. With the introduction of modern communications each locomotive was allocated a new five digit number comprising the two digit class number followed by a three digit serial number. These started to be applied in 1972 and several locomotives have carried more than one number in this scheme.

In this section, classes are listed in 1968 two digit class number order. Locomotives are listed in 1957 number order within each class apart from Classes 24, 25, 26, 31, 33, 37, 45 and 47 which are listed within sub-class groups (but still in 1957 number order within that sub-class). A number of diesel shunting locomotives were withdrawn prior to the classification system being introduced and these are listed at the beginning of this section. Experimental and civil engineers' main line locomotives are listed in Sections 2.4 and 2.5.

UNCLASSIFIED   HUDSWELL-CLARKE   0-6-0

Built: 1955–61 by Hudswell-Clarke & Company, Leeds. 20 built.
Engine: Gardner 8L3 of 152 kW (204 hp) at 1200 rpm.
Transmission: Mechanical. SSS powerflow double synchro.
Maximum Tractive Effort: 85.7 kN (19 245 lbf).
Continuous Tractive Effort: 76 kN (17 069 lbf) at 3.72 mph.
Weight: 34 tonnes.   **Wheel Diameter:** 1067 mm.
Maximum Speed: 25 mph.

D 2511	Keighley & Worth Valley Railway	HC D 1202/1961

UNCLASSIFIED   NORTH BRITISH   0-4-0

Built: 1957–61 by North British Locomotive Company, Glasgow. 73 built.
Engine: MAN W6V 17.5/22A of 168 kW (225 hp) at 1100 rpm.
Transmission: Mechanical. Voith L33YU.
Maximum Tractive Effort: 89.4 kN (20 080 lbf).
Continuous Tractive Effort: 53.4 kN (12 000 lbf) at 4 mph.
Weight: 28 tonnes.   **Wheel Diameter:** 1067 mm.
Maximum Speed: 15 mph.

D 2767	Bo'ness & Kinneil Railway	NBL 28020/1960
D 2774	Strathspey Railway	NBL 28027/1960

CLASS 01   0-4-0

Built: 1956 by Andrew Barclay, Kilmarnock. 4 built.
Engine: Gardner 6L3 of 114 kW (153 hp) at 1200 rpm.
Transmission: Mechanical. Wilson SE4 epicyclic gearbox.
Maximum Tractive Effort: 56.8 kN (12 750 lbf). **Weight:** 25.5 tonnes.
Wheel Diameter: 965 mm.   **Maximum Speed:** 14 mph.

No train brakes.

11503–D 2953	Peak Rail	AB 395/1956
11506–D 2956	East Lancashire Railway	AB 398/1956

CLASS 02   0-4-0

Built: 1960–61 by Yorkshire Engine Company, Sheffield. 20 built.
Engine: Rolls Royce C6NFL of 127 kW (170 hp) at 1800 rpm.
Transmission: Hydraulic. Rolls Royce CF 10000.
Maximum Tractive Effort: 66.8 kN (15 000 lbf).
Continuous Tractive Effort: 61 kN (13 700 lbf) at 1.4 mph.
Weight: 28.6 tonnes.
Wheel Diameter: 1067 mm.   **Maximum Speed:** 30 mph.

D 2853–02003	Barrow Hill Roundhouse	YE 2812/1960
D 2854	Peak Rail	YE 2813/1960
D 2858	Midland Railway-Butterley	YE 2817/1960
D 2860	National Railway Museum, York (N)	YE 2843/1961
D 2866	Peak Rail	YE 2849/1961
D 2867	Battlefield Railway	YE 2850/1961
D 2868	Peak Rail	YE 2851/1961

▲ Class 01 D2953 at the Heritage Shunters Trust site at Rowsley, Peak Rail on 15 July 2015.
Robert Pritchard

▼ Class 03 D2090 (03090) gives brake van ride at the National Railway Museum, Shildon on 5 September 2015. **Robert Pritchard**

CLASS 03 0-6-0

Built: 1957–62 at Doncaster and Swindon. 230 built.
Engine: Gardner 8L3 of 152 kW (204 hp) at 1200 rpm. Replaced with Deutz VM V12 (300–350 hp) on D 2128 and D 2134 whilst in industrial use in Belgium. D 2128 has been re-engined with a Cummins engine and hydraulic transmission.
Transmission: Mechanical. Wilson CA5 epicyclic gearbox.
Maximum Tractive Effort: 68 kN (15 300 lbf).   **Weight:** 31 tonnes.
Wheel Diameter: 1092 mm.   **Maximum Speed:** 28 mph.

x   Dual (air/vacuum) braked.
a   Air braked only.
§   modified with cut down cab for working on Burry Port & Gwendraeth Valley Line.

11205–D 2018–03018		Mangapps Railway Museum	Swindon 1958
11207–D 2020–03020		Mangapps Railway Museum	Swindon 1958
11209–D 2022–03022		Swindon & Cricklade Railway	Swindon 1958
11210–D 2023		Kent & East Sussex Railway	Swindon 1958
11211–D 2024	No. 4	Kent & East Sussex Railway	Swindon 1958
D 2027–03027		Peak Rail	Swindon 1958
D 2037–03037		Royal Deeside Railway	Swindon 1959
D 2041		Colne Valley Railway	Swindon 1959
D 2046		Plym Valley Railway	Doncaster 1958
D 2051	*Unnumbered*	North Norfolk Railway	Doncaster 1959
D 2059–03059x		Isle of Wight Steam Railway	Doncaster 1959
D 2062–03062		East Lancashire Railway	Doncaster 1959
D 2063–03063x		North Norfolk Railway	Doncaster 1959
D 2066–03066x		Barrow Hill Roundhouse	Doncaster 1959
D 2069–03069		Vale of Berkeley Railway, Sharpness	Doncaster 1959
D 2072–03072		Lakeside & Haverthwaite Railway	Doncaster 1959
D 2073–03073x		Crewe Heritage Centre	Doncaster 1959
D 2078–03078x		Stephenson Railway Museum	Doncaster 1959
D 2079–03079		Derwent Valley Light Railway	Doncaster 1960
D 2081–03081		Mangapps Railway Museum	Doncaster 1960
D 2089–03089x		Mangapps Railway Museum	Doncaster 1960
D 2090–03090		National Railway Museum, Shildon (N)	Doncaster 1960
D 2094–03094x		Royal Deeside Railway	Doncaster 1960
D 2099–03099		Peak Rail	Doncaster 1960
D 2112–03112x		Rother Valley Railway	Doncaster 1960
D 2113–03113		Peak Rail	Doncaster 1960
D 2117		Lakeside & Haverthwaite Railway	Swindon 1959
D 2118–"03118"		Nottingham Transport Heritage Centre	Swindon 1959
D 2119–03119§		Epping Ongar Railway	Swindon 1959
D 2120–03120§		Fawley Hill Railway	Swindon 1959
D 2128–03128a–"03901"		Appleby-Frodingham RPS, Scunthorpe	Swindon 1960
D 2133		West Somerset Railway	Swindon 1960
D 2134–03134a		Royal Deeside Railway	Swindon 1960
D 2138		Midland Railway-Butterley	Swindon 1960
D 2139		Peak Rail	Swindon 1960
D 2141–03141§		Pontypool & Blaenavon Railway	Swindon 1960
D 2144–03144§x		Wensleydale Railway	Swindon 1960
D 2145–03145§		Moreton Park Railway	Swindon 1960
D 2148		Ribble Steam Railway	Swindon 1960
D 2152–03152§		Swindon & Cricklade Railway	Swindon 1960
D 2158–03158x	"MARGARET-ANN"	Titley Junction Station	Swindon 1960
D 2162–03162x		Llangollen Railway	Swindon 1960
D 2170–03170x		Epping Ongar Railway	Swindon 1960
D 2178		Gwili Railway	Swindon 1962
D 2180–03180x		Peak Rail	Swindon 1962
D 2182		Gloucestershire Warwickshire Railway	Swindon 1962
D 2184		Colne Valley Railway	Swindon 1962
D 2189–03189		Ribble Steam Railway	Swindon 1961
D 2192	"TITAN"	Dartmouth Steam Railway	Swindon 1961
D 2197–03197x		Mangapps Railway Museum	Swindon 1961

D 2199	Peak Rail	Swindon 1961
Dept 92–D 2371–03371x	Dartmouth Steam Railway	Swindon 1958
D 2399–03399x	Mangapps Railway Museum	Doncaster 1961

CLASS 04   0-6-0

Built: 1952–62. Drewry design built by Vulcan Foundry & Robert Stephenson & Hawthorns. 140 built.
Engine: Gardner 8L3 of 152 kW (204 hp) at 1200 rpm.
Transmission: Mechanical. Wilson CA5 epicyclic gearbox.
Maximum Tractive Effort: 69.7 kN (15 650 lbf) (* 75.0 kN (16 850 lbf)).
Weight: 32 tonnes.
Wheel Diameter: 1067 mm (* 991 mm).   **Maximum Speed:** 28 mph (* 25 mph).

11103–D 2203*		Embsay & Bolton Abbey Railway	DC/VF 2400/D145/1952
11106–D 2205*		Peak Rail	DC/VF 2486/D212/1953
11108–D 2207*		North Yorkshire Moors Railway	DC/VF 2482/D208/1953
11135–D 2229	Unnumbered	Peak Rail	DC/VF 2552/D278/1955
11215–D 2245		Battlefield Railway	DC/RSH 2577/7864/1956
11216–D 2246		South Devon Railway	DC/RSH 2578/7865/1956
D 2271	"GARDNER"	West Somerset Railway	DC/RSH 2615/7913/1958
D 2272		Peak Rail	DC/RSH 2616/7914/1958
D 2279		East Anglian Railway Museum	DC/RSH 2656/8097/1960
D 2280	Unnumbered	North Norfolk Railway	DC/RSH 2657/8098/1960
D 2284		Peak Rail	DC/RSH 2661/8102/1960
D 2298		Buckinghamshire Railway Centre	DC/RSH 2679/8157/1960
D 2302		Moreton Park Railway	DC/RSH 2683/8161/1960
D 2310	04110	Battlefield Railway	DC/RSH 2691/8169/1960
D 2324		Nemesis Rail, Burton-upon-Trent	DC/RSH 2705/8183/1961
D 2325		Mangapps Railway Museum	DC/RSH 2706/8184/1961
D 2334		Churnet Valley Railway	DC/RSH 2715/8193/1961
D 2337		Peak Rail	DC/RSH 2718/8196/1961

D 2279 is currently being overhauled at Andrew Briddon Locomotives, Darley Dale.

CLASS 05   0-6-0

Built: 1955–61 by Hunslet Engine Company, Leeds. 69 built.
Engine: Gardner 8L3 of 152 kW (204 hp) at 1200 rpm.
Transmission: Mechanical. Hunslet gearbox.
Maximum Tractive Effort: 64.6 kN (14 500 lbf). **Weight:** 31 tonnes.
Wheel Diameter: 1121 (* 1016) mm.   **Maximum Speed:** 18 mph.

11140–D 2554–05001–97803*	Isle of Wight Steam Railway	HE 4870/1956
D 2578	Moreton Park Railway	HE 5460/1958 rebuilt HE 6999/1968
D 2587	Peak Rail	HE 5636/1959 rebuilt HE 7180/1969
D 2595	Ribble Steam Railway	HE 5644/1960 rebuilt HE 7179/1969

CLASS 06   0-4-0

Built: 1958–60 by Andrew Barclay, Kilmarnock. 35 built.
Engine: Gardner 8L3 of 152 kW (204 hp) at 1200 rpm.
Transmission: Mechanical. Wilson CA5 epicyclic gearbox.
Maximum Tractive Effort: 88 kN (19 800 lbf). **Weight:** 37 tonnes.
Wheel Diameter: 1092 mm.   **Maximum Speed:** 23 mph.

D 2420–06003–97804	Peak Rail	AB 435/1959

▲ 07001 and Class 02 D2854 top-and-tail a brake van trip in the yard at Rowsley, Peak Rail on 15 July 2015. **Robert Pritchard**

▼ Class 09 D3668 (09004) is seen visiting the Avon Valley Railway for a diesel gala on 13 April 2014, seen at Bitton with the 15.02 to Avon Riverside. **Darren Ford**

CLASS 07 0-6-0

Built: 1962 by Ruston & Hornsby, Lincoln. 14 built.
Engine: Paxman 6RPHL Mk III of 205 kW (275 hp) at 1360 rpm.
Transmission: Electric. One AEI RTB 6652 traction motor.
Maximum Tractive Effort: 126 kN (28 240 lbf).
Continuous Tractive Effort: 71 kN (15 950 lbf) at 4.38 mph.
Power at Rail: 142 kW (190 hp).　　**Weight:** 43.6 tonnes.
Wheel Diameter: 1067 mm.　　**Maximum Speed:** 20 mph.

x　Dual (air/vacuum) braked.

D 2985–07001x	Peak Rail	RH 480698/1962
D 2989–07005x	Boden Rail Engineering, Washwood Heath	RH 480690/1962
D 2994–07010	Avon Valley Railway	RH 480695/1962
D 2995–07011x	St Leonards Railway Engineering	RH 480696/1962
D 2996–07012	Barrow Hill Roundhouse	RH 480697/1962
D 2997–07013x	East Lancashire Railway	RH 480698/1962

CLASS 08 0-6-0

Built: 1952–62. Built at Derby, Darlington, Crewe, Horwich & Doncaster. 996 built.
Engine: English Electric 6KT of 298 kW (400 hp) at 680 rpm.
Transmission: Electric. Two EE 506 axle-hung traction motors.
Maximum Tractive Effort: 156 kN (35 000 lbf).
Continuous Tractive Effort: 49.4 kN (11 100 lbf) at 8.8 mph.
Power at Rail: 194 kW (260 hp).　　**Weight:** 50 tonnes.
Wheel Diameter: 1372 mm.　　**Maximum Speed:** 15 mph.

x　Dual (air/vacuum) braked.
a　Air-braked only.
§　modified with cut down cab for working on Burry Port & Gwendraeth Valley Line.

D 3101 built without train brakes.

13000–D 3000		Peak Rail	Derby 1952
13002–D 3002		Plym Valley Railway	Derby 1952
13014–D 3014	"SAMSON"	Dartmouth Steam Railway	Derby 1952
13018–D 3018–08011	"HAVERSHAM"	Chinnor & Princes Risborough Railway	Derby 1953
13019–D 3019		Cambrian Railway Trust, Llynclys	Derby 1953
13022–D 3022–08015		Severn Valley Railway	Derby 1953
13023–D 3023–08016		Peak Rail	Derby 1953
13029–D 3029–08021		Tyseley Locomotive Works	Derby 1953
13030–D 3030–08022	"LION"	Cholsey & Wallingford Railway	Derby 1953
13044–D 3044–08032	"MENDIP"	Mid Hants Railway	Derby 1954
13059–D 3059–08046	"BRECHIN CITY"	Caledonian Railway	Derby 1954
13067–D 3067–08054		Embsay & Bolton Abbey Railway	Darlington 1953
13074–D 3074–08060	"UNICORN"	Cholsey & Wallingford Railway	Darlington 1953
13079–D 3079–08064		National Railway Museum, Shildon (N)	Darlington 1954
13101–D 3101		Great Central Railway	Derby 1955
13167–D 3167–08102		Lincolnshire Wolds Railway	Derby 1955
13174–D 3174–08108	"Dover Castle"	Kent & East Sussex Railway	Derby 1955
13180–D 3180–08114		Nottingham Transport Heritage Centre	Derby 1955
13190–D 3190–08123		Cholsey & Wallingford Railway	Derby 1955
13201–D 3201–08133		Severn Valley Railway	Derby 1955
13232–D 3232–08164		East Lancashire Railway	Darlington 1956
13236–D 3236–08168		Nemesis Rail, Burton-upon-Trent	Darlington 1956
13255–D 3255		North Side Works, Leavening	Derby 1956
13261–D 3261		Swindon & Cricklade Railway	Derby 1956
13265–D 3265–08195	"MARK"	Llangollen Railway	Derby 1956
13272–D 3272–08202		Avon Valley Railway	Derby 1956
13290–D 3290–08220		Nottingham Transport Heritage Centre	Derby 1956
13308–D 3308–08238	"Charlie"	Dean Forest Railway	Darlington 1956
13336–D 3336–08266		Keighley & Worth Valley Railway	Darlington 1957
D 3358–08288	*Unnumbered*	Mid Hants Railway	Derby 1957

D 3429–08359		Chasewater Light Railway	Crewe 1958
D 3462–08377		Mid Hants Railway	Darlington 1957
D 3551–08436 x		Swanage Railway	Derby 1958
D 3558–08443		Bo'ness & Kinneil Railway	Derby 1958
D 3559–08444		Bodmin & Wenford Railway	Derby 1958
D 3586–08471		Severn Valley Railway	Crewe 1958
D 3588–08473		Dean Forest Railway	Crewe 1958
D 3591–08476		Swanage Railway	Crewe 1958
D 3594–08479		East Lancashire Railway	Horwich 1958
D 3605–08490		Strathspey Railway	Horwich 1958
D 3662–08507 a		London & North Western Railway Heritage Company, Crewe	Doncaster 1958
D 3690–08528 x		Great Central Railway	Horwich 1959
D 3723–08556		North Yorkshire Moors Railway	Darlington 1959
D 3757–08590 x	"RED LION"	Midland Railway-Butterley	Crewe 1959
D 3759–08592–08993 x§		Keighley & Worth Valley Railway	Crewe 1959
D 3771–08604 x	604 "PHANTOM"	Didcot Railway Centre	Derby 1959
D 3798–08631 x	EAGLE C.U.R.C.	London & North Western Railway Heritage Company, Crewe	Derby 1959
D 3802–08635 x		Severn Valley Railway	Derby 1959
D 3854–08687–08995 x§		North Dorset Railway Trust, Shillingstone	Horwich 1959
D 3861–08694 x		Great Central Railway	Horwich 1959
D 3905–08737 x		London & North Western Railway Heritage Company, Crewe	Crewe 1960
D 3935–08767 x		North Norfolk Railway	Horwich 1961
D 3937–08769	"Gladys"	Dean Forest Railway	Derby 1960
D 3940–08772 x	CAMULODUNUM	North Norfolk Railway	Derby 1960
D 3941–08773 x		Embsay & Bolton Abbey Railway	Derby 1960
D 3948–08780 x	"FRED"	Southall Depot, London	Derby 1960
D 3993–08825 a		Chinnor & Princes Risborough Railway	Derby 1960
D 3998–08830 a		Peak Rail	Horwich 1960
D 4018–08850 x		North Yorkshire Moors Railway	Horwich 1961
D 4095–08881 x		Somerset & Dorset Railway Heritage Trust, Midsomer Norton Station	Horwich 1961
D 4126–08896 x		Severn Valley Railway	Horwich 1962
D 4141–08911 x	"MATEY"	National Railway Museum, York	Horwich 1962
D 4145–08915 x		Stephenson Railway Museum	Horwich 1962
D 4174–08944 x		East Lancashire Railway	Darlington 1962

D3854 is currently under overhaul at Rye Farm, Wishaw.

CLASS 09   0-6-0

Built: 1959–62. Built at Darlington & Horwich. 26 built.
Engine: English Electric 6KT of 298 kW (400 hp) at 680 rpm.
Transmission: Electric: Two EE506 axle-hung traction motors.
Power at Rail: 201 kW (269 hp).
Maximum Tractive Effort: 111 kN (25 000 lbf).
Continuous Tractive Effort: 39 kN (8800 lbf) at 11.6 mph.
Weight: 50 tonnes.   **Wheel Diameter:** 1372 mm.
Maximum Speed: 27 mph.

Dual (air/vacuum) braked.

D 3665–09001		Peak Rail	Darlington 1959
D 3668–09004		Swindon & Cricklade Railway	Darlington 1959
D 3721–09010		South Devon Railway	Darlington 1959
D 4100–09012	"Dick Hardy"	Severn Valley Railway	Horwich 1961
D 4103–09015		Rye Farm, Wishaw, Sutton Coldfield	Horwich 1961
D 4105–09017		National Railway Museum, York	Horwich 1961
D 4106–09018		Bluebell Railway	Horwich 1961
D 4107–09019		West Somerset Railway	Horwich 1961
D 4112–09024		East Lancashire Railway	Horwich 1961
D 4113–09025		Lavender Line	Horwich 1962
D 4114–09026		Lavender Line	Horwich 1962

CLASS 10   0-6-0

Built: 1955–62. Built at Darlington & Doncaster. 146 built.
Engine: Lister Blackstone ER6T of 261 kW (350 hp) at 750 rpm.
Transmission: Electric. Two GEC WT821 axle-hung traction motors.
Power at Rail: 198 kW (265 hp).
Maximum Tractive Effort: 156 kN (35 000 lbf). **Weight:** 47 tonnes.
Continuous Tractive Effort: 53.4 kN (12 000 lbf) at 8.2 mph.
Wheel Diameter: 1372 mm.   **Maximum Speed:** 20 mph.

D 3452		Bodmin & Wenford Railway	Darlington 1957
D 3489	"COLONEL TOMLINE"	Spa Valley Railway	Darlington 1958
D 4067	"10119" "Margaret Ethel – Thomas Alfred Naylor"	Great Central Railway	Darlington 1961
D 4092		Barrow Hill Roundhouse	Darlington 1962

CLASS 14   0-6-0

Built: 1964–65 at Swindon. 56 built.
Engine: Paxman Ventura 6YJXL of 485 kW (650 hp) at 1500 rpm.
Transmission: Hydraulic. Voith L217u.
Maximum Tractive Effort: 135 kN (30 910 lbf).
Continuous Tractive Effort: 109 kN (26 690 lbf) at 5.6 mph.
Weight: 51 tonnes.   **Wheel Diameter:** 1219 mm.
Maximum Speed: 40 mph.   **Train Heating:** None.

x   Dual (air/vacuum) braked

D 9500		Andrew Briddon Locomotives, Darley Dale	Swindon 1964
D 9502		East Lancashire Railway	Swindon 1964
D 9504		Kent & East Sussex Railway	Swindon 1964
D 9513	N.C.B. 38	Embsay & Bolton Abbey Railway	Swindon 1964
D 9516 x		Didcot Railway Centre	Swindon 1964
D 9518	NCB 7	West Somerset Railway	Swindon 1964
D 9520	45	Nene Valley Railway	Swindon 1964
D 9521		Dean Forest Railway	Swindon 1964
D 9523 x		Derwent Valley Light Railway	Swindon 1964
D 9524	14901	Churnet Valley Railway	Swindon 1964
D 9525		Peak Rail	Swindon 1965
D 9526		West Somerset Railway	Swindon 1965
D 9529	14029	Nene Valley Railway	Swindon 1965
D 9531 x	"ERNEST"	East Lancashire Railway	Swindon 1965
D 9537		East Lancashire Railway	Swindon 1965
D 9539		Peak Rail	Swindon 1965
D 9551		Severn Valley Railway	Swindon 1965
D 9553	54	Vale of Berkeley Railway, Sharpness	Swindon 1965
D 9555		Dean Forest Railway	Swindon 1965

D9523 is currently under overhaul at the Nene Valley Railway.

D9524 has a Rolls Royce Type DV8T of 336 kW (450 hp) engine which was fitted whilst in industrial use with BP. This engine was originally fitted to a Class 17. On loan from Andrew Briddon Locomotives, Darley Dale.

D9539 is on loan from the Ribble Steam Railway.

CLASS 15   Bo-Bo

Built: 1957–60 by BTH/Clayton Equipment Company. 44 built.
Engine: Paxman 16YHXL of 597 kW (800 hp) at 1250 rpm.
Transmission: Electric. Four BTH 137AZ axle-hung traction motors.
Maximum Tractive Effort: 178 kN (40 000 lbf).
Continuous Tractive Effort: 88 kN (19 700 lbf) at 11.3 mph.
Weight: 69 tonnes.   **Wheel Diameter:** 1003 mm.
Maximum Speed: 60 mph.   **Train Heating:** None.

D 8233–ADB968001	East Lancashire Railway	BTH 1131/1960

CLASS 17   Bo-Bo

Built: 1962–65 by Clayton Equipment Company. 117 built.
Engine: Two Paxman 6ZHXL of 336 kW (450 hp) at 1500 rpm.
Transmission: Electric. Four GEC WT421 axle-hung traction motors.
Power at Rail: 461 kW (618 hp).
Maximum Tractive Effort: 178 kN (40 000 lbf).
Continuous Tractive Effort: 80 kN (18 000 lbf) at 12.8 mph.
Weight: 69 tonnes.   **Wheel Diameter:** 1003 mm.
Maximum Speed: 60 mph.   **Train Heating:** None.

D 8568   Chinnor & Princes Risborough Railway   CE 4365U/69 1964

CLASS 20   Bo-Bo

Built: 1957–68 by English Electric at Vulcan Foundry, Newton-le-Willows or Robert Stephenson & Hawthorns, Darlington. 228 built.
Engine: English Electric 8SVT of 746 kW (1000 hp) at 850 rpm.
Transmission: Electric. Four EE 526/5D axle-hung traction motors.
Power at Rail: 574 kW (770 hp).
Maximum Tractive Effort: 187 kN (42 000 lbf).
Continuous Tractive Effort: 111 kN (25 000 lbf) at 11 mph.
Weight: 74 tonnes.   **Wheel Diameter:** 1092 mm.
Maximum Speed: 75 mph.   **Train Heating:** None.

Dual (air/vacuum) braked except D 8000.

D 8000–20050		National Railway Museum, York (N)	EE/VF 2347/D375 1957
D 8001–20001		Midland Railway-Butterley	EE/VF 2348/D376 1957
D 8007–20007		St Leonards Railway Engineering	EE/VF 2354/D382 1957
D 8020–20020		Bo'ness & Kinneil Railway	EE/RSH 2742/8052 1959
D 8031–20031		Keighley & Worth Valley Railway	EE/RSH 2753/8063 1960
D 8035–20035	2001	Gloucestershire Warwickshire Railway	EE/VF 2757/D482 1959
D 8048–20048		Midland Railway-Butterley	EE/VF 2770/D495 1959
D 8057–20057		Midland Railway-Butterley	EE/RSH 2963/8215 1961
D 8059–20059		Severn Valley Railway	EE/RSH 2965/8217 1961
D 8063–20063	2002	Battlefield Railway	EE/RSH 2969/8221 1961
D 8069–20069		Mid Norfolk Railway	EE/RSH 2975/8227 1961
D 8087–20087		East Lancashire Railway	EE/RSH 2993/8245 1961
D 8098–20098		Great Central Railway	EE/RSH 3004/8256 1961
D 8128–20228	2004	Barry Rail Centre	EE/VF 3599/D998 1966
D 8137–20137	Murray B. Hofmeyr	Gloucestershire Warwickshire Railway	EE/VF 3608/D1007 1966
D 8154–20154		Nottingham Transport Heritage Centre	EE/VF 3625/D1024 1966
D 8169–20169		Wensleydale Railway	EE/VF 3640/D1039 1966
D 8177–20177		Severn Valley Railway	EE/VF 3648/D1047 1966
D 8188–20188		Severn Valley Railway	EE/VF 3669/D1064 1967
D 8305–20205		Midland Railway-Butterley	EE/VF 3686/D1081 1967
D 8314–20214		Lakeside & Haverthwaite Railway	EE/VF 3695/D1090 1967
D 8327–20227		Midland Railway-Butterley	EE/VF 3685/D1080 1968

20001 is currently under overhaul at Boden Rail Engineering, Washwood Heath.

CLASS 24   Bo-Bo

Built: 1958–61 at Derby, Crewe & Darlington. 151 built.
Engine: Sulzer 6LDA28A of 870 kW (1160 hp) at 750 rpm.
Transmission: Electric. Four BTH 137BY axle-hung traction motors.
Power at Rail: 629 kW (843 hp).
Maximum Tractive Effort: 178 kN (40 000 lbf).
Continuous Tractive Effort: 95 kN (21 300 lbf) at 4.38 mph.
Weight: 81 or 78 tonnes.   **Wheel Diameter:** 1143 mm.
Maximum Speed: 75 mph.   **Train Heating:** Steam.

▲ The sole preserved Class 17, D8568, at Kidderminster during a visit to the Severn Valley Railway on 18 September 2015. **Ian McLoughlin**

▼ Class 20 D8059 (20059) is seen stabled at Kidderminster on 11 May 2015. **Tony Christie**

Class 24/0. 81 tonnes.

D 5032–24032	North Yorkshire Moors Railway	Crewe 1959

Class 24/1. 78 tonnes.

D 5054–24054–ADB 968008 "PHIL SOUTHERN"	East Lancashire Railway	Crewe 1959
D 5061–24061–RDB 968007–97201 EXPERIMENT		
"Ian Johnson"	North Yorkshire Moors Railway	Crewe 1960
D 5081–24081	Gloucestershire Warwickshire Railway	Crewe 1960

D5054 is currently under overhaul at Barrow Hill Roundhouse.

CLASS 25   Bo-Bo

Built: 1961–67. Built at Darlington, Derby & Beyer Peacock, Manchester. 327 built.
Engine: Sulzer 6LDA28B of 930 kW (1250 hp) at 750 rpm.
Transmission: Electric. Four AEI 253AY axle-hung traction motors.
Power at Rail: 708 kW (949 hp).
Maximum Tractive Effort: 200 kN (45 000 lbf).
Continuous Tractive Effort: 93 kN (20 800 lbf) at 17.1 mph.
Weight: 72–76 tonnes.   **Wheel Diameter:** 1143 mm.
Maximum Speed: 90 mph.

Class 25/1. Dual (air/vacuum) braked except D 5217. Train heating: Steam.

D 5185–25035	"CASTELL DINAS BRAN"	Great Central Railway	Darlington 1963
D 5207–25057		North Norfolk Railway	Derby 1963
D 5209–25059		Keighley & Worth Valley Railway	Derby 1963
D 5217–25067		Nemesis Rail, Burton-upon-Trent	Derby 1963
D 5222–25072		Caledonian Railway	Derby 1963

Class 25/2. Dual (air/vacuum) braked except D 5233. Train heating: Steam: D 5233, D 7585/94. None: D 7523/35/41.

D 5233–25083		Caledonian Railway	Derby 1963
D 7523–25173		Epping Ongar Railway	Derby 1965
D 7535–25185	"MERCURY"	Dartmouth Steam Railway	Derby 1965
D 7541–25191		South Devon Railway	Derby 1965
D 7585–25235		Bo'ness & Kinneil Railway	Darlington 1964
D 7594–25244		Kent & East Sussex Railway	Darlington 1964

Class 25/3. Dual (air/vacuum) braked. Train heating: None.

D 7612–25262–25901		South Devon Railway	Derby 1966
D 7615–25265		Nemesis Rail, Burton-upon-Trent	Derby 1966
D 7628–25278	"SYBILLA"	North Yorkshire Moors Railway	BP 8038/1965
D 7629–25279		Ecclesbourne Valley Railway	BP 8039/1965
D 7633–25283–25904		Dean Forest Railway	BP 8043/1965
D 7659–25309–25909		RMS Locotec, Washwood Heath	BP 8069/1966
D 7663–25313		Wensleydale Railway	Derby 1966
D 7671–25321		Midland Railway-Butterley	Derby 1967
D 7672–25322–25912	TAMWORTH CASTLE	Churnet Valley Railway	Derby 1967

CLASS 26   Bo-Bo

Built: 1958–59 by the Birmingham Railway Carriage & Wagon Company. 47 built.
Engine: Sulzer 6LDA28A of 870 kW (1160 hp) at 750 rpm.
Transmission: Electric. Four Crompton-Parkinson C171A1 (§ C171D3) axle-hung traction motors.
Power at Rail: 671 kW (900 hp).
Maximum Tractive Effort: 187 kN (42 000 lbf).
Continuous Tractive Effort: 133 kN (30 000 lbf) at 14 mph.
Weight: 72–75 tonnes.   **Wheel Diameter:** 1092 mm.
Maximum Speed: 75 mph.
Train Heating: Built with steam. Removed from D 5300/01/02/04 in 1967.

Dual (air/vacuum) braked.

▲ The North Yorkshire Moors Railway's Class 25 D7628 (25278) passes Green End, between Grosmont and Goathland, with a train for Pickering on 29 October 2014. **Robert Falconer**

▼ D5343 (26043) approaches Winchcombe with the 14.10 Cheltenham Racecourse–Laverton during the Gloucestershire Warwickshire Railway's diesel gala on 25 July 2014. **Nigel Gibbs**

Class 26/0.

D 5300–26007	Barrow Hill Roundhouse	BRCW DEL/45/1958
D 5301–26001	Caledonian Railway	BRCW DEL/46/1958
D 5302–26002	Strathspey Railway	BRCW DEL/47/1958
D 5304–26004	Nemesis Rail, Burton-upon-Trent	BRCW DEL/49/1958
D 5310–26010	Llangollen Railway	BRCW DEL/55/1959
D 5311–26011	Nemesis Rail, Burton-upon-Trent	BRCW DEL/56/1959
D 5314–26014	Caledonian Railway	BRCW DEL/59/1959

Class 26/1.§

D 5324–26024		Bo'ness & Kinneil Railway	BRCW DEL/69/1959
D 5325–26025		Strathspey Railway	BRCW DEL/69/1959
D 5335–26035		Caledonian Railway	BRCW DEL/80/1959
D 5338–26038	"Tom Clift 1954–2012"	Bo'ness & Kinneil Railway	BRCW DEL/83/1959
D 5340–26040		Waverley Route Heritage Association, Whitrope	BRCW DEL/85/1959
D 5343–26043		Gloucestershire Warwickshire Railway	BRCW DEL/88/1959

CLASS 27   Bo-Bo

Built: 1961–62 by the Birmingham Railway Carriage & Wagon Company, Birmingham. 69 built.
Engine: Sulzer 6LDA28B of 930 kW (1250 hp) at 750 rpm.
Transmission: Electric. Four GEC WT459 axle-hung traction motors.
Power at Rail: 696 kW (933 hp).
Maximum Tractive Effort: 178 kN (40 000 lbf).
Continuous Tractive Effort: 111 kN (25 000 lbf) at 14 mph.
Weight: 72–75 tonnes.   **Wheel Diameter:** 1092 mm.
Maximum Speed: 90 mph.
Train Heating: Built with steam (except D 5370 – no provision). Replaced with electric on D 5386 and D 5410 but subsequently removed.

Dual (air/vacuum) braked except D 5353.

D 5347–27001	Bo'ness & Kinneil Railway	BRCW DEL/190/1961
D 5351–27005	Bo'ness & Kinneil Railway	BRCW DEL/194/1961
D 5353–27007	Mid Hants Railway	BRCW DEL/196/1961
D 5370–27024–ADB 968028	Caledonian Railway	BRCW DEL/213/1962
D 5386–27103–27212–27066	Barrow Hill Roundhouse	BRCW DEL/229/1962
D 5394–27106–27050	Strathspey Railway	BRCW DEL/237/1962
D 5401–27112–27056	Great Central Railway	BRCW DEL/244/1962
D 5410–27123–27205–27059	UK Rail Leasing, Leicester Depot	BRCW DEL/253/1962

27059 is currently under overhaul at the East Somerset Railway.

CLASS 28   METROVICK   Co-Bo

Built: 1958–59 by Metropolitan Vickers, Manchester. 20 built.
Engine: Crossley HSTVee 8 of 896 kW (1200 hp) at 625 rpm.
Transmission: Electric. Five MV 137BZ axle-hung traction motors.
Power at Rail: 671 kW (900 hp).
Maximum Tractive Effort: 223 kN (50 000 lbf).   **Weight:** 99 tonnes.
Continuous Tractive Effort: 111 kN (25 000 lbf) at 13.5 mph.
Wheel Diameter: 1003 mm.   **Train Heating:** Steam.
Maximum Speed: 75 mph.

D 5705–S 15705–TDB 968006	East Lancashire Railway	MV 1958

CLASS 31   A1A-A1A

Built: 1957–62 by Brush Electrical Engineering Company, Loughborough. 263 built.
Engine: Built with Mirrlees JVS12T of 1020 kW (1365 hp). Re-engined 1964–69 with English Electric 12SVT of 1100 kW (1470 hp) at 850 rpm.
Transmission: Electric. Four Brush TM73-68 axle-hung traction motors.
Power at Rail: 872 kW (1170 hp).
Maximum Tractive Effort: 190 kN (42 800 lbf).
Continuous Tractive Effort: 99 kN (22 250 lbf) at 19.7 mph.
Weight: 106.7–111 tonnes.   **Wheel Diameter:** 1092 mm.
Maximum Speed: 90 mph or 80 mph (D5500). D5518, D5522, D5526, and D5533 were originally 80 mph but have been regeared for 90 mph.
Train Heating: Built with steam heating.

D5500, D5518, D5522, D5526 and D5547 were built without roof-mounted headcode boxes. They were subsequently fitted to D5518.

Class 31/0. Electro-magnetic control.

D5500–31018	National Railway Museum, York (N)	BE 71/1957

Class 31/1. Electro-pneumatic control. Dual (air/vacuum) braked.

D5518–31101		Avon Valley Railway	BE 89/1958
D5526–31108		Midland Railway Butterley	BE 125/1959
D5537–31119		Embsay & Bolton Abbey Railway	BE 136/1959
D5546–31128	CHARYBDIS	Nemesis Rail, Burton-upon-Trent	BE 145/1959
D5548–31130	Calder Hall Power Station	Avon Valley Railway	BE 147/1959
D5580–31162		Nottingham Transport Heritage Centre	BE 180/1960
D5581–31163		Chinnor & Princes Risborough Railway	BE 181/1960
D5627–31203	"Steve Organ G.M."	Pontypool & Blaenavon Railway	BE 227/1960
D5630–31206		Rushden Transport Museum	BE 230/1960
D5631–31207		North Norfolk Railway	BE 231/1960
D5634–31210		Dean Forest Railway	BE 234/1960
D5662–31235		Mid Norfolk Railway	BE 262/1960
D5683–31255		Colne Valley Railway	BE 284/1961
D5800–31270	"Athena"	Peak Rail	BE 301/1961
D5801–31271	"Stratford 1840–2001"	Nene Valley Railway	BE 302/1961
D5821–31289	"PHOENIX"	Rushden Transport Museum	BE 322/1961
D5862–31327	Phillips-Imperial	Strathspey Railway	BE 398/1962

Class 31/4. Electro-pneumatic control. Dual (air/vacuum) braked. Fitted with Electric Train Supply equipment (steam heating removed when electric supply fitted, except D5522, D5669 and D5814 from which it was removed later).

D5522–31418	Midland Railway-Butterley	BE 121/1959
D5533–31115–31466	East Lancashire Railway	BE 132/1959
D5547–31129–31461	Nemesis Rail, Burton-upon-Trent	BE 146/1959
D5557–31139–31438–31538	Epping Ongar Railway	BE 156/1959
D5600–31179–31435	Embsay & Bolton Abbey Railway	BE 200/1960
D5695–31265–31430–31530 Sister Dora	Mangapps Railway Museum	BE 296/1961
D5814–31414–31514	Ecclesbourne Valley Railway	BE 315/1961
D5830–31297–31463–31563	Great Central Railway	BE 366/1962

31162 and 31271 are on loan from the Midland Railway-Butterley.

31466 is on loan from the Dean Forest Railway.

▲ The A1A Group's 31271 is seen at Peterborough (Nene Valley Railway) after arrival with a train from Wansford on 20 September 2015. **Alisdair Anderson**

▼ Hymek D7017 climbs away from Bishops Lydeard with a demonstration freight for Williton on the evening of 6 June 2015. **David Hunt**

CLASS 33   Bo-Bo

Built: 1961–62 by the Birmingham Railway Carriage & Wagon Company, Birmingham. 98 built.
Engine: Sulzer 8LDA28A of 1160 kW (1550 hp) at 750 rpm.
Transmission: Electric. Four Crompton-Parkinson C171C2 axle-hung traction motors.
Power at Rail: 906 kW (1215 hp).
Maximum Tractive Effort: 200 kN (45 000 lbf).
Continuous Tractive Effort: 116 kN (26 000 lbf) at 17.5 mph.
Weight: 78 tonnes.   **Wheel Diameter:** 1092 mm.
Maximum Speed: 85 mph.   **Train Heating:** Electric.

Dual (air/vacuum) braked.

Class 33/0.

D 6501–33002	Sea King	South Devon Railway	BRCW DEL/93/1960
D 6508–33008	Eastleigh	Battlefield Railway	BRCW DEL/100/1960
D 6515–33012		Swanage Railway	BRCW DEL/107/1960
D 6530–33018		Mangapps Railway Museum	BRCW DEL/122/1960
D 6534–33019	Griffon	Battlefield Railway	BRCW DEL/126/1960
D 6539–33021	"Captain Charles"	Churnet Valley Railway	BRCW DEL/131/1960
D 6553–33035	Spitfire	Barrow Hill Roundhouse	BRCW DEL/145/1961
D 6564–33046	Merlin	East Lancashire Railway	BRCW DEL/156/1961
D 6566–33048		West Somerset Railway	BRCW DEL/170/1961
D 6570–33052	Ashford	Kent & East Sussex Railway	BRCW DEL/174/1961
D 6571–33053		Mid Hants Railway	BRCW DEL/175/1961
D 6575–33057	Seagull	West Somerset Railway	BRCW DEL/179/1961
D 6583–33063	"R.J. Mitchell DESIGNER OF THE SPITFIRE"	Spa Valley Railway	BRCW DEL/187/1962
D 6585–33065	Sealion	Spa Valley Railway	BRCW DEL/189/1962

Class 33/1. Fitted for push-pull operation. Triple (vacuum, air and electro-pneumatic) braked.

D 6513–33102	"Sophie"	Churnet Valley Railway	BRCW DEL/105/1960
D 6514–33103	"SWORDFISH"	Ecclesbourne Valley Railway	BRCW DEL/106/1960
D 6521–33108	"VAMPIRE"	Barrow Hill Roundhouse	BRCW DEL/113/1960
D 6525–33109	Captain Bill Smith RNR	East Lancashire Railway	BRCW DEL/117/1960
D 6527–33110		Bodmin & Wenford Railway	BRCW DEL/119/1960
D 6528–33111		Swanage Railway	BRCW DEL/120/1960
D 6535–33116	Hertfordshire Railtours	Great Central Railway (N)	BRCW DEL/127/1960
D 6536–33117		East Lancashire Railway	BRCW DEL/128/1960

Class 33/2. Built to the former loading gauge of the Tonbridge–Battle line.

D 6586–33201		Swanage Railway	BRCW DEL/157/1962
D 6587–33202	"Dennis G. Robinson"	Epping Ongar Railway	BRCW DEL/158/1962
D 6593–33208		Battlefield Railway	BRCW DEL/164/1962

33103 is on loan from Nemesis Rail, Burton-upon-Trent.

33202 is on loan from the Mangapps Railway Museum.

33202 also carried the names The Burma Star and METEOR.

CLASS 35   HYMEK   B-B

Built: 1961–64 by Beyer Peacock, Manchester. 101 built.
Engine: Bristol Siddley Maybach MD 870 of 1269 kW (1700 hp) at 1500 rpm.
Transmission: Hydraulic. Mekydro K184U.
Maximum Tractive Effort: 207 kN (46 600 lbf).
Continuous Tractive Effort: 151 kN (33 950 lbf) at 12.5 mph.
Weight: 77 tonnes.   **Wheel Diameter:** 1143 mm.
Maximum Speed: 90 mph.   **Train Heating:** Steam.

D 7017	West Somerset Railway	BP 7911/1962
D 7018	West Somerset Railway	BP 7912/1962
D 7029	Severn Valley Railway	BP 7923/1962
D 7076	East Lancashire Railway	BP 7980/1963

CLASS 37   Co-Co

Built: 1960–66 by English Electric Company at Vulcan Foundry, Newton-le-Willows or Robert Stephenson & Hawthorns, Darlington. 309 built.
Engine: English Electric 12CSVT of 1300 kW (1750 hp) at 850 rpm unless stated otherwise.
Transmission: Electric. Six English Electric 538/A.
Power at Rail: 932 kW (1250 hp).
Maximum Tractive Effort: 247 kN (55 500 lbf).
Continuous Tractive Effort: 156 kN (35 000 lbf) at 13.6 mph.
Weight: 103–108 tonnes.   **Wheel Diameter:** 1092 mm.
Maximum Speed: 80 mph.
Train heating: Built with steam (* built without heating, but steam later fitted to D 6961, D 6963 and D 6964). Provision of steam heating was removed from D 6823, D 6842, D 6852, D 6859, D 6869, D 6915, D 6916 and D 6927 soon after delivery and may never have been used. D 6948 has been restored with steam heating.

Dual (air/vacuum) braked.

Class 37/0.

D 6608–37308–37274*		Dean Forest Railway	EE/VF 3568/D997/1966
D 6703–37003	"Dereham Neatherd High School 1912–2012"	Mid Norfolk Railway	EE/VF 2866/D582/1960
D 6723–37023	Stratford TMD	Allely's Heavy Haulage, Studley	EE/VF 2886 D602/1961
D 6725–37025	Inverness TMD	Bo'ness & Kinneil Railway	EE/VF 2888/D604/1961
D 6729–37029		Epping Ongar Railway	EE/VF 2892/D608/1961
D 6737–37037–37321	"Loch Treig"	South Devon Railway	EE/VF 2900/D616/1962
D 6742–37042		Eden Valley Railway	EE/VF 3034/D696/1962
D 6775–37075		Keighley & Worth Valley Railway	EE/RSH 3067/8321/1962
D 6797–37097	"Old Fettercairn"	Caledonian Railway	EE/VF 3226/D751/1962
D 6808–37108–37325	Lanarkshire Steel	Crewe Heritage Centre	EE/VF 3237/D762/1963

▲ D6732 (37032/37353) arrives at Sheringham on the North Norfolk Railway with a train from Holt on 17 May 2014.   **Tony Christie**

D 6809–37109		East Lancashire Railway	EE VF 3238/D763/1963
D 6842–37142		Bodmin & Wenford Railway	EE/VF 3317/D816/1963
D 6852–37152–37310	British Steel Ravenscraig	Peak Rail	EE/VF 3327/D826/1963
D 6890–37190–37314	Dalzell	Midland Railway-Butterley	EE/RSH 3368/8411/1964
D 6915–37215		Gloucestershire Warwickshire Railway	EE/VF 3393/D859/1964
D 6916–37216	Great Eastern	Pontypool & Blaenavon Railway	EE/VF 3394/D860 1964
D 6927–37227		Nemesis Rail, Burton-upon-Trent	EE/VF 3413/D871/1964
D 6940–37240*		Llangollen Railway	EE/VF 3497/D928/1964
D 6948–37248*	Loch Arkaig	Gloucestershire Warwickshire Railway	EE/VF 3505/D936/1964
D 6950–37250*		Wensleydale Railway	EE/VF 3507/D938/1964
D 6955–37255*		Nemesis Rail, Burton-upon-Trent	EE/VF 3512/D943/1965
D 6961–37261*		Bo'ness & Kinneil Railway	EE/VF 3521/D950/1965
D 6963–37263*		Tyseley Locomotive Works	EE/VF 3523/D952/1965
D 6964–37264*		North Yorkshire Moors Railway	EE/VF 3524/D953/1965
D 6975–37275*	Stainless Pioneer	South Devon Railway	EE/VF 3535/D964/1965
D 6994–37294*		Embsay & Bolton Abbey Railway	EE/VF 3554/D983/1965

Class 37/3. Fitted with regeared CP7 bogies. Details as Class 37/0 except:
Maximum Traction Effort: 250 kN (56 180 lbf).
Continuous Tractive Effort: 184 kN (41 250 lbf) at 11.4 mph.

D 6700–37119–37350	NATIONAL RAILWAY MUSEUM	National Railway Museum, York (N)	EE/VF 2863/D579/1960
D 6709–37009–37340		Nottingham Transport Heritage Centre	EE/VF 2872/D588/1961
D 6732–37032–37353		North Norfolk Railway	EE/VF 2895/D611/1962
D 6859–37159–37372		Barrow Hill Roundhouse	EE/RSH 3337/8390/1963

Class 37/4. Main generator replaced by alternator. Fitted with Electric Train Supply equipment and regeared CP7 bogies. Details as Class 37/0 except:
Transmission: Electric. Six English Electric 538/5A.
Power at rail: 935 kW (1254 hp).
Maximum Tractive Effort: 256 kN (57 440 lbf).
Continous Tractive Effort: 184 kN (41 250 lbf) at 11.4 mph.

D 6607–37307–37403*	Isle of Mull	Bo'ness & Kinneil Railway	EE/VF 3567/D996/1965
D 6971–37271–37418*	Pectinidae	East Lancashire Railway	EE/VF 3531/D960/1965
D 6976–37276–37413*	Loch Eil Outward Bound	East Lancashire Railway	EE/VF 3536/D965/1965

Class 37/5. Main generator replaced by alternator. Regeared CP7 bogies. Details as Class 37/0 except:
Maximum Traction Effort: 248 kN (55 590 lbf).
Continuous Tractive Effort: 184 kN (41 250 lbf) at 10.2 mph.

D 6817–37117–37521	English China Clays	Barrow Hill Roundhouse	EE/VF 3246/D771/1963
D 6823–37123–37679		East Lancashire Railway	EE/RSH 3268/8383/1963
D 6869–37169–37674	Saint Blaise Church 1445–1995	Wensleydale Railway	EE/VF 3347/D833/1963

Class 37/7. Main generator replaced by alternator. Regeared CP7 bogies. Ballast weights added. Details as Class 37/0 except:
Main Alternator: Brush BA1005A.
Maximum Traction Effort: 276 kN (62 000 lbf).
Continuous Tractive Effort: 184 kN (41 250 lbf) at 10.2 mph.

D6724–37024–37714	Thornaby TMD	Great Central Railway	EE/VF 2887/D603/1961

37372 is undergoing conversion to a replica Class 23 "Baby Deltic", none of which were preserved.

D 6703 carried the name First East Anglian Regiment for a short time in 1963 but was never officially named.
37037 also carried the name Gartcosh.
37248 also carried the name Midland Railway Centre.
37275 also carried the name Oor Wullie.
37403 also carried the names Ben Cruachan and Glendarroch.
37413 also carried the name The Scottish Railway Preservation Society.
37418 also carried the names An Comunn Gaidhealach and East Lancashire Railway.

CLASS 40 1Co-Co1

Built: 1958–62 by English Electric at Vulcan Foundry, Newton-le-Willows & Robert Stephenson & Hawthorns, Darlington. 200 built.
Engine: English Electric 16SVT MkII of 1492 kW (2000 hp) at 850 rpm.
Transmission: Electric. Six EE 526/5D axle-hung traction motors.
Power at Rail: 1156 kW (1550 hp).
Maximum Tractive Effort: 231 kN (52 000 lbf).
Continuous Tractive Effort: 137 kN (30 900 lbf) at 18.8 mph.
Weight: 132 tonnes. **Wheel Diameters:** 914/1143 mm.
Maximum Speed: 90 mph. **Train Heating:** Steam.

Dual (air/vacuum) braked except D 306.

D 200–40122		National Railway Museum, York (N)	EE/VF 2367/D395	1958
D 212–40012–97407	AUREOL	Barrow Hill Roundhouse	EE/VF 2667/D429	1959
D 213–40013	ANDANIA	Barrow Hill Roundhouse	EE/VF 2668/D430	1959
D 306–40106	"ATLANTIC CONVEYOR"	East Lancashire Railway	EE/RSH 2726/8136	1960
D 318–40118–97408		Tyseley Locomotive Works	EE/RSH 2853/8148	1961
D 335–40135–97406		East Lancashire Railway	EE/VF 3081/D631	1961
D 345–40145		East Lancashire Railway	EE/VF 3091/D641	1961

D 212 is on loan from the Midland Railway-Butterley.

▲ 40106 "ATLANTIC CONVEYOR" passes Bewdley Bridge with the 13.42 Bridgnorth–Kidderminster on 4 October 2014. **Tom McAtee**

CLASS 41   PROTOTYPE HST POWER CAR

Built: 1972 at Derby. 2 built. Two prototype High Speed Diesel Train (HSDT) power cars (41001/002) were constructed to a locomotive lot (No. 1501) whilst the intermediate vehicles (10000, 10100, 11000–002 and 12000–002) were constructed to coaching stock lots. On 10 July 1974 the power cars were reclassified as coaching stock and issued with a coaching stock lot number. All prototype HSDT vehicles were thus categorised as multiple unit stock and renumbered into the 4xxxx series, Class No. 252 being allocated for the complete set. 41001 has been restored to original Class 41 condition and is used as a conventional locomotive.
Engine: Paxman Valenta 12RP200L of 1680 kW (2250 hp) at 1500 rpm.
Traction Motors: Four Brush TMH 68-46.
Power at Rail: 1320 kW (1770 hp).
Maximum Tractive Effort: 80 kN (17 980 lbf).
Continuous Tractive Effort: 46 kN (10 340 lbf) at 64.5 mph.
Weight: 67 tonnes.   **Wheel Diameter:** 1020 mm.
Maximum Speed: 125 mph.   **Train Heating:** Electric.

Air braked.

41001–43000–ADB 975812   Nottingham Transport Heritage Centre (N)   Derby 1972

CLASS 42   WARSHIP   B-B

Built: 1958–61 at Swindon. 38 built.
Engines: Two Bristol Siddley Maybach MD650 of 821 kW (1100 hp) at 1530 rpm.
Transmission: Hydraulic. Mekydro K 104U.
Maximum Tractive Effort: 223 kN (52 400 lbf).
Continuous Tractive Effort: 209 kN (46 900 lbf) at 11.5 mph.
Weight: 80 tonnes.   **Wheel Diameter:** 1033 mm.
Maximum Speed: 90 mph.   **Train Heating:** Steam.

| D 821 | GREYHOUND | Severn Valley Railway | Swindon 1960 |
| D 832 | ONSLAUGHT | West Somerset Railway | Swindon 1961 |

D 821 is currently being overhauled at Old Oak Common Depot, London.

D 832 is on loan from the East Lancashire Railway.

CLASS 44   PEAK   1Co-Co1

Built: 1959–60 at Derby. 10 built.
Engine: Sulzer 12LDA28A of 1720 kW (2300 hp) at 750 rpm.
Transmission: Electric. Six Crompton Parkinson C171B1 axle-hung traction motors.
Power at Rail: 1342 kW (1800 hp).
Maximum Tractive Effort: 222 kN (50 000 lbf).
Continuous Tractive Effort: 129 kN (29 100 lbf) at 23.2 mph.
Weight: 135 tonnes.   **Wheel Diameters:** 914/1143 mm.
Maximum Speed: 90 mph.
Train Heating: Built with steam but facility removed in 1962.

| D 4–44004 | GREAT GABLE | Midland Railway-Butterley | Derby 1959 |
| D 8–44008 | PENYGHENT | Peak Rail | Derby 1959 |

CLASS 45   1Co-Co1

Built: 1960–63 at Crewe and Derby. 127 built.
Engine: Sulzer 12LDA28B of 1860 kW (2500 hp) at 750 rpm.
Transmission: Electric. Six Crompton Parkinson C172A1 axle-hung traction motors.
Power at Rail: 1491 kW (2000 hp).
Maximum Tractive Effort: 245 kN (55 000 lbf).
Continuous Tractive Effort: 133 kN (30 000 lbf) at 25 mph.
Weight: 135 or 138 tonnes.
Wheel Diameters: 914/1143 mm.   **Maximum Speed:** 90 mph.
Train Heating: Built with steam.

Dual (air/vacuum) braked.

▲ 45060 "SHERWOOD FORESTER" leaves Harmans Cross for Swanage during the railway's diesel gala on 7 May 2015. **Tom McAtee**

▼ 47715 "Haymarket" approaches Redmire with the Wensleydale Railway's 15.15 Leeming Bar–Redmire on 30 May 2016. **Robert Pritchard**

Class 45/0. Weight 138 tonnes.

D 14–45015		Battlefield Railway	Derby 1960
D 53–45041	ROYAL TANK REGIMENT	Great Central Railway	Crewe 1962
D 100–45060	SHERWOOD FORESTER	Barrow Hill Roundhouse	Crewe 1961

Class 45/1. Steam heating replaced with Electric train supply equipment. Weight 135 tonnes.

D 22–45132		Epping Ongar Railway	Derby 1961
D 40–45133		Midland Railway-Butterley	Derby 1961
D 61–45112	THE ROYAL ARMY ORDNANCE CORPS	Nemesis Rail, Burton-upon-Trent	Crewe 1962
D 67–45118	THE ROYAL ARTILLERYMAN	RVEL, Derby	Crewe 1962
D 86–45105		Barrow Hill Roundhouse	Crewe 1961
D 99–45135	3rd CARABINIER	East Lancashire Railway	Crewe 1961
D 120–45108		Midland Railway-Butterley	Crewe 1961
D 123–45125	"LEICESTERSHIRE AND DERBYSHIRE YEOMANRY"	Great Central Railway	Crewe 1961
D 135–45149		Gloucestershire Warwickshire Railway	Crewe 1961

45041 is on loan from the Midland Railway-Butterley.

CLASS 46　　　　　　　　　　　　　1Co-Co1

Built: 1961–63 at Derby. 56 built.
Engine: Sulzer 12LDA28B of 1860 kW (2500 hp) at 750 rpm.
Transmission: Electric. Six Brush TM73-68 MkIII axle-hung traction motors.
Power at Rail: 1460 kW (1960 hp).
Maximum Tractive Effort: 245 kN (55 000 lbf).
Continuous Tractive Effort: 141 kN (31 600 lbf) at 22.3 mph.
Weight: 141 tonnes.　　　　　　**Wheel Diameters:** 914/1143 mm.
Maximum Speed: 90 mph.
Train Heating: Steam.

Dual (air/vacuum) braked.

D 147–46010		Nottingham Transport Heritage Centre	Derby 1961
D 172–46035–97403	Ixion	Crewe Heritage Centre	Derby 1962
D 182–46045–97404		Midland Railway-Butterley	Derby 1962

CLASS 47　　　　　　　　　　　　　　Co-Co

Built: 1963–67 at Crewe and Brush Electrical Engineering Company, Loughborough. 512 built.
Engine: Sulzer 12LDA28C of 1920 kW (2580 hp) at 750 rpm.
Transmission: Electric. Six Brush TG 160-60 axle-hung traction motors.
Power at Rail: 1550 kW (2080 hp).
Maximum Tractive Effort: 267 kN (60 000 lbf). (§ 245 kN (55 000 lbf)).
Continuous Tractive Effort: 133 kN (33 000 lbf) at 26 mph.
Weight: 119–121 tonnes.　　　　　　**Wheel Diameter:** 1143 mm.
Maximum Speed: 95 mph.
Train Heating: Built with steam (except Class 47/3).

D 1705 was built with a Sulzer 12LVA24 engine but replaced with a 12LDA28C in 1972.

Dual (air/vacuum) braked.

Class 47/0.

D 1524–47004	Old Oak Common Traction & Rolling Stock Depot	Embsay & Bolton Abbey Railway	BE 419/1963
D 1693–47105		Gloucestershire Warwickshire Railway	BE 455/1963
D 1705–47117	"SPARROWHAWK"	Great Central Railway	BE 467/1965
D 1842–47192		Crewe Heritage Centre	Crewe 1965
D 1855–47205		Northampton & Lamport Railway	Crewe 1965
D 1994–47292		Nottingham Transport Heritage Centre	Crewe 1966

Class 47/3. Built with no train heating.

D1787–47306	The Sapper	Bodmin & Wenford Railway	BE 549/1964
D1886–47367		Mid Norfolk Railway	BE 648/1965
D1895–47376	Freightliner 1995	Gloucestershire Warwickshire Railway	BE 657/1965

Class 47/4. Fitted with Electric Train Supply Equipment. D1500, D1501 & D1516 built with dual heat. Steam heating removed from others when electric train supply equipment fitted (except D1107 which had its steam heating removed later).

D1107–47524	Res Gestae	Churnet Valley Railway	Crewe 1966
D1500–47401§	North Eastern	Midland Railway-Butterley	BE 342/1962
D1501–47402§	Gateshead	East Lancashire Railway	BE 343/1962
D1516–47417§		Midland Railway-Butterley	BE 358/1963
D1566–47449	"ORION"	Llangollen Railway	Crewe 1964
D1606–47029–47635	Jimmy Milne	Epping Ongar Railway	Crewe 1964
D1619–47038–47564–47761	COLOSSUS	Midland Railway-Butterley	Crewe 1964
D1643–47059–47631–47765	Ressaldar	Nottingham Transport Heritage Centre	Crewe 1965
D1654–47070–47620–47799	Prince Henry	Eden Valley Railway	Crewe 1965
D1656–47072–47609–47798	Prince William	National Railway Museum, York (N)	Crewe 1965
D1661–47077–47613–47840	NORTH STAR	West Somerset Railway	Crewe 1965
D1662–47484	ISAMBARD KINGDOM BRUNEL	Rye Farm, Wishaw, Sutton Coldfield	Crewe 1965
D1713–47488	Rail Riders	Nemesis Rail, Burton-upon-Trent	BE 475/1964
D1726–47134–47622–47841	The Institution of Mechanical Engineers	London & North Western Railway Heritage Company, Crewe	BE 497/1964
D1755–47541–47773	The Queen Mother	Tyseley Locomotive Works	BE 483/1964
D1762–47167–47580–47732	County of Essex	Mid Norfolk Railway	BE 524/1964
D1778–47183–47579–47793	James Nightall G.C.	Mangapps Railway Museum	BE 540/1964
D1909–47232–47665–47785	Fiona Castle	Wensleydale Railway	BE 671/1965
D1921–47244–47640	University of Strathclyde	Battlefield Railway	BE 683/1966
D1927–47250–47600–47744	Royal Mail Cheltenham	Nemesis Rail, Burton-upon-Trent	BE 689/1966
D1933–47255–47596	Aldeburgh Festival	Mid Norfolk Railway	BE 695/1966
D1935–47257–47650–47805	Bristol Bath Road	London & North Western Railway Heritage Company, Crewe	BE 697/1966
D1944–47501	Craftsman	London & North Western Railway Heritage Company, Crewe	BE 706/1966
D1946–47503–47771	Heaton Traincare Depot	Colne Valley Railway	BE 708/1966
D1966–47266–47629–47828	Severn Valley Railway	Dartmoor Railway	Crewe 1965
D1970–47269–47643		Bo'ness & Kinneil Railway	Crewe 1965
D1973–47272–47593–47790	Galloway Princess	London & North Western Railway Heritage Company, Crewe	Crewe 1965

Class 47/7. Fitted with push-pull equipment. Electric train supply equipment fitted & steam heating removed. **Maximum Speed:** 100 mph.

D1932–47493–47701	Waverley	Nemesis Rail, Burton-upon-Trent	BE 694/1966
D1945–47502–47715	Haymarket	Wensleydale Railway	BE 707/1966
D1948–47505–47712	ARTEMIS	Crewe Heritage Centre	BE 610/1966

47401 also carried the name Star of the East.
47488 also carried the name DAVIES THE OCEAN.
47600/744 also carried the names Dewi Saint/Saint David, Saint Edwin and The Cornish Experience.
47635 also carried the name The Lass O' Ballochmyle.
47701 also carried the names Saint Andrew and Old Oak Common Traction & Rolling Stock Depot.
47712 also carried the names Lady Diana Spencer and Dick Whittington.
47715 also carried the name "POSEIDON".
47732 also carried the name Restormel.
47771 also carried the name The Geordie.
47773 also carried the name Reservist.
47785 also carried the name The Statesman.
47790 also carried the names York Intercity Control and Saint David/Dewi Sant.
47793 also carried the names Christopher Wren and Saint Augustine.
47798 also carried the name FIRE FLY.

▲ 50035 "Ark Royal" heads away from Corfe Castle for Swanage during the Swanage Railway's 2015 diesel gala on 7 May 2015. **Tom McAtee**

▼ Main line certified D1015 "WESTERN CHAMPION" passes South Brent with the 07.37 London Paddington–Okehampton railtour on 7 May 2016. **Tony Christie**

47799 also carried the name Windsor Castle.
47841 also carried the name Spirit of Chester.

47785 was also numbered 47820 for a time, 47790 was also numbered 47673 for a time, 47798 was also numbered 47834 for a time and 47799 was also numbered 47835 for a time.

CLASS 50   Co-Co

Built: 1967–68 by English Electric at Vulcan Foundry, Newton-le-Willows. 50 built.
Engine: English Electric 16CVST of 2010 kW (2700 hp) at 850 rpm.
Transmission: Electric. Six EE 538/5A axle-hung traction motors.
Power at Rail: 1540 kW (2070 hp).
Maximum Tractive Effort: 216 kN (48 500 lbf).
Continuous Tractive Effort: 147 kN (33 000 lbf) at 18.8 mph.
Weight: 117 tonnes.   **Wheel Diameter:** 1092 mm.
Maximum Speed: 100 mph.
Train Heating: Electric.

Dual (air/vacuum) braked.

D 400–50050	Fearless	Boden Rail Engineering, Washwood Heath	
			EE/VF 3770/D1141 1967
D 402–50002	Superb	South Devon Railway	EE/VF 3772/D1143 1967
D 407–50007	Hercules	Boden Rail Engineering, Washwood Heath	
			EE/VF 3777/D1148 1968
D 408–50008	Thunderer	UK Rail Leasing, Leicester Depot	EE/VF 3778/D1149 1968
D 415–50015	Valiant	East Lancashire Railway	EE/VF 3785/D1156 1968
D 417–50017	Royal Oak	Boden Rail Engineering, Washwood Heath	
			EE/VF 3787/D1158 1968
D 419–50019	Ramillies	Mid Norfolk Railway	EE/VF 3789/D1160 1968
D 421–50021	Rodney	Arlington Fleet Services, Eastleigh Works	
			EE/VF 3791/D1162 1968
D 426–50026	Indomitable	Arlington Fleet Services, Eastleigh Works	
			EE/VF 3796/D1167 1968
D 427–50027	Lion	Mid Hants Railway	EE/VF 3797/D1168 1968
D 429–50029	Renown	Peak Rail	EE/VF 3799/D1170 1968
D 430–50030	Repulse	Peak Rail	EE/VF 3800/D1171 1968
D 431–50031	Hood	Severn Valley Railway	EE/VF 3801/D1172 1968
D 433–50033	Glorious	Tyseley Locomotive Works	EE/VF 3803/D1174 1968
D 435–50035	Ark Royal	Severn Valley Railway	EE/VF 3805/D1176 1968
D 442–50042	Triumph	Bodmin & Wenford Railway	EE/VF 3812/D1183 1968
D 444–50044	Exeter	Severn Valley Railway	EE/VF 3814/D1185 1968
D 449–50049–50149	Defiance	Severn Valley Railway	EE/VF 3819/D1190 1968

50007 also carried the name SIR EDWARD ELGAR.

CLASS 52   WESTERN   C-C

Built: 1961–64 at Crewe and Swindon. 74 built.
Engines: Two Bristol Siddley Maybach MD655 of 1007 kW (1350 hp) at 1500 rpm.
Transmission: Hydraulic. Voith L630rV.
Maximum Tractive Effort: 297.3 kN (66 770 lbf).
Continuous Tractive Effort: 201.2 kN (45 200 lbf) at 14.5 mph.
Weight: 111 tonnes.   **Wheel Diameter:** 1092 mm.
Maximum Speed: 90 mph.   **Train Heating:** Steam.

Dual (air/vacuum) braked.

D 1010	WESTERN CAMPAIGNER	West Somerset Railway	Swindon 1962
D 1013	WESTERN RANGER	Severn Valley Railway	Swindon 1962
D 1015	WESTERN CHAMPION	Severn Valley Railway	Swindon 1963
D 1023	WESTERN FUSILIER	National Railway Museum, York (N)	Swindon 1963
D 1041	WESTERN PRINCE	East Lancashire Railway	Crewe 1962
D 1048	WESTERN LADY	Midland Railway-Butterley	Crewe 1962
D 1062	WESTERN COURIER	Severn Valley Railway	Crewe 1963

CLASS 55   DELTIC   Co-Co

Built: 1961–62 by English Electric at Vulcan Foundry, Newton-le-Willows. 22 built.
Engine: Two Napier Deltic T18-25 of 1230 kW (1650 hp) at 1500 rpm.
Transmission: Electric. Six EE 538 axle-hung traction motors.
Power at Rail: 1969 kW (2640 hp).
Maximum Tractive Effort: 222 kN (50 000 lbf).
Continuous Tractive Effort: 136 kN (30 500 lbf) at 32.5 mph.
Weight: 105 tonnes.   **Wheel Diameter:** 1092 mm.
Maximum Speed: 100 mph.
Train Heating: Built with steam, electric subsequently fitted.

Dual (air/vacuum) braked.

D 9000–55022	ROYAL SCOTS GREY	North Yorkshire Moors Railway	EE/VF 2905/D557 1961
D 9002–55002	THE KING'S OWN YORKSHIRE LIGHT INFANTRY		
		National Railway Museum, York (N)	EE/VF 2907/D559 1961
D 9009–55009	ALYCIDON	Barrow Hill Roundhouse	EE/VF 2914/D566 1961
D 9015–55015	TULYAR	Barrow Hill Roundhouse	EE/VF 2920/D572 1961
D 9016–55016	GORDON HIGHLANDER	Boden Rail Engineering, Washwood Heath	
			EE/VF 2921/D573 1961
D 9019–55019	ROYAL HIGHLAND FUSILIER		
		Barrow Hill Roundhouse	EE/VF 2924/D576 1961

CLASS 56   Co-Co

Built: 1976–84 by Electroputere, Craiova, Romania and BREL Doncaster & Crewe. 135 built.
Engine: Ruston-Paxman 16RK3CT of 2460 kW (3250 hp) at 900 rpm.
Transmission: Electric. Six Brush TM73-62 axle-hung traction motors.
Power at Rail: 1790 kW (2400 hp).
Maximum Tractive Effort: 275 kN (61 800 lbf).
Continuous Tractive Effort: 240 kN (53 950 lbf) at 32.5 mph.
Weight: 125 tonnes.   **Wheel Diameter:** 1143 mm.
Maximum Speed: 80 mph.
Train Heating: None.

Air braked.

56006		UK Rail Leasing, Leicester Depot	EP 755/1977
56045–56301	British Steel Shelton	UK Rail Leasing, Leicester Depot	Doncaster 1978
56097		Nottingham Transport Heritage Centre	Doncaster 1981

CLASS 58   Co-Co

Built: 1983–87 by BREL Doncaster. 50 built.
Engine: Ruston-Paxman 12RK3ACT of 2460 kW (3300 hp) at 1000 rpm
Transmission: Electric. Brush TM73-62 traction motors.
Power at Rail: 1780 kW (2387 hp).
Maximum Tractive Effort: 275 kN (61 800 lbf).
Continuous Tractive Effort: 240 kN (53 950 lbf) at 32.5 mph.
Weight: 130 tonnes.   **Wheel Diameter:** 1120 mm.
Maximum Speed: 80 mph.   **Train Heating:** None.

Air braked.

58016	UK Rail Leasing, Leicester Depot	Doncaster 1984

CLASS 98/1   0-6-0

Built: 1987 by Brecon Mountain Railway. 1 built for use on Aberystwyth–Devil's Bridge line.
Engine: Caterpillar 3304T of 105 kW (140 hp).
Transmission: Hydraulic. Twin Disc torque converter.
Gauge: 1′ 11½″.   **Weight:** 12.75 tonnes.
Maximum Speed: 15 mph.   **Wheel Diameter:** 610 mm.

10	Vale of Rheidol Railway	BMR 1987

▲ Visiting the Bluebell Railway, Deltic 55019 "ROYAL HIGHLAND FUSILIER" powers the 13.15 East Grinstead–Sheffield Park near Horsted Keynes on 18 April 2015. **Aubrey Evans**

▼ 56006 and 56098 (not a preserved locomotive) double head the 11.30 Peterborough Nene Valley–Wansford at Longueville Junction on 10 April 2016. **Nigel Gibbs**

2.4. EXPERIMENTAL DIESEL LOCOMOTIVES

PROTOTYPE DELTIC   Co-Co

Built: 1955 by English Electric. Used by BR 1959–61.
Engine: Two Napier Deltic T18-25 of 1230 kW (1650 hp) at 1500 rpm.
Transmission: Electric. Six EE 526A axle-hung traction motors.
Power at Rail: 1976 kW (2650 hp).
Maximum Tractive Effort: 267 kN (60 000 lbf).
Continuous Tractive Effort: 104 kN (23 400 lbf) at 43.5 mph.
Weight: 107.7 tonnes.   **Wheel Diameter:** 1092 mm.
Maximum Speed: 105 mph.   **Train Heating:** Steam.

DELTIC   National Railway Museum, Shildon (N)   EE 2003/1955

PROTOTYPE ENGLISH ELECTRIC SHUNTER   0-6-0

Built: 1957 by English Electric at Vulcan Foundry, Newton-le-Willows. Used by BR 1957–60.
Engine: English Electric 6RKT of 373 kW (500 hp) at 750 rpm.
Transmission: Electric.
Power at Rail:
Maximum Tractive Effort: 147 kN (33 000 lbf).
Continuous Tractive Effort: (lbf) at   mph.
Weight: 48 tonnes.   **Wheel Diameter:** 1219 mm.
Maximum Speed: 35 mph.

D 226–D 0226   "VULCAN"   Keighley & Worth Valley Railway   EE/VF 2345/D226 1956

PROTOTYPE NORTH BRITISH SHUNTER   0-4-0

Built: 1954 by North British Locomotive Company, Glasgow. Used by BR Western Region (27414)
and BR London Midland & Southern regions (27415). Subsequently sold for industrial use.
Engine: Paxman 6 VRPHXL of 160 kW (225 hp) at 1250 rpm.
Transmission: Hydraulic. Voith L24V.   **Weight:**
Maximum Tractive Effort: 112 kN (22 850 lbf). **Maximum Speed:** 12 mph.
Wheel Diameter: 1016 mm.

No train brakes.

BR	Present		
–	TOM	Telford Steam Railway	NBL 27414/1954
–	TIGER	Bo'ness & Kinneil Railway	NBL 27415/1954

PROTOTYPE NORTH BRITISH SHUNTER   0-4-0

Built: 1958 by North British Locomotive Company, Glasgow. Used by BR Western Region at Old
Oak Common in 1958. Subsequently sold for industrial use.
Engine: MAN W6V 17.5/22 of 168 kW (225 hp).
Transmission: Hydraulic. Voith L24V.   **Weight:**
Maximum Tractive Effort: 112 kN (22 850 lbf). **Maximum Speed:** 12 mph.
Wheel Diameter: 940 mm.

No train brakes.

BR	Present		
–	D1	The Pallot Heritage Steam Museum, Jersey	NBL 27734/1958

2.5. CIVIL ENGINEERS' DIESEL LOCOMOTIVES

CLASS 97/6　　　　　　　　　　　　　　　　　　　0-6-0

Built: 1952–59 by Ruston & Hornsby at Lincoln for BR Western Region Civil Engineers. 5 built.
Engine: Ruston 6VPH of 123 kW (165 hp).
Transmission: Electric. One British Thomson Houston RTA5041 traction motor.
Maximum Tractive Effort: 75 kN (17 000 lbf).　　**Weight:** 31 tonnes.
Maximum Speed: 20 mph.　　　　　　　　　　**Wheel Diameter:** 978 mm.

PWM 650–97650	Lincolnshire Wolds Railway	RH 312990/1952
PWM 651–97651	Swindon & Cricklade Railway	RH 431758/1959
PWM 654–97654	Peak Rail	RH 431761/1959

▲ Ruston PWM 651/97651 makes its passenger debut at the Swindon & Cricklade Railway mixed
traction weekend on 16 April 2016.　　　　　　　　　　　　　　　　**Darren Ford**

PLATFORM 5 MAIL ORDER

NARROW GAUGE STEAM LOCOMOTIVES
OF GREAT BRITAIN & IRELAND
By Peter Nicholson

This completely new book from Platform 5 Publishing is the definitive guide to all narrow gauge steam locomotives known to exist in Great Britain and Ireland of track gauges 1ft 6in to 4ft 6in. It fills a gap between 'Preserved Locomotives of British Railways' which contains details of preserved standard gauge steam locomotives still in existence, and 'Miniature Railways of Great Britain and Ireland' which deals predominantly with locomotives of gauges from 7¼in to 18in.

Locomotives are listed by builder so that it can be easily seen how many of each type or builder are in existence. For every locomotive details of builder's number, year of manufacture, type, class, gauge, location and running number/name are provided. Detailed footnotes provide further information about each locomotive's origin and history.

The information contained has been collated over many years of personal observation and correspondence since the mid-1960s. Also includes 64 colour illustrations, a locomotive names index and a full list of heritage railways, museums and collections where locomotives can be observed. 80 pages. Published 2014.

£14.95 *TR Subscriber Price* **£11.95**

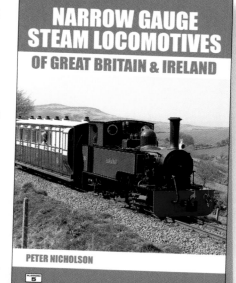

3. ELECTRIC LOCOMOTIVES

GENERAL

Electric railways have existed in Great Britain for over 100 years. Several early railway companies pioneered this form of traction, most notably the North Eastern Railway with a small fleet of electric locomotives for hauling heavy coal and steel trains in County Durham using overhead wires to supply the electric, but it was the need for mass movement of passengers into and around metropolitan areas that led to the rapid growth of electrification in the inter-war years. Early systems employed direct current normally supplied from a third rail; several different voltages were trialled but 750 V DC favoured by the Southern Railway, at the time Britain's largest electrified network, eventually became the standard. After World War II technological advances led to alternating current supplied from overhead wires becoming the norm; several suburban networks and all of Britain's electrified main lines now operate from 25 kV AC overhead supply.

For further information about wheel arrangement, dimensions, tractive effort, brakes and numbering systems please refer to Section 2: Diesel Locomotives.

3.1. PRE-GROUPING DESIGN ELECTRIC LOCOMOTIVES

LSWR   Bo

Built: 1898. Siemens design for operation on the Waterloo & City line.
System: 750 V DC third rail.   **Train Heating:** None.
Traction Motors: Two Siemens 45 kW (60 hp). **Weight:**
Wheel Diameter: 3' 4".

BR	*SR*		
DS75	75S	National Railway Museum, Shildon (N)	SM 6/1898

NORTH EASTERN RAILWAY CLASS ES1   Bo-Bo

Built: 1905. Used on Newcastle Quay Branch. 2 built.
System: 600 V DC overhead or third rail.   **Train Heating:** None.
Traction Motors: 4 BTH design.   **Weight:** 46 tonnes.
Wheel Diameter: 915 mm.

BR	*LNER*	*NER*		
26500	1–4075–6480	1	National Railway Museum, Shildon (N)	BE 1905

▲ LSWR 75S at the National Railway Museum, Shildon on 5 September 2015. **Robert Pritchard**

▼ Class EM2 1505 on display at the Museum of Science & Industry, Manchester on 25 October 2014. **Robert Pritchard**

3.2. PRE-GROUPING DESIGN BATTERY-ELECTRIC LOCOMOTIVE

NORTH STAFFORDSHIRE RAILWAY   2-A

Built: 1917. This is an electric shunting locomotive with batteries powering its two electric motors. No. 1 was used for 46 years to shunt wagons at the T Bolton & Son Works and adjacent station at Oakamoor.
Battery: 108 cells giving an output of 61 kW (82 hp).
Transmission: Wilson four-speed gearbox driving a rear jackshaft.
Maximum Tractive Effort: 50 kN (15 300 lbf).   **Wheel Diameter:** 940 mm.

NSR	*LMS*		
1	BEL 2	National Railway Museum, York (N)	Stoke 1917

3.3. LNER DESIGN ELECTRIC LOCOMOTIVES

LNER/BR CLASS EM1 (BR CLASS 76)   Bo+Bo

Built: 1941–53 at Doncaster (26000) and Gorton (others) for Manchester–Sheffield/Wath-upon-Dearne. 58 built.
System: 1500 V DC overhead.
Traction Motors: 4 MV 186 axle-hung.
Max Rail Power: 2460 kW (3300 hp).
Continuous Rating: 970 kW (1300 hp).
Maximum Tractive Effort: 200 kN (45 000 lbf).
Continuous Tractive Effort: 39 kN (8800 lbf) at 56 mph.
Weight: 88 tonnes.   **Wheel Diameter:** 1270 mm.
Maximum Speed: 65 mph.   **Train Heating:** Steam.

26020–E26020–76020	National Railway Museum, York (N)	Gorton 1027/1951

BR CLASS EM2 (BR CLASS 77)   Co-Co

Built: 1953–55 at Gorton for BR to LNER design for Manchester–Sheffield/Wath-upon-Dearne. 7 built. Sold to NS (Netherlands Railways) 1969.
System: 1500 V DC overhead.
Traction Motors: 6 MV 146 axle-hung.
Max Rail Power: 1716 kW (2300 hp).
Maximum Tractive Effort: 200 kN (45 000 lbf).
Continuous Tractive Effort: 78 kN (15 600 lbf) at 23 mph.
Weight: 102 tonnes.   **Wheel Diameter:** 1092 mm.
Maximum Speed: 90 mph.
Train Heating: Steam whilst on BR, electric fitted by NS.

Air brakes.

BR	*NS*			
27000–E27000	1502	ELECTRA	Midland Railway-Butterley	Gorton 1065/1953
27001–E27001	1505	ARIADNE	Museum of Science & Industry, Manchester	Gorton 1066/1954
27003–E27003	1501	(DIANA)	Netherlands National Railway Museum, Blerick Yard storage shed	Gorton 1068/1954

3.4. BRITISH RAILWAYS ELECTRIC LOCOMOTIVES

NUMBERING SYSTEM

Numbering of electric locomotives from 1957 was similar to that of diesel locomotives, except that the numbers were prefixed with an "E" instead of a "D". Locomotives of pre-nationalisation design continued to be numbered in the 2xxxx series, although LNER design Classes EM1 and EM2 (see section 3.3) later acquired an "E" prefix to their existing numbers. As with diesels, electric locomotives were later allocated a two-digit class number followed by a three-digit serial number.

In this section classes are listed in 1968 two-digit class number order. Locomotives are listed in 1957 number order within each class. For further details of British Railways Numbering and Classification System for diesel and electric locomotives, please refer to section 2.3.

CLASS 71   Bo-Bo

Built: 1958–60 at Doncaster. 24 built.
System: 660–750 V DC third rail or overhead.
Traction Motors: English Electric 532.
Continuous Rating: 1715 kW (2300 hp).
Maximum Tractive Effort: 191 kN (43000 lbf).
Continuous Tractive Effort: 55 kN (12400 lbf) at 69.6 mph.
Weight: 76.2 tonnes.   **Wheel Diameter:** 1219 mm.
Maximum Speed: 90 mph.   **Train Heating:** Electric

Dual (air/vacuum) braked.

E 5001–71001	Barrow Hill Roundhouse (N)	Doncaster 1959

CLASS 73/0 ELECTRO-DIESEL   Bo-Bo

Built: 1962 at Eastleigh. 6 built.
System: 660–750 V DC third rail.
Engine: English Electric 4SRKT of 447 kW (600 hp) at 850 rpm.
Traction Motors: English Electric 546/1B.
Continuous Rating: Electric 1060 kW (1420 hp).
Maximum Tractive Effort: Electric 187 kN (42 000 lbf). Diesel 152 kN (34 100 lbf).
Continuous Tractive Effort: Diesel 72 kN (16 100 lbf) at 10 mph.
Weight: 76.3 tonnes.   **Wheel Diameter:** 1016 mm.
Maximum Speed: 80 mph.   **Train Heating:** Electric.

Triple (vacuum, air and electro-pneumatic) braked.

E 6001–73001–73901		Dean Forest Railway	Eastleigh 1962
E 6002–73002		Dean Forest Railway	Eastleigh 1962
E 6003–73003	Sir Herbert Walker	Swindon & Cricklade Railway	Eastleigh 1962

CLASS 73/1 ELECTRO-DIESEL   Bo-Bo

Built: 1965–67 by English Electric at Vulcan Foundry, Newton-le-Willows. 43 built.
System: 660–750 V DC third rail.
Engine: English Electric 4SRKT of 447 kW (600 hp) at 850 rpm.
Traction Motors: English Electric 546/1B.
Continuous Rating: Electric 1060 kW (1420 hp).
Maximum Tractive Effort: Electric 179 kN (40 000 lbf). Diesel 152 kN (34 100 lbf).
Continuous Tractive Effort: Diesel 60 kN (13 600 lbf) at 11.5 mph.
Weight: 76.8 tonnes.   **Wheel Diameter:** 1016 mm.
Maximum Speed: 90 mph.   **Train Heating:** Electric.

Fitted for push-pull operation. Triple (vacuum, air and electro-pneumatic) braked.

E6016–73110		Nottingham Transport Heritage Centre	EE/VF 3578/E348 1966
E6020–73114	Stewarts Lane Traction & Maintenance Depot	Battlefield Railway	EE/VF 3582/E352 1966
E6022–73116–73210	Selhurst	Mid Norfolk Railway	EE/VF 3584/E354 1966
E6024–73118	The Romney, Hythe and Dymchurch Railway	Barry Rail Centre	EE/VF 3586/E356 1966
E6036–73129	City of Winchester	Gloucestershire Warwickshire Railway	EE/VF 3598/E368 1966
E6037–73130	City of Portsmouth	Finmere Station, Oxfordshire	EE/VF 3709/E369 1966
E6047–73140		Spa Valley Railway	EE/VF 3719/E379 1966

CLASS 81   Bo-Bo

Built: 1959–64 by the Birmingham Railway Carriage & Wagon Company, Birmingham. 25 built.
System: 25 kV AC overhead.
Traction Motors: AEI 189 frame mounted.
Continuous Rating: 2390 kW (3200 hp).
Maximum Tractive Effort: 222 kN (50 000 lbf).
Continuous Tractive Effort: 76 kN (17 000 lbf) at 71 mph.
Weight: 79 tonnes.   **Wheel Diameter:** 1219 mm.
Maximum Speed: 100 mph.   **Train Heating:** Electric.

Dual (air/vacuum) braked.

E3003–81002	Barrow Hill Roundhouse	BRCW 1085/1960

▲ 73001 passes Burrs on the East Lancashire Railway with a train for Bury on 23 April 2015.
Tom McAtee

CLASS 82   Bo-Bo

Built: 1960–62 by Beyer Peacock, Manchester. 10 built.
System: 25 kV AC overhead.
Traction Motors: AEI 189 frame mounted.
Continuous Rating: 2460 kW (3300 hp).
Maximum Tractive Effort: 222 kN (50 000 lbf).
Continuous Tractive Effort: 76 kN (17 000 lbf) at 73 mph.
Weight: 80 tonnes.   **Wheel Diameter:** 1219 mm.
Maximum Speed: 100 mph.   **Train Heating:** Electric.

Dual (air/vacuum) braked.

E3054–82008	Barrow Hill Roundhouse	BP 7893/1961

CLASS 83   Bo-Bo

Built: 1960–62 by English Electric at Vulcan Foundry, Newton-le-Willows. 15 built.
System: 25 kV AC overhead.
Traction Motors: English Electric 532A frame mounted.
Continuous Rating: 2200 kW (2950 hp).
Maximum Tractive Effort: 169 kN (38 000 lbf).
Continuous Tractive Effort: 68 kN (15 260 lbf) at 73 mph.
Weight: 76 tonnes.   **Wheel Diameter:** 1219 mm.
Maximum Speed: 100 mph.   **Train Heating:** Electric.

Dual (air/vacuum) braked.

E3035–83012	Barrow Hill Roundhouse	EE 2941/VF E277/1961

CLASS 84   Bo-Bo

Built: 1960–61 by North British Locomotive Company, Glasgow. 10 built.
System: 25 kV AC overhead.
Traction Motors: GEC WT501 frame mounted.
Continuous Rating: 2312 kW (3100 hp).
Maximum Tractive Effort: 222 kN (50 000 lbf).
Continuous Tractive Effort: 78 kN (17 600 lbf) at 66 mph.
Weight: 76.6 tonnes.   **Wheel Diameter:** 1219 mm.
Maximum Speed: 100 mph.   **Train Heating:** Electric.

Dual (air/vacuum) braked.

E 3036–84001	Barrow Hill Roundhouse (N)	NBL 27793/1960

CLASS 85   Bo-Bo

Built: 1961–65 at Doncaster. 40 built.
System: 25 kV AC overhead.
Traction Motors: AEI 189 frame mounted.
Continuous Rating: 2390 kW (3200 hp).
Maximum Tractive Effort: 222 kN (50 000 lbf).
Continuous Tractive Effort: 76 kN (17 000 lbf) at 71 mph.
Weight: 82.5 tonnes.   **Wheel Diameter:** 1219 mm.
Maximum Speed: 100 mph.   **Train Heating:** Electric.

Dual (air/vacuum) braked.

E3061–85006–85101	"Doncaster Plant 150 1853–2003"	Barrow Hill Roundhouse	Doncaster 1961

CLASS 86   Bo-Bo

Built: 1965–66 at Doncaster or English Electric Company at Vulcan Foundry, Newton-le-Willows. 100 built.
System: 25 kV AC overhead.

Traction Motors: AEI 282AZ axle hung.
Continuous Rating: 2680 kW (3600 hp).
Maximum Tractive Effort: 258 kN (58 000 lbf).
Continuous Tractive Effort: 89 kN (20 000 lbf).
Weight: 83 tonnes.　　　　　　　**Wheel Diameter:** 1156 mm.
Maximum Speed: 100 mph.　　　　**Train Heating:** Electric.

Dual (air/vacuum) braked.

Class 86/0:

E 3199–86001–86401	Northampton Town	Willesden Depot, London	EE/VF3491/E337 1966

Class 86/1: Rebuilt with Class 87-type bogies and traction motors. Details as Class 86/0 except:
Traction Motors: GEC 412AZ frame mounted.
Continuous Rating: 5860 kW (5000 hp).
Continuous Tractive Effort: 95 kN (21 300 lbf).
Weight: 87 tonnes.
Wheel Diameter: 1150 mm.
Maximum Speed: 110 mph.

E 3191–86201–86101	Sir William A Stanier FRS	Willesden Depot, London	EE/VF3483/E329 1965

Class 86/2: Rebuilt with resilient wheels and Flexicoil suspension. Details as Class 86/0 except:
Traction Motors: AEI 282BZ axle hung.
Continuous Rating: 3010 kW (4040 hp).
Maximum Tractive Effort: 207 kN (46 500 lbf).
Continuous Tractive Effort: 85 kN (19 200 lbf).
Weight: 85 tonnes.

E 3137–86045–86259	"Les Ross"	Willesden Depot, London	Doncaster 1966

86259 also carried the names Peter Pan and Greater MANCHESTER THE LIFE & SOUL OF BRITAIN.

CLASS 87　　　　　　　　　　　　　　　　　　　　Bo-Bo

Built: 1973–75 by BREL at Crewe. 36 built.
System: 25 kV AC overhead.
Traction motors: GEC G412Az frame mounted.
Continuous Rating: 3730 kW (5000 hp).
Maximum Tractive Effort: 258 kN (58000 lbf).
Continuous Tractive Effort: 95 kN (21 300 lbf) at 87 mph.
Weight: 83.5 tonnes.　　　　　　　**Wheel Diameter:** 1150 mm.
Maximum Speed: 110 mph.　　　　　**Train Heating:** Electric.

Air braked.

87001	Royal Scot	National Railway Museum, York (N)	Crewe 1973
87002	Royal Sovereign	Willesden Depot, London	Crewe 1973
87035	Robert Burns	Crewe Heritage Centre	Crewe 1974

87001 also carried the name STEPHENSON and 87002 also carried the name "The AC Locomotive Group".

CLASS 89　　　　　　　　　　　　　　　　　　　　Co-Co

Built: 1987 by BREL at Crewe. 1 built.
System: 25 kV AC overhead.
Traction motors: Brush TM 2201A. Frame mounted.
Continuous Rating: 4350 kW (6550 hp).
Maximum Tractive Effort: 205 kN (46 000 lbf).
Continuous Tractive Effort: 105 kN (23 600 lbf) at 92 mph.
Weight: 104 tonnes.　　　　　　　**Wheel Diameter:** 1150 mm.
Maximum Speed: 125 mph.　　　　　**Train Heating:** Electric.

Air braked.

89001	Avocet	Barrow Hill Roundhouse	Crewe 1987

4. GAS TURBINE VEHICLES

GENERAL

The potential for gas turbines as a source of propulsion for railway vehicles was first explored in the immediate post-war period; the trials were not successful and the idea was dropped. The oil crisis of the early 1970s led to a re-examination of the concept for the ill-fated Experimental Advanced Passenger Train project. Again, the trials were unsuccessful and the idea of using gas-turbines for railways in the UK has yet to be revisited.

LOCOMOTIVE   A1A-A1A

Built: 1950 by Brown Boveri in Switzerland.
Power Unit: Brown Boveri gas turbine of 1828 kW (2450 hp).
Transmission: Electric. Four traction motors.
Maximum Tractive Effort: 140 kN (31 500 lbf).
Continuous Tractive Effort: 55 kN (12 400 lbf) at 64 mph.
Weight: 117.1 tonnes.   **Wheel Diameter:** 1232 mm.
Maximum Speed: 90 mph.   **Train Heating:** Steam.

18000	Didcot Railway Centre	BBC 4559/1950

EXPERIMENTAL ADVANCED PASSENGER TRAIN (APT-E)

Built: 1972 at Derby Litchurch Lane.
Power Units: Eight Leyland 350 automotive gas turbines of 222 kW (298 hp).
Traction Motors: Four GEC 253AY. Articulated unit.

PC1	National Railway Museum, Shildon (N)	Derby 1972
PC2	National Railway Museum, Shildon (N)	Derby 1972
TC1	National Railway Museum, Shildon (N)	Derby 1972
TC2	National Railway Museum, Shildon (N)	Derby 1972

▲ The experimental APT-E on display at the National Railway Museum, Shildon on 5 September 2015.   **Robert Pritchard**

5. MULTIPLE UNIT VEHICLES

GENERAL

During the early years of the 20th Century attempts were made to develop what can best be described as self-propelled carriages.

The GWR and GNSR produced Steam Railmotors which were a combination of steam locomotive and carriage. These were powerful enough to move themselves as well as an additional carriage referred to as a trailer.

Steam Railmotors did not prove successful and many were subsequently converted to Auto-trailers for use with conventional locomotives.

More successful was the development by the NER of the petrol electric railcar. This being one of several schemes to transfer bus technology to rail vehicles that took place prior to nationalisation, the most successful being on the GWR where the concept was developed and the result was a fleet of distinctive diesel railcars.

During the 1950s British Railways developed the idea of diesel railcars as part of their search for cheaper vehicles to operate on lightly-used lines. Numerous new designs appeared, the preservation of which has expanded enormously in recent years.

The earliest electric multiple units were introduced in the late 19th century, their development largely driven by the difficulties associated with operating steam traction underground. The early 20th century saw rapid development of the technology and by the 1923 grouping, the SR, LMS and LNER each inherited sections of electrified lines. Further expansion, particularly by the Southern Railway, saw vast quantities of electric multiple units constructed, and a growing number of vehicles are finding their way into preservation, albeit often for use as hauled coaching stock.

The sub-sections with this section are arranged by means of propulsion in the order that such means was first introduced or became most commonly in use. Where appropriate multiple sub-sections are provided for common means of propulsion, further divided between pre-grouping companies, the "Big Four" and British Railways. Within each sub-section multiple units are listed in numerical order of the owning company unless otherwise stated in the sub-section introduction.

PREFIXES AND SUFFIXES

Coaching stock vehicles used to carry regional prefix letters to denote the owning region. These were removed in the 1980s. These are not shown. Pre-nationalisation number series vehicles carried both prefix and suffix letters, the suffix denoting the pre-nationalisation number series. The prefixes and suffixes are shown for these vehicles.

DIMENSIONS

Dimensions are shown as length (over buffers or couplers) x width (over bodysides including door handles).

SEATING CAPACITIES

These are shown as nF/nS nT relating to First and Second Class seats and lavatories respectively, eg a car with 12 First Class seats, 51 Second Class seats and one lavatory would be shown as 12/51 1T. Prior to 3 June 1956 Second class was referred to as "Third" Class and is now referred to as "Standard" class. Certain old vehicles are thus shown as Third Class.

BOGIES

All vehicles are assumed to have two four-wheeled bogies unless otherwise stated.

▲ GWR Steam Railmotor No. 93 leaves Southall with a special train to Brentford on 19 October 2014. **Robert Pritchard**

▼ BR green-liveried Class 115 DMU DMBS 51880+TCL 59678+DMBS 51859 waits to return to Minehead from Blue Anchor on 6 June 2015. **Tony Christie**

5.1. STEAM RAILMOTORS

GWR STEAM RAILMOTOR

Original Class Built: 1905–08. 35 built. Converted to Autotrailer 212 in 1935. Converted back to Steam Rail Motor in 2011 with new replica steam propulsion unit. It sometimes operates with GWR Autotrailer No. 92 which was returned to service in 2013.

Boiler Pressure: 160 lbf/sq in.
Weight: 45.55 tons.
Wheel Diameters: 4′ 0″ (driving), 3′ 7½″.
Valve Gear: Walschaerts.
Cylinders: 12″ x 16″ (O).
Tractive Effort: 6530 lbf.
Seats: –/61.

93	Didcot Railway Centre	Rebuilt Llangollen 2011

5.2. PETROL-ELECTRIC RAILCARS

NER PETROL ELECTRIC AUTOCAR

Built: 1903 as a petrol-electric autocar for the North Eastern Railway; this vehicle is now being restored to its rebuilt 1923 form as a diesel railcar using the chassis from GNR B 2391 and the original body and mechanical parts from a Class 416 BR EMU including power bogie. It will operate with NER trailer autocoach 3453.

Original Class Built: York 1903 (2 built).
Weight: 35 tons.
Transmission:
Wheel Diameters:
Engine: New engine being built to 225 hp.
Seats: –/48 (–/52 as built).

To be fitted with vacuum and air brakes.

3170	Embsay & Bolton Abbey Railway	Undergoing rebuilding

5.3. GWR DIESEL RAILCARS

UNCLASSIFIED   PARK ROYAL

Built: 1934 by Park Royal. Single cars with two driving cabs.
Engines: Two AEC 90 kW (121 hp).
Transmission: Mechanical.
Body: 19.58 x 2.70 m.
Weight: 26.6 tonnes.
Seats: –/44.
Max. Speed: 75 mph.

BR	GWR		
W 4 W	4	National Railway Museum, York (N)	PR 1934

UNCLASSIFIED   GWR

Built: 1940 at Swindon. Single cars with two driving cabs.
Engines: Two AEC 78 kW (105 hp).
Transmission: Mechanical.
Body: 20.21 x 2.70 m.
Weight: 36.2 tonnes.
Seats: –/48.
Max. Speed: 40 mph.

BR	GWR		
W 20 W	20	Kent & East Sussex Railway	Swindon 1940
W 22 W	22	Didcot Railway Centre	Swindon 1941

5.4. BRITISH RAILWAYS DIESEL MULTIPLE UNITS

NUMBERING SYSTEM

Early BR Diesel Multiple Units were numbered in the 79xxx series, but when it was evident that this series did not contain enough numbers the 5xxxx series was allocated to this type of vehicle and the few locomotive-hauled non-corridor coaches which were in the 5xxxx series were renumbered into the 4xxxx series. Power cars in the 50xxx series and driving trailers in the 56xxx series were eventually renumbered into the 53xxx and 54xxx series respectively to avoid conflicting numbers with Class 50 and 56 diesel locomotives.

Diesel Electric Multiple Unit power cars were numbered in the 60000–60499 series, trailers in the 60500–60799 series and driving trailers in the 60800–60999 series.

In this section classes are listed in three-digit class number order. Multiple unit vehicles are listed in original five-digit number order within each class. Unclassified multiple units are listed at the end of each sub-section.

TYPE CODES

The former BR operating departments used a series of Type Codes to describe the various types of multiple unit in service. The type codes relating to diesel multiple units are listed below and are used in sections 5.4.1. and 5.4.2. Please note that type codes used for diesel electric multiple units (section 5.4.3.) were drawn from the series used for electric multiple units, details of which can be found in Appendix IV.

DMBC	Driving Motor Brake Composite
DMBS	Driving Motor Brake Second
DMCL	Driving Motor Composite with Lavatory
DMPMV	Driving Motor Parcels & Miscellaneous Van
DMS	Driving Motor Second
DMSL	Driving Motor Second with Lavatory
DTCL	Driving Trailer Composite with Lavatory
DTPMV	Driving Trailer Parcels & Miscellaneous Van
DTS	Driving Trailer Second
TBSL	Trailer Brake Second with Lavatory
TC	Trailer Composite
TCK	Trailer Composite side corridor with Lavatory (seating in compartments)
TCL	Trailer Composite with Lavatory
TRCBL	Trailer Composite with Buffet and Lavatory
TRCsoBL	Trailer semi-open Composite with Buffet and Lavatory
TRSBL	Trailer Second with Buffet and Lavatory
TS	Trailer Second
TSK	Trailer Second side corridor with Lavatory (seating in compartments)
TSL	Trailer Second with Lavatory
TSso	Trailer semi-open Second

Brake vehicles contain luggage space and a guards/conductors compartment.

Second is now referred to as Standard.

Some DMU vehicles are usually used as hauled stock and these are denoted by a letter "h" after the number.

5.4.1. DIESEL MECHANICAL/HYDRAULIC MULTIPLE UNITS

All vehicles in this section have a Maximum Speed of 70 mph. All vehicles have mechanical transmission unless stated. Unless otherwise stated all multiple units are gangwayed within each set, with seating in open saloons.

CLASS 100 — GRCW 2-CAR UNITS

Built: 1957–58.
Original formation: DMBS–DTCL.
Engines: Two AEC 220 of 112 kW (150 hp).

DMBS	18.49 x 2.82 m	30.5 tonnes	–/52
DTCL	18.49 x 2.82 m	25.5 tonnes	12/54 1T

51118	DMBS	Midland Railway-Butterley	GRCW 1957
56097	DTCL	Midland Railway-Butterley	GRCW 1957
56301	DTCL	Mid Norfolk Railway	GRCW 1957
56317	DTCL	Alley's Heavy Haulage, Studley	GRCW 1958

CLASS 101 — METRO-CAMMELL UNITS

Built: 1958–59. Various formations.
Engines: Two AEC 220 of 112 kW (150 hp).

DMBS	18.49 x 2.82 m	32.5 tonnes	–/52 or –/49.
DMCL	18.49 x 2.82 m	32.5 tonnes	12/53 or 12/46 1T.
DMSL	18.49 x 2.82 m	32.5 tonnes	–/72 1T (originally DMCL 12/53 1T)
DTCL	18.49 x 2.82 m	25.5 tonnes	12/53 1T
DTSL	18.49 x 2.82 m	25.5 tonnes	–72 1T (originally DTCL 12/53 1T)
TSL	18.49 x 2.82 m	25.5 tonnes	–/71 1T (§ –/58 1T, † –/72 1T) (§† originally TCL 12/53 1T)

50160–53160	DMSL	North Yorkshire Moors Railway	MC 1956
50164–53164	DMSL	North Yorkshire Moors Railway	MC 1956
50170–53170	DMSL	Ecclesbourne Valley Railway	MC 1957
50193–53193–977898	DMCL	Great Central Railway	MC 1957
50203–53203–977897	DMBS	Great Central Railway	MC 1957
50204–53204	DMBS	North Yorkshire Moors Railway	MC 1957
50222–53222–977693	DMBS	Barry Rail Centre	MC 1957
50253–53253	DMBS	Ecclesbourne Valley Railway	MC 1957
50256–53256	DMBS	East Kent Light Railway	MC 1957
50266–53266	DMSL	Great Central Railway	MC 1957
50321–53321–977900	DMCL	Great Central Railway	MC 1958
50338–53338–977694	DMCL	Barry Rail Centre	MC 1958
50746–53746	DMSL	Wensleydale Railway	MC 1957
51187	DMBS	Cambrian Railway Trust, Llynclys	MC 1958
51188	DMBS	Ecclesbourne Valley Railway	MC 1958
51189	DMBS	Keighley & Worth Valley Railway	MC 1958
51192	DMBS	North Norfolk Railway (N)	MC 1958
51205	DMBS	Cambrian Railway Trust, Llynclys	MC 1958
51210	DMBS	Wensleydale Railway	MC 1958
51213	DMBS	East Anglian Railway Museum	MC 1958
51226	DMBS	Mid Norfolk Railway	MC 1958
51228	DMBS	North Norfolk Railway	MC 1958
51427–977899	DMBS	Great Central Railway	MC 1959
51434 "MATTHEW SMITH 1974–2002"	DMBS	Mid Norfolk Railway	MC 1959
51499	DMSL	Mid Norfolk Railway	MC 1959
51503	DMCL	Mid Norfolk Railway	MC 1959
51505	DMSL	Ecclesbourne Valley Railway	MC 1959
51511	DMSL	North Yorkshire Moors Railway	MC 1959
51512	DMSL	Cambrian Railway Trust, Llynclys	MC 1959
51803	DMSL	Keighley & Worth Valley Railway	MC 1959

56055–54055	DTSL	Cambrian Railway Trust, Llynclys	MC 1957
56062–54062	DTSL	North Norfolk Railway	MC 1957
56342–54342–042222	DTCL	Midland Railway-Butterley	MC 1958
56343–54343	DTSL	East Kent Light Railway	MC 1958
56347–54347 h	DTSL	Foxfield Railway	MC 1958
56352–54352	DTSL	North Norfolk Railway (N)	MC 1958
56356–54356–6300h "HEBRIDEAN"	DTCL	Barry Rail Centre	MC 1959
56358–54358	DTSL	East Anglian Railway Museum	MC 1959
56408	DTSL	Spa Valley Railway	MC 1958
59117§	TSL	Mid Norfolk Railway	MC 1958
59303	TSL	Ecclesbourne Valley Railway	MC 1957
59539†	TSL	North Yorkshire Moors Railway	MC 1959

CLASS 103 — PARK ROYAL 2-CAR UNITS

Built: 1958.
Original formation: DMBS–DTCL.
Engines: Two AEC 220 of 112 kW (150 hp).

DMBS	18.49 x 2.82 m	34 tonnes	–/52
DTCL	18.49 x 2.82 m	27 tonnes	16/48 1T

50413	DMBS	Helston Railway	PR 1958
56160–DB 975228	DTCL	Denbigh & Mold Junction Railway	PR 1958
56169	DTCL	Helston Railway	PR 1958

CLASS 104 — BRCW UNITS

Built: 1957–58. Various formations.
Engines: Two BUT (Leyland) of 112 kW (150 hp).

DMBS	18.49 x 2.82 m	31.5 tonnes	–/52
TCL	18.49 x 2.82 m	24.5 tonnes	12/54 1T
TBSL	18.49 x 2.82 m	25.5 tonnes	–/51 1T
DMCL	18.49 x 2.82 m	31.5 tonnes	12/54 (* 12/51) 1T
DTCL	18.49 x 2.82 m	24.5 tonnes	12/54 1T

50437–53437	DMBS	East Lancashire Railway	BRCW 1957
50447–53447	DMBS	Llangollen Railway	BRCW 1957
50454–53454	DMBS	Llangollen Railway	BRCW 1957
50455–53455	DMBS	East Lancashire Railway	BRCW 1957
50479–53479	DMBS	Telford Steam Railway	BRCW 1958
50494–53494	DMCL	East Lancashire Railway	BRCW 1957
50517–53517	DMCL	East Lancashire Railway	BRCW 1957
50528–53528	DMCL	Llangollen Railway	BRCW 1958
50531–53531	DMCL	Telford Steam Railway	BRCW 1958
50556–53556*	DMCL	Telford Steam Railway	BRCW 1958
56182–54182–977554	DTCL	North Norfolk Railway	BRCW 1958
59137	TCL	East Lancashire Railway	BRCW 1957
59228	TBSL	Telford Steam Railway	BRCW 1958

CLASS 105 — CRAVENS 2-CAR UNITS

Built: 1957–59.
Various formations: DMBS–DTCL or DMCL.
Engines: Two AEC 220 of 112 kW (150 hp).

DMBS	18.49 x 2.82 m	29.5 tonnes	–/52
DTCL	18.49 x 2.82 m	23.5 tonnes	12/51 1T

51485	DMBS	East Lancashire Railway	Cravens 1959
56121	DTCL	East Lancashire Railway	Cravens 1957
56456–54456	DTCL	Llangollen Railway	Cravens 1959

CLASS 107   DERBY HEAVYWEIGHT 3-CAR UNITS

Built: 1960–61.
Original formation: DMBS–TSL–DMCL.
Engines: Two BUT (Leyland) of 112 kW (150 hp).

DMBS	18.49 x 2.82 m	35 tonnes	–/52
DMCL	18.49 x 2.82 m	35.5 tonnes	12/53 1T
TSL	18.49 x 2.82 m	28.5 tonnes	–/71 1T

51990–977830	DMBS	Strathspey Railway	Derby 1960
51993–977834	DMBS	Tanat Valley Light Railway	Derby 1961
52005–977832	DMBS	Tanat Valley Light Railway	Derby 1961
52006	DMBS	Avon Valley Railway	Derby 1961
52008	DMBS	Strathspey Railway	Derby 1961
52012–977835	DMCL	Tanat Valley Light Railway	Derby 1960
52025–977833	DMCL	Avon Valley Railway	Derby 1961
52029	DMCL	Gloucestershire Warwickshire Railway	Derby 1961
52030–977831	DMCL	Strathspey Railway	Derby 1961
52031	DMCL	Tanat Valley Light Railway	Derby 1961
59791	TSL	Tanat Valley Light Railway	Derby 1961

CLASS 108   DERBY LIGHTWEIGHT UNITS

Built: 1958–61. Various formations.
Engines: Two Leyland of 112 kW (150 hp).

DMBS	18.49 x 2.79 m	29.5 tonnes	–/52
TBSL	18.49 x 2.79 m	21.5 tonnes	–/50 1T
TSL	18.49 x 2.79 m	21.5 tonnes	–/68 1T
DMCL	18.49 x 2.79 m	28.5 tonnes	12/53 1T
DMSL	18.49 x 2.79 m	28.5 tonnes	–/71 1T (originally DMCL 12/53 1T)
DTCL	18.49 x 2.79 m	21.5 tonnes	12/53 1T

50599–53599	DMBS	Ecclesbourne Valley Railway	Derby 1958
50619–53619	DMBS	Dean Forest Railway	Derby 1958
50628–53628	DMBS	Keith & Dufftown Railway	Derby 1958
50632–53632	DMSL	Pontypool & Blaenavon Railway	Derby 1958
50645–53645	DMSL	Nottingham Transport Heritage Centre	Derby 1958
50926–53926–977814	DMBS	Nottingham Transport Heritage Centre	Derby 1959
50928–53928	DMBS	Keighley & Worth Valley Railway	Derby 1959
50933–53933	DMBS	Severn Valley Railway	Derby 1960
50971–53971	DMBS	Kent & East Sussex Railway	Derby 1959
50980–53980	DMBS	Bodmin & Wenford Railway	Derby 1959
51562	DMCL	East Kent Light Railway (N)	Derby 1959
51565	DMCL	Keighley & Worth Valley Railway	Derby 1959
51566	DMCL	Dean Forest Railway	Derby 1959
51567-977854	DMCL	Midland Railway-Butterley	Derby 1959
51568	DMCL	Keith & Dufftown Railway	Derby 1959
51571	DMCL	Kent & East Sussex Railway	Derby 1960
51572	DMCL	Wensleydale Railway	Derby 1960
51907	DMBS	Llangollen Railway	Derby 1960
51909	DMBS	East Somerset Railway	Derby 1960
51914	DMBS	Dean Forest Railway	Derby 1960
51919	DMBS	Garw Valley Railway	Derby 1960
51922	DMBS	East Kent Light Railway (N)	Derby 1960
51933	DMBS	Swanage Railway	Derby 1960
51937–977806	DMBS	Midland Railway-Butterley	Derby 1960
51941	DMBS	Severn Valley Railway	Derby 1960
51942	DMBS	Mid Norfolk Railway	Derby 1961
51947	DMBS	Bodmin & Wenford Railway	Derby 1961
51950	DMBS	Telford Steam Railway	Derby 1961
52044	DMCL	Pontypool & Blaenavon Railway	Derby 1960
52048	DMCL	Garw Valley Railway	Derby 1960

52053–977807	DMCL	Keith & Dufftown Railway	Derby 1960
52054	DMCL	Bodmin & Wenford Railway	Derby 1960
52062	DMCL	Telford Steam Railway	Derby 1961
52064	DMCL	Severn Valley Railway	Derby 1961
56207–54207 h	DTCL	Appleby-Frodingham RPS, Scunthorpe	Derby 1958
56208–54208	DTCL	Severn Valley Railway	Derby 1958
56223–54223	DTCL	Llangollen Railway	Derby 1959
56224–54224	DTCL	Keith & Dufftown Railway	Derby 1959
56270–54270	DTCL	Mid Norfolk Railway	Derby 1959
56271–54271	DTCL	East Somerset Railway	Derby 1960
56274–54274	DTCL	Wensleydale Railway	Derby 1960
56279–54279	DTCL	Lavender Line	Derby 1960
56484–54484	DTCL	Midland Railway-Butterley	Derby 1960
56490–54490	DTCL	Llangollen Railway	Derby 1960
56491–54491	DTCL	Keith & Dufftown Railway	Derby 1960
56492–54492	DTCL	Dean Forest Railway	Derby 1960
56495–54495	DTCL	Kirklees Light Railway	Derby 1960
56504–54504	DTCL	Swanage Railway	Derby 1960
59245 h	TBSL	Appleby-Frodingham RPS, Scunthorpe	Derby 1958
59250	TBSL	Severn Valley Railway	Derby 1958
59387	TSL	Dean Forest Railway	Derby 1958

50628 and 56491 are named "SPIRIT OF DUFFTOWN" and 51568 & 52053 are named "SPIRIT OF BANFFSHIRE".

CLASS 109   D WICKHAM 2-CAR UNITS

Built: 1957.
Original formation: DMBS–DTCL.
Engines: Two BUT (Leyland) of 112 kW (150 hp).

DMBS	18.49 x 2.82 m	27.5 tonnes	–/52	
DTCL	18.49 x 2.82 m	20.5 tonnes	16/50 1T	

50416–DB 975005	DMBS	Llangollen Railway	Wkm 1957
56171–DB 975006	DTCL	Llangollen Railway	Wkm 1957

CLASS 110   BRCW CALDER VALLEY 3-CAR UNITS

Built: 1961–62.
Original formation: DMBC–TSL–DMCL.
Engines: Two Rolls-Royce C6NFLH38D of 134 kW (180 hp).

DMBC	18.48 x 2.82 m	32.5 tonnes	12/33
DMCL	18.48 x 2.82 m	32.5 tonnes	12/54 1T
TSL	18.48 x 2.82 m	24.5 tonnes	–/72 1T

51813	DMBC	Wensleydale Railway	BRCW 1961
51842	DMCL	Wensleydale Railway	BRCW 1961
52071	DMBC	Lakeside & Haverthwaite Railway	BRCW 1962
52077	DMCL	Lakeside & Haverthwaite Railway	BRCW 1961
59701	TSL	East Lancashire Railway	BRCW 1961

59701 is on loan from the Wensleydale Railway.

CLASS 111   METRO-CAMMELL TRAILER BUFFET

Built: 1960. Used to augment other units as required.

TRSBL	18.49 x 2.82 m	25.5 tonnes	–/53 1T	

59575	TRSBL	Great Central Railway	MC 1960

CLASS 114   DERBY HEAVYWEIGHT 2-CAR UNITS

Built: 1956–57.
Original formation: DMBS–DTCL. Some rebuilt for parcels use, formation DMPMV–DTPMV.
Engines: Two Leyland Albion of 149 kW (200 hp).

DMBS	20.45 x 2.82 m	38 tonnes	–/62
DMPMV	20.45 x 2.82 m	41.5 tonnes	
DTCL	20.45 x 2.82 m	30 tonnes	12/62 1T
DTPMV	20.45 x 2.82 m	30 tonnes	

50015–53015–55929–977775	DMPMV	Midland Railway-Butterley	Derby 1957
50019–53019	DMBS	Midland Railway-Butterley	Derby 1957
56006–54006	DTCL	Midland Railway-Butterley	Derby 1956
56015–54015–54904–977776	DTPMV	Midland Railway-Butterley	Derby 1957
56047–54047	DTCL	Strathspey Railway	Derby 1957

55929 and 54904 were allocated departmental numbers 977715 and 977716 but these were never carried and they subsequently became 977775 and 977776.

CLASS 115   DERBY SUBURBAN 4-CAR UNITS

Built: 1960. Non-gangwayed when built, but gangways subsequently fitted.
Original formation: DMBS–TSso–TCL–DMBS.
Engines: Two Leyland Albion of 149 kW (200 hp).

DMBS	20.45 x 2.82 m	38.5 tonnes	–/74 (originally –/78)
TCL	20.45 x 2.82 m	30.5 tonnes	28/38 (originally 30/40) 2T
TSso	20.45 x 2.82 m	29.5 tonnes	–/98 (originally –/106)

59678 has been converted to TRCBL seating 28/32 by the West Somerset Railway.

BR	Present			
51655		DMBS	Thomas Muir (Rosyth), Port of Rosyth	Derby 1960
51669		DMBS	Spa Valley Railway	Derby 1960
51677		DMBS	European Metal Recycling, Kingsbury	Derby 1960
51849		DMBS	Spa Valley Railway	Derby 1960
51859		DMBS	West Somerset Railway	Derby 1960
51880		DMBS	West Somerset Railway	Derby 1960
51886		DMBS	Buckinghamshire Railway Centre	Derby 1960
51887		DMBS	West Somerset Railway	Derby 1960
51899		DMBS	Buckinghamshire Railway Centre	Derby 1960
59659 h	"9659"	TSso	Midland Railway-Butterley	Derby 1960
59664 h		TCL	Somerset & Dorset Railway Heritage Trust, Midsomer Norton Station	Derby 1960
59678		TCL	West Somerset Railway	Derby 1960
59719 h		TCL	Dartmouth Steam Railway	Derby 1960
59740	"9740"	TSso	South Devon Railway	Derby 1960
59761		TCL	Buckinghamshire Railway Centre	Derby 1960

59740 has been converted to a static cafe at Staverton.

CLASS 116   DERBY SUBURBAN 3-CAR UNITS

Built: 1957–58. Non-gangwayed when built, but gangways subsequently fitted.
Original formation: DMBS–TS or TC–DMS.
Engines: Two Leyland of 112 kW (150 hp).

DMBS	20.45 x 2.82 m	36.5 tonnes	–/65
DMS	20.45 x 2.82 m	36.5 tonnes	–/89 (originally –/95)
TS§	20.45 x 2.82 m	29 tonnes	–/98 (originally –/102)
TC	20.45 x 2.82 m	29 tonnes	20/68 (originally 28/74)

§   converted from TC seating 28/74.

51131	DMBS	Battlefield Railway	Derby 1958
51138	DMBS	Nottingham Transport Heritage Centre	Derby 1958

51151	DMS	Nottingham Transport Heritage Centre	Derby 1958
59003 h "ZOE"	TS	Dartmouth Steam Railway	Derby 1957
59004 h "EMMA"	TS	Dartmouth Steam Railway	Derby 1957
59444 h	TC	Chasewater Light Railway	Derby 1958

51138 was allocated departmental number 977921 but this was never carried.

CLASS 117 — PRESSED STEEL SUBURBAN 3-CAR UNITS

Built: 1960. Non-gangwayed when built, but gangways subsequently fitted.
Original formation: DMBS–TCL–DMS.
Engines: Two Leyland of 112 kW (150 hp).

DMBS	20.45 x 2.82 m	36.5 tonnes	–/65
TCL	20.45 x 2.82 m	30.5 tonnes	22/48 (originally 24/50) 2T
DMS	20.45 x 2.82 m	36.5 tonnes	–/89 (originally –/91)

51339	DMBS	East Lancashire Railway	PS 1960
51342	DMBS	Epping Ongar Railway	PS 1960
51346	DMBS	Swanage Railway	PS 1960
51347	DMBS	Gwili Railway	PS 1960
51351	DMBS	Pontypool & Blaenavon Railway	PS 1960
51352	DMBS	Quinton Rail Technology Centre, Long Marston	PS 1960
51353	DMBS	Wensleydale Railway	PS 1960
51354	DMBS	Peak Rail	PS 1960
51356	DMBS	Swanage Railway	PS 1960
51360	DMBS	Gloucestershire Warwickshire Railway	PS 1960
51363	DMBS	Gloucestershire Warwickshire Railway	PS 1960
51365	DMBS	Plym Valley Railway	PS 1960
51367	DMBS	Strathspey Railway	PS 1960
51370	DMBS	Titley Junction Station, Herefordshire	PS 1960
51371–977987	DMBS	Quinton Rail Technology Centre, Long Marston	PS 1960
51372	DMBS	Titley Junction Station, Herefordshire	PS 1960
51375–977992	DMS	Chinnor & Princes Risborough Railway	PS 1960
51376	DMS	Quinton Rail Technology Centre, Long Marston	PS 1960
51381	DMS	Mangapps Railway Museum	PS 1960
51382	DMS	East Lancashire Railway	PS 1960
51384	DMS	Epping Ongar Railway	PS 1960
51388	DMS	Swanage Railway	PS 1960
51392	DMS	Swanage Railway	PS 1960
51396	DMS	Peak Rail	PS 1960
51397	DMS	Pontypool & Blaenavon Railway	PS 1960
51400	DMS	Wensleydale Railway	PS 1960
51401	DMS	Gwili Railway	PS 1960
51402	DMS	Strathspey Railway	PS 1960
51405	DMS	Gloucestershire Warwickshire Railway	PS 1960
51407	DMS	Plym Valley Railway	PS 1960
51412	DMS	Titley Junction Station, Herefordshire	PS 1960
51413–977988	DMBS	Quinton Rail Technology Centre, Long Marston	PS 1960
59486	TCL	Swanage Railway	PS 1960
59488	TCL	Dartmouth Steam Railway	PS 1960
59492	TCL	Swanage Railway	PS 1960
59493 h	TCL	West Somerset Railway	PS 1960
59494 h "CHLOE"	TCL	Dartmouth Steam Railway	PS 1960
59500	TCL	Wensleydale Railway	PS 1960
59501	TCL	Nottingham Transport Heritage Centre	PS 1960
59503 h "NINA"	TCL	Dartmouth Steam Railway	PS 1960
59505	TCL	Quinton Rail Technology Centre, Long Marston	PS 1960
59506 h	TCL	Quinton Rail Technology Centre, Long Marston	PS 1960
59507 h "ELLA"	TCL	Dartmouth Steam Railway	PS 1960
59508	TCL	Gwili Railway	PS 1960
59509 h	TCL	Wensleydale Railway	PS 1960
59510	TCL	Gloucestershire Warwickshire Railway	PS 1960
59511	TCL	Strathspey Railway	PS 1960
59513 h "HEIDI"	TCL	Dartmouth Steam Railway	PS 1960

59514	TCL	Swindon & Cricklade Railway	PS 1960
59515 h	TCL	Yeovil Railway Centre	PS 1960
59517 h "EMILY"	TCL	Dartmouth Steam Railway	PS 1960
59520	TCL	Dartmoor Railway	PS 1960
59521 h	TCL	Helston Railway	PS 1960
59522 h	TCL	Chasewater Light Railway	PS 1960

51346, 51356, 51388, 51392, 59486 and 59492 are currently undergoing overhaul at Arlington Fleet Services, Eastleigh Works

59488 has been converted into a static Visitor Centre at Kingswear Station.

CLASS 118 — BRCW SUBURBAN 3-CAR UNITS

Built: 1960. Non-gangwayed when built, but gangways subsequently fitted.
Original formation: DMBS–TCL–DMS.
Engines: Two Leyland of 112 kW (150 hp).

DMS	20.45 x 2.82 m	36.5 tonnes	–/89 (originally –/91)
51321–977753	DMS	Battlefield Railway	BRCW 1960

CLASS 119 — GRCW CROSS-COUNTRY 3-CAR UNITS

Built: 1959.
Original formation: DMBC–TRSBL–DMSL.
Engines: Two Leyland of 112 kW (150 hp).

DMBC	20.45 x 2.82 m	37.5 tonnes	18/16
DMSL	20.45 x 2.82 m	38.5 tonnes	–/68 2T
51073	DMBC	Ecclesbourne Valley Railway	GRCW 1959
51074	DMBC	Swindon & Cricklade Railway	GRCW 1959
51104	DMSL	Swindon & Cricklade Railway	GRCW 1959

CLASS 120 — SWINDON CROSS-COUNTRY 3-CAR UNITS

Built: 1958.
Original formation: DMBC–TRSBL–DMSL.

TRSBL	20.45 x 2.82 m	31.5 tonnes	–/60 2T
59276	TRSBL	Great Central Railway	Swindon 1958

CLASS 121 — PRESSED STEEL SINGLE UNITS & DRIVING TRAILERS

Built: 1960–61. Non-gangwayed single cars with two driving cabs plus driving trailers used for augmentation. The driving trailers were latterly fitted with gangways for coupling to power cars of other classes.
Engines: Two Leyland of 112 kW (150 hp).

DMBS	20.45 x 2.82 m	38 tonnes	–/65
DTS	20.45 x 2.82 m	30 tonnes	–/89 (originally –/91)
55023	DMBS	Chinnor & Princes Risborough Railway	PS 1960
55024–977858	DMBS	Chinnor & Princes Risborough Railway	PS 1960
55027–977975	DMBS	Ecclesbourne Valley Railway	PS 1960
55028–977860	DMBS	Swanage Railway	PS 1960
55029–977968	DMBS	Rushden Transport Museum	PS 1960
55031–977976	DMBS	Ecclesbourne Valley Railway	PS 1960
55032–977842	DMBS	Wensleydale Railway	PS 1960
55033–977826	DMBS	Colne Valley Railway	PS 1960
56287–54287	DTS	Colne Valley Railway	PS 1961
56289–54289	DTS	East Lancashire Railway	PS 1961

55028 is currently undergoing overhaul at Arlington Fleet Services, Eastleigh Works.

▲ Displaying the somewhat optimistic destination of London Euston, the Wensleydale Railway's Class 117 DMS 51400 is paired with Class 121 55032 as it leaves Redmire with the 11.00 to Leeming Bar on 29 December 2015. **Robert Pritchard**

▼ Class 122 DMBS 55006 pauses at Carrog on the Llangollen Railway with the 12.22 Corwen East–Llangollen on 21 June 2015. **David Jackman**

CLASS 122   GRCW SINGLE-CAR UNITS

Built: 1958. Non-gangwayed single cars with two driving cabs.
Engines: Two AEC 220 of 112 kW (150 hp).

DMBS   20.45 x 2.82 m   36.5 tonnes   –/65

55000	DMBS	South Devon Railway	GRCW 1958
55001–DB975023	DMBS	East Lancashire Railway	GRCW 1958
55003	DMBS	Gloucestershire Warwickshire Railway	GRCW 1958
55005	DMBS	Battlefield Railway	GRCW 1958
55006	DMBS	Ecclesbourne Valley Railway	GRCW 1958
55009	DMBS	Mid Norfolk Railway	GRCW 1958
55012	DMBS	Weardale Railway	GRCW 1958
55019–DB975042	DMBS	Llanelli & Mynydd Mawr Railway	GRCW 1958

CLASS 126   SWINDON INTER-CITY UNITS

Built: 1956–59. 51017, 51043 and 59404 for Ayrshire services and 79443 for Glasgow–Edinburgh services. Various formations.
Engines: Two AEC 220 of 112 kW (150 hp).

DMBSL	20.45 x 2.82 m	38.5 tonnes	–/52 1T
DMSL	20.45 x 2.82 m	38.5 tonnes	–/64 1T
TCK	20.45 x 2.82 m	32.3 tonnes	18/32 2T
TRCsoBL	20.45 x 2.82 m	34 tonnes	18/12 1T (First Class seating in compartments)

51017	DMSL	Bo'ness & Kinneil Railway	Swindon 1959
51043	DMBSL	Bo'ness & Kinneil Railway	Swindon 1959
59404	TCK	Bo'ness & Kinneil Railway	Swindon 1959
79443	TRCsoBL	Bo'ness & Kinneil Railway	Swindon 1957

59404 was converted by BR to a TSK –/56 but has been restored as a TCK.

CLASS 127   DERBY SUBURBAN 4-CAR UNITS

Built: 1959. Non-gangwayed.
Original formation: DMBS–TSL–TS–DMBS. Some DMBS rebuilt as DMPMV, normal formation DMPMV(A)–DMPMV(B).
Engines: Two Rolls-Royce C8 of 177 kW (238 hp).
Transmission: Hydraulic.

DMBS	20.45 x 2.82 m	40.6 tonnes	–/76
DMPMV (A)	20.45 x 2.82 m	40 tonnes	
DMPMV (B)	20.45 x 2.82 m	40 tonnes	
TSL	20.45 x 2.82 m	30.5 tonnes	–/86 2T

51591–55966		DMPMV(A)	Midland Railway-Butterley	Derby 1959
51610–55967	"GLEN ORD"	DMPMV(B)	Midland Railway-Butterley	Derby 1959
51616	"ALF BENNEY"	DMBS	Great Central Railway	Derby 1959
51618		DMBS	Llangollen Railway	Derby 1959
51622		DMBS	Great Central Railway	Derby 1959
51625–55976		DMPMV(A)	Midland Railway-Butterley	Derby 1959
59603 h		TSL	Chasewater Light Railway	Derby 1959
59609		TSL	Midland Railway-Butterley	Derby 1959

UNCLASSIFIED   DERBY LIGHTWEIGHT 2-CAR UNIT

Built: 1955. Original formation: DMBS–DTCL.
Engines: Two BUT (AEC) of 112 kW (150 hp).

DMBS	18.49 x 2.82 m	27.4 tonnes	–/61
DTCL	18.49 x 2.82 m	21.3 tonnes	9/53 1T

79018–DB975007	DMBS	Ecclesbourne Valley Railway	Derby 1955
79612–DB975008	DTCL	Ecclesbourne Valley Railway	Derby 1955

UNCLASSIFIED — DERBY LIGHTWEIGHT SINGLE-CAR UNIT

Built: 1956. Non-gangwayed single cars with two driving cabs.
Engines: Two AEC of 112 kW (150 hp).

DMBS	18.49 x 2.82 m	27 tonnes	–/57	
79900–DB 975010 IRIS	DMBS	Ecclesbourne Valley Railway		Derby 1956

5.4.2. FOUR-WHEELED DIESEL RAILBUSES

A small number of diesel railbuses appeared in the 1950s as a result of the Modernisation Plan. These were intended for use on very lightly loaded branch line services. Within a few years of their introduction many of the services for which they were designed ceased and they were withdrawn.

Faced with the need to find replacements for the ageing DMU fleet in the late 1970s, the concept was again investigated. As a result a number of prototypes emerged which it was hoped would lead to substantial orders from both BR and overseas railways. Although BR purchased large numbers of 2-car and 3-car railbuses no significant overseas orders materialised.

See Diesel Mechanical/Hydraulic Multiple Units section for details of Type Codes.

CLASS 140 — DERBY/LEYLAND BUS PROTOTYPE 2-CAR RAILBUS

Built: 1981.
Formation: DMSL–DMS.
Engine: Leyland TL11 of 152 kW (205 hp)
Transmission: Mechanical. Self-Changing Gears 4-speed gearbox.
Maximum Speed: 75 mph.

Air braked.

DMSL	16.20 x 2.50 m	23.2 tonnes	–/50 1T	
DMS	16.20 x 2.50 m	23.0 tonnes	–/52	
55500	DMS	(ex-unit 140 001)	Keith & Dufftown Railway	Derby 1981
55501	DMSL	(ex-unit 140 001)	Keith & Dufftown Railway	Derby 1981

CLASS 141 — BREL/LEYLAND BUS 2-CAR RAILBUS

Built: 1983–84. Modified by Andrew Barclay 1988–89.
Formation: DMS–DMSL.
Engine: Leyland TL11 of 152 kW (205 hp) (* Cummins L10 of 165 kW (225 hp)).
Transmission: Mechanical, Self Changing gears (* Hydraulic, Voith T211r).
Maximum Speed: 75 mph.

Air braked.

DMS	15.45 x 2.50 m	26.0 tonnes	–/50	
DMSL	15.45 x 2.50 m	26.5 tonnes	–/44 1T	
55503	DMS	(ex-unit 141 103)	Weardale Railway	BREL Leyland 1984
55508	DMS	(ex-unit 141 108)	Colne Valley Railway	BREL Leyland 1984
55510	DMS	(ex-unit 141 110)	Weardale Railway	BREL Leyland 1984
55513 *	DMS	(ex-unit 141 113)	Midland Railway-Butterley	BREL Leyland 1984
55523	DMSL	(ex-unit 141 103)	Weardale Railway	BREL Leyland 1984
55528	DMSL	(ex-unit 141 108)	Colne Valley Railway	BREL Leyland 1984
55533 *	DMSL	(ex-unit 141 113)	Midland Railway-Butterley	BREL Leyland 1984

In addition a further 28 Class 141 vehicles have been exported for use abroad:

The following vehicles have been sold to Iranian Islamic Republic Railways: 55502, 55505, 55507, 55509, 55511, 55514, 55515, 55516, 55517, 55518, 55519, 55520, 55522, 55525, 55527, 55529, 55531, 55534, 55535, 55536, 55537, 55538, 55539 and 55540.

The following vehicles have been sold to Connexion, Utrecht, Netherlands: 55506, 55512, 55526 and 55532.

UNCLASSIFIED — WAGGON UND MASCHINENBAU

Built: 1958. 5 built.
Engine: Buessing of 112 kW (150 hp) at 1900 rpm (§ AEC 220 of 112 kW (150 hp)).
Transmission: Mechanical.
Maximum Speed: 70 mph.

DMS	13.95 x 2.67 m	15 tonnes	–/56	
79960		Ribble Steam Railway	WMD 1265/1958
79962		Keighley & Worth Valley Railway	WMD 1267/1958
79963		East Anglian Railway Museum	WMD 1268/1958
79964§		Keighley & Worth Valley Railway	WMD 1298/1958

79960 is on loan from the North Norfolk Railway.

UNCLASSIFIED — AC CARS

Built: 1958. 5 built.
Engine: AEC 220 of 112 kW (150 hp) (§ engine removed).
Transmission: Mechanical.
Maximum Speed: 70 mph.

DMS	11.33 x 2.82 m	11 tonnes	–/46	
79976§		Great Central Railway	AC 1958
79978		Colne Valley Railway	AC 1958

UNCLASSIFIED — BR DERBY/LEYLAND

Built: 1977. Used by BR and in the USA.
Engine: Leyland 510 of 149 kW (200 hp) (fitted 1979).
Transmission: Mechanical. Self Changing Gears.
Maximum Speed: 75 mph.

Air braked.

DMS	12.32 x 2.50 m	16.67 tonnes	–/40	
R1-RDB 975874		Wensleydale Railway (N)	RTC Derby 1977

UNCLASSIFIED — BREL DERBY/LEYLAND/WICKHAM

Built: 1980. Built for the US Federal Railroad Administration. Trialled by BR before export.
Engine: Leyland 690 of 149 kW (200 hp).
Transmission: Mechanical. Self Changing Gears.
Maximum Speed: 75 mph.

Air braked.

DMS	15.30 x 2.50 m	19.8 tonnes	–/56	
R3.01		Connecticut Trolley Museum, East Windsor, CT, USA	Wkm 1980

UNCLASSIFIED — BREL DERBY/LEYLAND

Built: 1981. Used by BR. Subsequently sold to Northern Ireland Railways.
Engine: Leyland 690 of 149 kW (200 hp).
Transmission: Mechanical. Self Changing Gears SE4 epicyclic gearbox and cardan shafts to SCG RF28 final drive.
Maximum Speed: 75 mph.
Gauge: Built as 1435 mm but converted to 1600 mm when sold to Northern Ireland Railways.

Air braked.

DMS	15.30 x 2.50 m		19.96 tonnes	–/56	
R3.03–RDB 977020		RB3	Downpatrick Steam Railway, NI	RTC Derby 1981

UNCLASSIFIED — BREL-LEYLAND

Built: 1984. Built for demonstration purposes. RE 002 used in mainland Europe. RE 004 used in the USA.
Engine: Leyland TL11 of 152 kW (205 hp).
Transmission: Mechanical.
Maximum Speed: 75 mph.

Air braked.

DMS	x 2.50 m	37.5 tonnes	–/64 (* –/40)

RE 002		Riverstown Mill Railway, Dundalk, Ireland	BREL Leyland 1984
RE 004*	RB 004	Waverley Route Heritage Association, Whitrope	BREL Leyland 1984

UNCLASSIFIED — WICKHAM TRACK RECORDING CAR

Built: 1958 for BR Research. Later known as the Wickham Self-propelled Laboratory. Preserved as passenger-carrying Railbus and fitted with 28 seats.
Engine: Meadows 6HDC500 of 71 kW (97 hp) at 1800 rpm.
Transmission: Mechanical, to one axle only. 4 speed epicyclic gearbox Type R11.
Maximum Speed: 55 mph.

999507-RDB 999507	Lavender Line	Wkm 8025/1958

5.4.3. DIESEL ELECTRIC MULTIPLE UNITS

At the time of the 1955 Modernisation Plan much of the then Southern Region was already operating from third rail electric supply, with just a handful of lines not so equipped. Complete electrification was out of the question, so much thought was given to how to replace steam power on these lines. The solution was the Diesel Electric Multiple Unit; essentially an electric multiple unit design fitted with a diesel engine to enable operation on non-electrified lines.

In the early 1980s BR desperately needed to replace its ageing fleet of diesel multiple units and returned to the DEMU concept as a possible solution. Two prototype units were built but the high cost of the vehicles proved to be too expensive and the project was dropped. Most of the Southern Region lines for which DEMUs had originally been acquired either closed or were the subject of a later electrification programme.

For details of Type Codes see Appendix IV.

CLASS 201   "HASTINGS" — 6-CAR DIESEL-ELECTRIC UNITS

Built: 1957 by BR Eastleigh Works on frames constructed at Ashford. Special narrow-bodied units built to the former loading gauge of the Tonbridge–Battle line. Gangwayed within set.
Original formation: DMBSO–TSOL–TSOL–TFK–TSOL–DMBSO.
Engines: English Electric 4SRKT of 370 kW (500 hp).
Transmission: Two EE 507 traction motors on the power car inner bogie.
Maximum Speed: 75 mph.

DMBSO	18.35 x 2.50 m	54 tonnes	–/22
TSOL	18.35 x 2.50 m	29 tonnes	–/52 2T
TFK	18.36 x 2.50 m	30 tonnes	42/– 2T

60000	"Hastings"	DMBSO	(ex-unit 1001)	St Leonards Railway Engineering	Eastleigh 1957
60001		DMBSO	(ex-unit 1001)	St Leonards Railway Engineering	Eastleigh 1957
60500		TSOL	(ex-unit 1001)	St Leonards Railway Engineering	Eastleigh 1957
60501		TSOL	(ex-unit 1001)	St Leonards Railway Engineering	Eastleigh 1957
60502		TSOL	(ex-unit 1001)	St Leonards Railway Engineering	Eastleigh 1957
60700		TFK	(ex-unit 1001)	St Leonards Railway Engineering	Eastleigh 1957

CLASS 202 "HASTINGS" 6-CAR DIESEL-ELECTRIC UNITS

Built: 1957–58 by BR Eastleigh Works on frames constructed at Ashford. Special narrow-bodied units built to the former loading gauge of the Tonbridge–Battle line. Gangwayed within set.
Original formation: DMBSO–TSOL–TSOL (or TRSKB)–TFK–TSOL–DMBSO.
Engines: English Electric 4SRKT of 370 kW (500 hp).
Transmission: Two EE 507 traction motors on the power car inner bogie.
Maximum Speed: 75 mph.

DMBSO	20.34 x 2.50 m	55 tonnes	–/30
TSOL	20.34 x 2.50 m	29 tonnes	–/60 2T
TFK	20.34 x 2.50 m	31 tonnes	48/– 2T
TRSKB	20.34 x 2.50 m	34 tonnes	–/21

60016–60116	DMBSO	(ex-unit 1012)	St Leonards Railway Engineering	Eastleigh 1957
60018–60118	DMBSO	(ex-units 1013–203 101)	St Leonards Railway Engineering	Eastleigh 1957
60019	DMBSO	(ex-units 1013–203 101)	St Leonards Railway Engineering	Eastleigh 1957
60527	TSOL	(ex-units 1013–203 101)	St Leonards Railway Engineering	Eastleigh 1957
60528	TSOL	(ex-units 1013–202 001)	St Leonards Railway Engineering	Eastleigh 1957
60529	TSOL	(ex-units 1013–202 001)	St Leonards Railway Engineering	Eastleigh 1957
60708	TFK	(ex-unit 1012)	St Leonards Railway Engineering	Eastleigh 1957
60709	TFK	(ex-units 1013–203 101)	St Leonards Railway Engineering	Eastleigh 1957
60750–RDB 975386	TRSKB	(ex-unit 1032)	Electric Railway Museum, Coventry	Eastleigh 1958

60116 carries the name "Mountfield" and 60118 carries the name "Tunbridge Wells".

60018, 60019, 60527, 60709 were also formed in unit 202 001.

CLASS 205 "HAMPSHIRE" 2- & 3-CAR DIESEL-ELECTRIC UNITS

Built: 1957–59 by BR Eastleigh Works on frames constructed at Ashford. Non-gangwayed (* subsequently fitted with gangways).
Original formation: DMBSO–TSO–DTCsoL or DMBSO–DTCsoL.
Engines: English Electric 4SRKT of 370 kW (500 hp).
Transmission: Two EE 507 traction motors on the power car inner bogie.
Maximum Speed: 75 mph.

DMBSO	20.34 x 2.82 m	56 tonnes	–/52 (* –/39)
TSO	20.28 x 2.82 m	30 tonnes	–/104
DTCsoL	20.34 x 2.82 m	32 tonnes	19/50 2T (§ 13/50 2T) (originally 13/62 2T)
DTSOL	20.34 x 2.82 m	32 tonnes	–/76 2T (originally DTCsoL 13/62 2T)

60100–60154	DMBSO	(ex-unit 1101–205 001)	East Kent Light Railway	Eastleigh 1957
60108	DMBSO	(ex-unit 1109–205 009)	Eden Valley Railway	Eastleigh 1957
60110*	DMBSO	(ex-units 1111–205 205)	Epping Ongar Railway	Eastleigh 1957
60117	DMBSO	(ex-unit 1118–205 018)	Dartmoor Railway	Eastleigh 1957
60122	DMBSO	(ex-unit 1123–205 023)	Lavender Line	Eastleigh 1959
60124	DMBSO	(ex-unit 1125–205 025)	Mid Hants Railway	Eastleigh 1959
60658	TSO	(ex-unit 1109–205 009)	Eden Valley Railway	Eastleigh 1959
60669	TSO	(ex-unit 1124–205 024)	Swindon & Cricklade Railway	Eastleigh 1959
60800§	DTCsoL	(ex-unit 1101–205 001)	East Kent Light Railway	Eastleigh 1957
60808	DTCsoL	(ex-unit 1109–205 009)	Eden Valley Railway	Eastleigh 1957
60810	DTSOL	(ex-units 1111–205 205)	Epping Ongar Railway	Eastleigh 1957
60820	DTCsoL	(ex-unit 1121–205 008)	Lavender Line	Eastleigh 1958
60822	DTCsoL	(ex-unit 1123–205 023)	Swindon & Cricklade Railway	Eastleigh 1959
60824§	DTCsoL	(ex-unit 1125–205 025)	Mid Hants Railway	Eastleigh 1959

Unit 205 205 (60110–60810) was also numbered 205 101 for a time.

60820 was reformed into unit 1108 (later 205 008) in 1974.

60820 was originally used on the Hastings–Ashford line and the Bexhill West and New Romney branches. The four units 1119–1122 originally used on these services were referred to as "HASTINGS" when based at St Leonards depot.

CLASS 205   "BERKSHIRE" 3-CAR DIESEL-ELECTRIC UNITS

Built: 1960–62 by BR Eastleigh Works on frames constructed at Ashford. Non-gangwayed.
Original formation: DMBSO–TSO–DTCsoL.
Engines: English Electric 4SRKT of 370 kW (500 hp).
Transmission: Two EE 507 traction motors on the power car inner bogie.
Maximum Speed: 75 mph.

DMBSO	20.34 x 2.82 m	56 tonnes	–/42
TSO	20.28 x 2.82 m	30 tonnes	–/104
DTCsoL	20.34 x 2.82 m	32 tonnes	13/62 2T

60145–977939	DMBSO	(ex-unit 1127–205 027)	St Leonards Railway Engineering	Eastleigh 1962
60146	DMBSO	(ex-unit 1128–205 028)	Dartmoor Railway	Eastleigh 1962
60149–977940	DMBSO	(ex-unit 1131–205 031)	St Leonards Railway Engineering	Eastleigh 1962
60150	DMBSO	(ex-unit 1132–205 032)	Dartmoor Railway	Eastleigh 1962
60151	DMBSO	(ex-unit 1133–205 033)	Lavender Line	Eastleigh 1962
60673	TSO	(ex-unit 1128–205 028)	Dartmoor Railway	Eastleigh 1962
60677	TSO	(ex-unit 1132–205 032)	Dartmoor Railway	Eastleigh 1962
60678	TSO	(ex-unit 1133–205 033)	Cold Norton Play School, Essex	Eastleigh 1962
60827	DTCsoL	(ex-unit 1128–205 028)	Dartmoor Railway	Eastleigh 1962
60828	DTCsoL	(ex-units 1129–205 018)	Dartmoor Railway	Eastleigh 1962
60831	DTCsoL	(ex-unit 1132–205 032)	Dartmoor Railway	Eastleigh 1962
60832	DTCsoL	(ex-unit 1133–205 033)	Lavender Line	Eastleigh 1962

60828 was also formed in unit 205 029 for a time.

CLASS 207   "OXTED"   3-CAR DIESEL-ELECTRIC UNITS

Built: 1962 by BR Eastleigh Works on frames constructed at Ashford. Reduced body width to allow operation through Somerhill Tunnel. Non-gangwayed (* subsequently fitted with gangways).
Original formation: DMBSO–TCsoL–DTSO.
Engines: English Electric 4SRKT of 370 kW (500 hp).
Transmission: Two EE 507 traction motors on the power car inner bogie.
Maximum Speed: 75 mph.

DMBSO	20.34 x 2.74 m	56 tonnes	–/42 (* –/40)
DTSO	20.32 x 2.74 m	32 tonnes	–/76 (* –/75)
TCsoL	20.34 x 2.74 m	31 tonnes	24/42

60127*	DMBSO	(ex-units 1302–207 203)	Swindon & Cricklade Railway	Eastleigh 1962
60130*	DMBSO	(ex-units 1305–207 202)	East Lancashire Railway	Eastleigh 1962
60142	DMBSO	(ex-unit 1317–207 017)	Spa Valley Railway	Eastleigh 1962
60616	TCsoL	(ex-unit 1317–207 017)	Spa Valley Railway	Eastleigh 1962
60901*	DTSO	(ex-units 1302–207 201)	Swindon & Cricklade Railway	Eastleigh 1962
60904*	DTSO	(ex-units 1305–207 202)	East Lancashire Railway	Eastleigh 1962
60916	DTSO	(ex-unit 1317–207 017)	Spa Valley Railway	Eastleigh 1962

Unit 207 202 (including 60130 and 60904) was also numbered 207 005 and 207 102 for a time and unit 207 203 (including 60127 and 60901) was also numbered 207 002 and 207 103 for a time.

CLASS 210 DERBY PROTOTYPE 3 & 4-CAR DIESEL-ELECTRIC UNITS

Built: 1981 by BR Derby Works.
Original formation: DMBSO–TSO–TSOL–DTSO or DMSO–TSO–DTSO.
Engines: MTU 12V396TC11 of 850 kW.
Transmission:
Maximum Speed: 75 mph.

DTSO	20.52 x 2.82 m	29 tonnes	–/74

54000–60300–67300	DTSO	Electric Railway Museum, Coventry	Derby 1981

Formerly part of units 210 001, 7001 and 316 999.

5.5. SOUTHERN RAILWAY ELECTRIC MULTIPLE UNITS

In this section classes are listed in order of the lowest numbered example of the class to be still in existence. Within classes vehicles are listed in numerical order of original number.

For details of type codes see Appendix IV.

CLASS 487 — WATERLOO & CITY LINE UNITS

Built: 1940. No permanent formations.
System: 630 V DC third rail.
Traction Motors: Two EE 500 of 140 kW (185 hp).　**Maximum Speed:** 35 mph.

| DMBSO | 14.33 x 2.64 m | 29 tons | –/40 |

| *BR* | *SR* | | | |
| S 61 S | 61 | DMBSO | London Transport Depot Museum, Acton (N) | EE 1940 |

1285 CLASS (later 3 Sub) — SUBURBAN UNITS

Built: 1925. Non-gangwayed.
Original Formation: DMBS–TS–DMBS.
System: 630 V DC third rail.
Traction Motors: Two MV 167 kW (225 hp).　**Maximum Speed:** 75 mph.

| DMBS | 18.90 x 2.44 m | 39 tons | –/70 |

| *BR* | *SR* | | | | |
| S 8143 S | 8143 | DMBS | (ex-unit 1293, later 4308) | National Railway Museum, York (N) | MC 1925 |

4 Cor — "NELSONS" — PORTSMOUTH EXPRESS STOCK

Built: 1937–38.
Original Formation: DMBSO–TSK–TCK–DMBSO.
System: 630 V DC third rail.
Traction Motors: Two EE 167 kW (225 hp) per power car.
Maximum Speed: 75 mph.

DMBSO	19.54 x 2.88 m	46.5 tons	–/52
TSK	19.54 x 2.85 m	32.65 tons	–/68
TCK	19.54 x 2.85 m	32.6 tons	30/24

BR	*SR*				
S 10096 S	10096	TSK	(ex-unit 3142)	East Kent Light Railway	Eastleigh 1937
S 11161 S	11161	DMBSO	(ex-unit 3142)	East Kent Light Railway	Eastleigh 1937
S 11179 S	11179	DMBSO	(ex-unit 3131)	National Railway Museum, Shildon (N)	Eastleigh 1937
S 11187 S	11187	DMBSO	(ex-unit 3135)	East Kent Light Railway	Eastleigh 1937
S 11201 S	11201	DMBSO	(ex-unit 3142)	Rye Farm, Wishaw, Sutton Coldfield	Eastleigh 1937
S 11825 S	11825	TCK	(ex-unit 3142)	East Kent Light Railway	Eastleigh 1937

S 11161 S was originally in unit 3065 and S11825S in unit 3135.

4 Sub (later Class 405) — SUBURBAN UNITS

Built: 1941–51. Non-gangwayed.
Original Formation: DMBSO–TS–TSO–DMBSO.
System: 630 V DC third rail.
Traction Motors: Two EE507 of 185 kW (250 hp).　**Maximum Speed:** 75 mph.

DMBSO	19.05 x 2.82 m	42 tons	–/82
TS	18.90 x 2.82 m	27 tons	–/120
TSO	18.90 x 2.82 m	26 tons	–/102

▲ 4 Cor "Nelsons" EMU 3142, led by DMBSO 11187 is seen at Shepherdswell on the East Kent Light Railway on 7 September 2014. **Phil Barnes**

▼ Some DMU and EMU vehicles can be found in unlikely places. One such vehicle is Class 411 TSOL 70547 which is at Garden Art Plus, an antique garden ornament shop in Hungerford, Berkshire. The vehicle is seen here on 20 April 2016. **Tony Bartlett**

S 10239 S	TS	(ex-units 4413–4732)	Electric Railway Museum, Coventry	Eastleigh 1947
S 10400 S–977364	TS	(ex-unit 4349)	Finmere Station, Oxfordshire	Eastleigh 1946
S 12354 S	TSO	(ex-units 4381–4732)	Electric Railway Museum, Coventry	Eastleigh 1948
S 12795 S	DMBSO	(ex-unit 4732)	Electric Railway Museum, Coventry	Eastleigh 1951
S 12796 S	DMBSO	(ex-unit 4732)	Electric Railway Museum, Coventry	Eastleigh 1951

S10400 was converted to a de-icing trailer in 1960. It also carried the number DS 70087.

2 Bil   SEMI-FAST UNITS

Built: 1937.
Original Formation: DMBSK–DTCK.
System: 630 V DC third rail.
Traction Motors: Two EE of 205 kW (275 hp).   **Maximum Speed:** 75 mph.

DMBSK	19.24 x 2.85 m	43.5 tons	–/52
DTCK	19.24 x 2.85 m	31.25 tons	24/30

BR	SR				
S 10656 S	10656	DMBSK	(ex-unit 1890–2090)	National Railway Museum, Shildon (N)	Eastleigh 1937
S 12123 S	12123	DTCK	(ex-unit 1890–2090)	National Railway Museum, Shildon (N)	Eastleigh 1937

4 DD   DOUBLE-DECK SUBURBAN UNITS

Built: 1949. Non-gangwayed.
Original Formation: DMBS–TS–TS–DMBS.
System: 630 V DC third rail.
Traction Motors: Two EE of 185 kW (250 hp).   **Maximum Speed:** 75 mph.

DMBS	19.24 x 2.85 m	39 tons	–/121

S 13003 S	DMBS	(ex-unit 4002–4902)	Hope Farm, Sellindge	Lancing 1949
S 13004 S	DMBS	(ex-unit 4002–4902)	Northamptonshire Ironstone Railway	Lancing 1949

4 EPB (later Class 415)   SUBURBAN UNITS

Built: 1951–57. Non-gangwayed.
Original Formation: DMBSO–TS–TSO–DMBSO.
System: 630 V DC third rail.
Traction Motors: Two EE507 of 185 kW (250 hp).   **Maximum Speed:** 75 mph.

DMBSO	19.05 x 2.82 m	42 tons	–/82
TSO	18.90 x 2.82 m	26 tons	–/102

S 14351 S	DMBSO	(ex-unit 5176)	Northamptonshire Ironstone Railway	Eastleigh 1955
S 14352 S	DMBSO	(ex-unit 5176)	Northamptonshire Ironstone Railway	Eastleigh 1955
S 15354 S	TSO	(ex-unit 5176)	Electric Railway Museum, Coventry	Eastleigh 1955
S 15396 S	TSO	(ex-unit 5176)	Northamptonshire Ironstone Railway	Eastleigh 1956

S 15396 S was originally formed in unit 5208.

2 EPB (later Class 416/1)   SUBURBAN UNITS

Built: 1959. Non-gangwayed.
Original Formation: DMBSO–DTSO.
System: 630 V DC third rail.
Traction Motors: Two EE of 185 kW (250 hp).   **Maximum Speed:** 75 mph.

DMBSO	19.05 x 2.82 m	40 tons	–/82
DTSO	18.90 x 2.82 m	30 tons	–/92

S 14573 S	DMBSO	(ex-unit 5667–6307)	Electric Railway Museum, Coventry	Eastleigh 1959
S 16117 S	DTSO	(ex-unit 5667–6307)	Electric Railway Museum, Coventry	Eastleigh 1959

5.6. PULLMAN CAR COMPANY ELECTRIC MULTIPLE UNITS

For details of Type Codes see Appendix IV.

GENERAL

Pullman cars owned by the Pullman Car Company operated as parts of EMU formations on the Southern Railway (later BR Southern Region). In addition the three Brighton Belle EMU sets were composed entirely of Pullman vehicles.

All vehicles are used as hauled stock except * – static exhibits.

6 Pul

Built: 1932. 6-car sets incorporating one Pullman kitchen composite.
Original Formation: DMBSO–TSK–TCK–TPCK–TCK–DMBSO.

TPCK		20.40 x 2.77 m		43 tons		12/16 2T	
RUTH	S 264 S	TPCK	(ex-unit 2017–3042)	British Pullman, Stewarts Lane, London	MC 1932
BERTHA	S 278 S	TPCK	(ex-unit 2012–3001)	West Coast Railway Co, Carnforth	MC 1932

5 BEL   BRIGHTON BELLE UNITS

Built: 1932. 5-car all Pullman sets.
Original Formation: DMPBSOL–TPSOL–TPFKOL–TPFKOL–DMPBSOL.
System: 630 V DC Third rail.
Traction Motors: Four BTH of 167 kW (225 hp).

TPFKOL	20.40 x 2.77 m	42 tons	20/–
TPSOL	20.40 x 2.77 m	41 tons	–/56
DMPBSOL	20.62 x 2.77 m	62 tons	–/48

HAZEL	S279S	TPFKOL	(ex-unit 2051–3051)	Barrow Hill Roundhouse	MC 1932
AUDREY	S280S	TPFKOL	(ex-unit 2052–3052)	British Pullman, Stewarts Lane, London	MC 1932
GWEN	S281S	TPFKOL	(ex-unit 2053–3053)	British Pullman, Stewarts Lane, London	MC 1932
DORIS	S282S	TPFKOL	(ex-unit 2051–3051)	Barrow Hill Roundhouse	MC 1932
MONA	S283S	TPFKOL	(ex-unit 2053–3053)	British Pullman, Stewarts Lane, London	MC 1932
VERA	S284S	TPFKOL	(ex-unit 2052–3052)	British Pullman, Stewarts Lane, London	MC 1932
CAR No. 85	S285S	TPSOL	(ex-unit 2053–3053)	Barrow Hill Roundhouse	MC 1932
CAR No. 86	S286S	TPSOL	(ex-unit 2051–3051)	British Pullman, Stewarts Lane, London	MC 1932
CAR No. 87	S287S	TPSOL	(ex-unit 2052–3052)	Barrow Hill Roundhouse	MC 1932
CAR No. 88	S288S	DMPBSOL	(ex-unit 2051–3051)	Barrow Hill Roundhouse	MC 1932
CAR No. 89*	S289S	DMPBSOL	(ex-unit 2051–3051)	Little Mill Inn, Rowarth, Derbyshire	MC 1932
CAR No. 91	S291S	DMPBSOL	(ex-unit 2052–3052)	Barrow Hill Roundhouse	MC 1932
CAR No. 92	S292S	DMPBSOL	(ex-unit 2053–3053)	British Pullman, Stewarts Lane, London	MC 1932
CAR No. 93	S293S	DMPBSOL	(ex-unit 2053–3053)	British Pullman, Stewarts Lane, London	MC 1932

The following vehicles are part of the Brighton Belle project: Nos. S279S, S282S, S285S, S287S, S288S, S291S.

5.7. LMS & CONSTITUENT COMPANIES' ELECTRIC MULTIPLE UNITS

In this section classes and vehicles within classes are listed in LMS number order.

For details of Type Codes see Appendix IV.

LNWR   EUSTON–WATFORD STOCK

Built: 1915. Oerlikon design. Non-gangwayed.
Original Formation: DMBSO–TSO–DTSO.
System: 630 V DC third rail. Used on Euston–Watford line.
Traction Motors: Four Oerlikon 179 kW (240 hp).
Maximum Speed:

DMBSO	17.60 x 2.73 m		54.75 tonnes	–/48

BR	LMS	LNWR			
M 28249 M	5751–28249	31 E	DMBSO	National Railway Museum, York (N)	MC 1915

CLASS 502   LIVERPOOL–SOUTHPORT STOCK

Built: 1939. Non-gangwayed.
Original Formation: DMBSO–TSO–DTSO (originally DTCO).
System: 630 V DC third rail.
Traction Motors: Four EE 175 kW.   **Maximum Speed:** 65 mph.

DMBSO	21.18 x 2.90 m		42.5 tonnes	–/88
DTSO	21.18 x 2.90 m		25.5 tonnes	–/79 (built as DTCO 53/25)

BR	LMS			
M 28361 M	28361	DMBSO	Merseyside Transport Trust, Burscough	Derby 1939
M 29896 M	29896	DTSO	Merseyside Transport Trust, Burscough	Derby 1939

CLASS 503   MERSEY WIRRAL STOCK

Built: 1938. Non-gangwayed.
Original Formation: DMBSO–TSO (originally TCO)–DTSO.
System: 630 V DC third rail.
Traction Motors: 4 BTH 100 kW.   **Maximum Speed:** 65 mph.

DMBSO	18.48 x 2.77 m		36.5 tonnes	–/56
TSO	17.77 x 2.77 m		20.5 tonnes	–/58 (built as TCO 40/19)
DTSO	18.85 x 2.77 m		21.5 tonnes	–/66

BR	LMS			
M 28690 M	28690	DMBSO	Electric Railway Museum, Coventry	Derby 1938
M 29720 M	29720	TSO	Electric Railway Museum, Coventry	Derby 1938
M 29289 M	29289	DTSO	Electric Railway Museum, Coventry	Derby 1938

MSJ&A STOCK

Built: 1931. Non-gangwayed.
Original Formation: DMBS–TC–DTS.
System: 1500 V DC overhead. Used on Manchester South Junction and Altrincham line until it was converted to 25 kV AC. This line is now part of the Manchester Metrolink system.
Traction Motors: **Maximum Speed:** 65 mph.

TC	17.60 x 2.85 m		31 tonnes.	24/72

BR	LMS	MSJ&A			
M 29666 M	29666	117	TC	Midland Railway-Butterley	MC 1931
M 29670 M	29670	121	TC	Midland Railway-Butterley	MC 1931

5.8. LNER & CONSTITUENT COMPANIES' ELECTRIC MULTIPLE UNITS

In this section classes and vehicles within classes are listed in LNER number order. The sole surviving tramway vehicle is listed at the end.

For details of Type Codes see Appendix IV.

NORTH EASTERN RAILWAY   DMLV

Built: 1904. Driving motor luggage van for North Tyneside line. After withdrawal from capital stock, this vehicle was used as a rail de-icing car.
System: 675 V DC third rail.
Traction Motors: **Maximum Speed:**

DMLV   17.40 x 2.77 m   46.5 tonnes

BR	LNER	NER			
DE 900730	23267	3267	DMLV	Stephenson Railway Museum (N)	MC 1904

CLASS 306   LIVERPOOL STREET–SHENFIELD STOCK

Built: 1949. Non-gangwayed.
Original Formation: DMSO–TBSO–DTSO.
System: 25 kV AC overhead (originally 1500 V DC overhead).
Traction Motors: Four Crompton Parkinson of 155 kW.
Maximum Speed: 65 mph.

DMSO	18.41 x 2.90 m	51.7 tonnes	–/62	
TBSO	16.78 x 2.90 m	26.4 tonnes	–/46	
DTSO	16.87 x 2.90 m	27.9 tonnes	–/60	
E 65217 E	DMSO	(ex-unit 017)	East Anglian Railway Museum (N)	MC 1949
E 65417 E	TBSO	(ex-unit 017)	East Anglian Railway Museum (N)	MC 1949
E 65617 E	DTSO	(ex-unit 017)	East Anglian Railway Museum (N)	BRCW 1949

GRIMSBY & IMMINGHAM LIGHT RAILWAY TRAM   A1-1A

Built: 1915 by GCR Dukinfield.
Type: Single deck tram.
Seats: 64 + 8 tip-up.
Bogies: Brush.
Motors: 2 x 25 hp Dick Kerr DK9 of 18 kW.

14		Crich Tramway Village	GCR Dukinfield 1915

5.9. BRITISH RAILWAYS ELECTRIC MULTIPLE UNITS

NUMBERING SYSTEM

BR EMU power cars were usually numbered in the 6xxxx series beginning with 61000, whilst trailer cars were numbered in the 7xxxx series. Exceptions to this rule are the APT-P, battery EMU vehicles and trams.

In this section classes are listed in three-digit class number order. Multiple unit vehicles are listed in original five-digit number order within each class. Unclassified battery EMUs and trams are listed at the end of the section.

For details of type codes see Appendix IV.

CLASS 302 — BR

Built: 1958–60 for London Fenchurch Street–Shoeburyness services.
System: 25 kV AC overhead.
Original Formation: BDTSOL–MBS–TCsoL–DTS. Non-gangwayed.
Formation as Rebuilt: BDTCOL–MBSO–TSOL–DTSO. Gangwayed within set.
Traction Motors: Four English Electric EE 536A of 143.5 kW.
Maximum Speed: 75 mph.

DTSO	20.36 x 2.83 m	33.4 tonnes	–/88	
75033	DTSO	(ex-unit 302 201)	Mangapps Railway Museum	York 1958
75250	DTSO	(ex-unit 302 277)	Mangapps Railway Museum	York 1959

CLASS 303 — PRESSED STEEL

Built: 1959–61 for Glasgow area services. Gangwayed within set (originally non-gangwayed).
System: 25 kV AC overhead.
Original Formation: DTSO–MBSO–BDTSO.
Traction Motors: Four MV of 155 kW.
Maximum Speed: 75 mph.

Forms part of the National Museums of Scotland assets.

DTSO	20.18 x 2.83 m	34.4 tonnes	–/56 (originally –/83)
MBSO	20.18 x 2.83 m	56.4 tonnes	–/48 (originally –/70)
BDTSO	20.18 x 2.83 m	38.4 tonnes	–/56 (originally –/83)
61503	MBSO	(ex-unit 303 023)	Bo'ness & Kinneil Railway	PS 1960
75597	DTSO	(ex-unit 303 032)	Bo'ness & Kinneil Railway	PS 1960
75632	BDTSO	(ex-unit 303 032)	Bo'ness & Kinneil Railway	PS 1960

CLASS 307 — BR

Built: 1954–56 for London Liverpool Street–Southend Victoria services.
System: 1500 V DC overhead. Converted 1960–61 to 25 kV AC overhead.
Original Formation: BDTBS–MS–TCsoL–DTSOL. Non-gangwayed.
Formation as Rebuilt: BDTBSO–MSO–TSOL–DTCOL. Gangwayed within set.
Traction Motors: Four GEC WT344 of 130 kW.
Maximum Speed: 75 mph.

BDTBSO	20.18 x 2.83 m	43 tonnes	–/66	
DTCOL	20.18 x 2.83 m	33 tonnes	24/48 1T	
75023	BDTBSO	(ex-unit 307 123)	Electric Railway Museum, Coventry	Eastleigh 1956
75120–94320	DTCOL	(ex-unit 307 120)	Mid Norfolk Railway	Eastleigh 1956

75120 was rebuilt as propelling control vehicle.

CLASS 308   BR

Built: 1961 for London Liverpool Street–Clacton stopping services.
System: 25kV AC overhead.
Original Formation: BDTCOL–MBS–TCSoL–DTS. Non-gangwayed.
Formation as Rebuilt: BDTCOL–MBSO–TSOL–DTSO. Gangwayed within set.
Traction Motors: Four English Electric EE 536A of 143.5 kW.
Maximum Speed: 75mph.

BDTCOL	20.18 x 2.82 m	36.3 tonnes	24/52 1T
75881	BDTCOL (ex-unit 308 136) Electric Railway Museum, Coventry		York 1961

CLASS 309   BREL YORK

Built: 1962–63 for London Liverpool Street–Clacton express services.
System: 25kV AC overhead.
Original Formation: BDTCsoL–MBSK–TSOL or TRUB–DTCOL or DTCsoL.
Formation as Rebuilt: BDTCsoL–MBSOL–TSOL–DTSOL.
Traction Motors: Four GEC WT401 of 210kW.
Maximum Speed: 100mph.

MBSOL	20.18 x 2.82 m	57.7 tonnes	–/52 2T
BDTCsoL	20.18 x 2.82 m	40.0 tonnes	18/32 2T
DTSOL	20.18 x 2.82 m	36.6 tonnes	–/56 2T

61928–977966	MBSOL	(ex-unit 309 624)	Electric Railway Museum, Coventry	York 1962
61937–977963	MBSOL	(ex-unit 309 616)	Electric Railway Museum, Coventry	York 1962
75642–977962	BDTCsoL	(ex-unit 309 616)	Electric Railway Museum, Coventry	York 1962
75965–977965	BDTCsoL	(ex-unit 309 624)	Electric Railway Museum, Coventry	York 1962
75972–977967	DTSOL	(ex-unit 309 624)	Electric Railway Museum, Coventry	York 1962
75981–977964	DTSOL	(ex-unit 309 616)	Electric Railway Museum, Coventry	York 1963

61928 is named NEW DALBY.

CLASS 311   CRAVENS

Built: 1967 for Glasgow "South Side electrification" extension to Gourock and Wemyss Bay.
Non-gangwayed.
System: 25kV AC overhead.
Original Formation: DTSO(A)–MBSO–DTSO(B).
Traction Motors: Four AEI of 165kW.   **Maximum Speed:** 75mph.

MBSO	20.18 x 2.83 m	56.4 tonnes	–/70
DTSO(B)	20.18 x 2.83 m	38.4 tonnes	–/83

62174–977845	MBSO	(ex-unit 311 103)	Summerlee Museum of Scottish Industrial Life	Cravens 1967
76433–977844	DTSO(B)	(ex-unit 311 103)	Summerlee Museum of Scottish Industrial Life	Cravens 1967

CLASS 312   BREL YORK

Built: 1975–78 using Mark 2 bodyshell for outer-suburban services from London King's Cross and London Liverpool Street and in the West Midlands area. Gangwayed within set.
System: 25kV AC overhead.
Original Formation: BDTSOL–MBSO–TSO–DTCOL.
Traction Motors: Four English Electric 546 of 201.5kW.
Maximum Speed: 90mph.

TSO	20.18 x 2.82 m	30.5 tonnes	–/98
DTCOL	20.18 x 2.82 m	33.0 tonnes	25/47 1T

71205	TSO	(ex-units 312 112–312 792)	Electric Railway Museum, Coventry	York 1976
78037	DTCOL	(ex-units 312 112–312 792)	Electric Railway Museum, Coventry	York 1976

CLASS 370 PROTOTYPE ADVANCED PASSENGER TRAIN (APT-P)

Built: 1978–80. Designed to run as pairs of 6-car articulated units with two power cars in the middle, these electric trains featured active hydraulic tilt and proved to be a maintenance nightmare. The power cars were reasonably successful, and are partly the basis of the Class 91 electric locomotive.
System: 25 kV AC overhead.
Normal Formation of Trailer rake: DTSOL–TSOL–TSRBL–TUOL–TFOL–TBFOL.
Formation of Preserved Set: DTSOL–TBFOL–M–TRSBL–TBFOL–DTSOL.
Traction Motors: Four ASEA LJMA 410F body mounted.
Wheel Dia: 853 mm.   **Maximum Speed:** 125 mph.

DTSOL	21.44 x 2.72 m	33.7 tonnes	–/52 1T
TBFOL	21.20 x 2.72 m	31.9 tonnes	25/– 1T
TRSBL	21.20 x 2.72 m	26.75 tonnes	–/28 1T
M	20.40 x 2.72 m	67.5 tonnes	

48103	DTSOL	Crewe Heritage Centre	Derby 1978
48106	DTSOL	Crewe Heritage Centre	Derby 1979
48602	TBFOL	Crewe Heritage Centre	Derby 1978
48603	TBFOL	Crewe Heritage Centre	Derby 1978
48404	TSRBL	Crewe Heritage Centre	Derby 1979
49002	M	Crewe Heritage Centre	Derby 1979
49006	M	Electric Railway Museum, Coventry	Derby 1980

CLASSES 410 & 411 (4 Bep & 4 Cep)   BR

Built: 1956–63 for Kent Coast electrification. Rebuilt 1979–84. Class 410 (4 Bep) was later reclassified Class 412.
System: 750 V DC third rail.
Original Formation: DMBSO–TCK–TSK (4 Cep) TRSB (4 Bep)–DMBSO.
Formation as Rebuilt: DMSO–TBCK–TSOL (4 Cep) TRSB (4 Bep)–DMSO.
Traction Motors: Two English Electric EE507 of 185 kW.
Maximum Speed: 90 mph.

DMSO	20.34 x 2.82 m	49 tonnes	–/56
TSOL	20.18 x 2.82 m	36 tonnes	–/64 2T
TBCK	20.18 x 2.82 m	34 tonnes	24/8 2T
TRSB	20.18 x 2.82 m	35.5 tonnes	–/24

61229	DMSO	(ex-units 7105–1537)	Arlington Fleet Services, Eastleigh Works	Eastleigh 1958
61230	DMSO	(ex-units 7105–1537)	Arlington Fleet Services, Eastleigh Works	Eastleigh 1958
61736	DMSO	(ex-units 7175–2304–1198)	Chinnor & Princes Risborough Railway	Eastleigh 1960
61737	DMSO	(ex-units 7175–2304–1198)	Chinnor & Princes Risborough Railway	Eastleigh 1960
61742	DMSO	(ex-units 7178–1589)	Dartmoor Railway	Eastleigh 1960
61743	DMSO	(ex-units 7178–1589–1399)	Dartmoor Railway	Eastleigh 1960
61798	DMSO	(ex-units 7016–2305)	Eden Valley Railway	Eastleigh 1961
61799	DMSO	(ex-units 7016–2305)	Eden Valley Railway	Eastleigh 1961
61804	DMSO	(ex-units 7019–2301)	Eden Valley Railway	Eastleigh 1961
61805	DMSO	(ex-units 7019–2301)	Eden Valley Railway	Eastleigh 1961
69013	TRSB	(ex-units 7014–2305)	East Kent Light Railway	Eastleigh 1958
70229	TSOL	(ex-units 7105–1537)	Eden Valley Railway	Eastleigh 1958
70235	TBCK	(ex-units 7105–1537)	East Kent Light Railway	Eastleigh 1958
70262	TSOL	(ex-units 7113–1524)	St Leonards Railway Engineering	Eastleigh 1958
70273	TSOL	(ex-units 7124–1530)	Dartmoor Railway	Eastleigh 1958
70284	TSOL	(ex-units 7135–1520)	Northamptonshire Ironstone Railway	Eastleigh 1959
70292	TSOL	(ex-units 7143–1554)	Quinton Rail Technology Centre, Long Marston	Eastleigh 1959
70296	TSOL	(ex-units 7147–1559)	Northamptonshire Ironstone Railway	Eastleigh 1959
70345	TBCK	(ex-units 7153–1500)	Hydraulic House, Sutton Bridge	Eastleigh 1959
70354	TBCK	(ex-units 7011–2305)	Eden Valley Railway	Eastleigh 1959
70508	TSOL	(ex-units 7159–1595–1399)	Dartmoor Railway	Eastleigh 1960
70510	TSOL	(ex-units 7161–1597)	Northamptonshire Ironstone Railway	Eastleigh 1960
70527	TSOL	(ex-units 7178–1589)	Whitwell & Reepham Station, Norfolk	Eastleigh 1960
70531	TSOL	(ex-units 7152–1610)	Quinton Rail Technology Centre, Long Marston	Eastleigh 1961
70539	TSOL	(ex-units 7190–1568)	Eden Valley Railway	Eastleigh 1961
70547	TSOL	(ex-units 7198–1569)	Garden Art Plus, Hungerford	Eastleigh 1961

70549	TSOL	(ex-units 7200–1567)	East Lancashire Railway	Eastleigh 1961
70573	TBCK	(ex-units 7175–2304)	Chinnor & Princes Risborough Railway	Eastleigh 1960
70576	TBCK	(ex-units 7178–1589)	Leicestershire County Museum store, Snibston	Eastleigh 1960
70607	TBCK	(ex-units 7019–2301)	Eden Valley Railway	Eastleigh 1961

69013 also carried the number 69345 after rebuild as a TRSB.

70547 was latterly formed in DEMU 207203 and 70549 was latterly formed in DEMU 207202.

CLASS 414 (2 Hap)   BR

Built: 1959 for the South Eastern Division of the former BR Southern Region. Non-gangwayed.
System: 750 V DC third rail.
Original Formation: DMBSO–DTCsoL.
Traction Motors: Two English Electric EE507 of 185 kW.
Maximum Speed: 90 mph.

DMBSO	20.44 x 2.82 m	42 tonnes		–/84
DTCsoL	20.44 x 2.82 m	32.5 tonnes		19/60 1T

61275	DMBSO	(ex-unit 6077–4308)	National Railway Museum, Shildon (N)	Eastleigh 1959
61287	DMBSO	(ex-unit 6089–4311)	Electric Railway Museum, Coventry	Eastleigh 1959
75395	DTCsoL	(ex-unit 6077–4308)	National Railway Museum, Shildon (N)	Eastleigh 1959
75407	DTCsoL	(ex-unit 6089–4311)	Electric Railway Museum, Coventry	Eastleigh 1959

CLASS 416/2 (2 EPB)   BR

Built: 1954–56. 65373 & 77558 were built for the South Eastern Division of BR Southern Region. 65321 and 77112 were former North Eastern Region vehicles originally used between Newcastle and South Shields but were transferred to join the rest of the class on the Southern Region when the South Tyneside line was de-electrified in 1963. Non-gangwayed.
System: 750 V DC third rail.
Original Formation: DMBSO–DTSso.
Traction Motors: Two English Electric EE507 of 185 kW.
Maximum Speed: 75 mph.

DMBSO	20.44 x 2.82 m	42 tonnes		–/82
DTSso	20.44 x 2.82 m	30.5 tonnes		–/102

65302–977874	DMBSO	(ex-units 5703–6203–930204)	Finmere Station, Oxfordshire	Eastleigh 1954
65304–977875	DMBSO	(ex-units 5703–6205–930204)	Finmere Station, Oxfordshire	Eastleigh 1954
65321–977505	DMBSO	(ex-units 5791–6291–930 053)	Electric Railway Museum, Coventry	Eastleigh 1955
65373	DMBSO	(ex-unit 5759–6259)	East Kent Light Railway	Eastleigh 1956
65379–977925	DMBSO	(ex-units 5765–6265–930206)	Finmere Station, Oxfordshire	Eastleigh 1956
65382–977924	DMBSO	(ex-units 5765–6268–930206)	Finmere Station, Oxfordshire	Eastleigh 1956
77112–977508	DTSso	(ex-units 5793–6293–930 054)	Electric Railway Museum, Coventry	Eastleigh 1955
77558	DTSso	(ex-unit 5759–6259)	East Kent Light Railway	Eastleigh 1956

CLASS 419 (MLV)   BR

Built: 1959–61. Motor luggage vans for Kent Coast electrification. Fitted with traction batteries to allow operation on non-electrified lines.
System: 750 V DC third rail.
Traction Motors: Two English Electric EE507 of 185 kW.
Maximum Speed: 90 mph.

Also fitted with vacuum brakes for hauling parcels trains.

DMLV	20.45 x 2.82 m	45.5 tonnes

68001	(ex-units 9001–931091)	East Kent Light Railway	Eastleigh 1959
68002	(ex-units 9002–931092)	Southall Depot	Eastleigh 1959
68003	(ex-units 9003–931093)	Eden Valley Railway	Eastleigh 1961

68004	(ex-units 9004–931 094)	Mid Norfolk Railway	Eastleigh 1961
68005	(ex-units 9005–931 095)	Eden Valley Railway	Eastleigh 1961
68008	(ex-units 9008–931 098)	East Kent Light Railway	Eastleigh 1961
68009	(ex-units 9009–931 099)	East Kent Light Railway	Eastleigh 1961
68010	(ex-units 9010–931 090)	Eden Valley Railway	Eastleigh 1961

CLASS 420 & 421 (4 Big & 4 Cig)   BR

Built: 1963–71 for the Central Division of BR Southern Region. Class 420 (4 Big) was later reclassified Class 422.
System: 750 V DC third rail.
Original Formation: DTCsoL–MBSO–TSO (4 Cig), TRSB (4 Big)–DTCsoL.
Traction Motors: Four English Electric EE507 of 185 kW.
Maximum Speed: 90 mph.

MBSO	20.18 x 2.82 m	49 tonnes	–/56
TSO	20.18 x 2.82 m	31.5 tonnes	–/72
DTCsoL	20.23 x 2.82 m	35 tonnes	24/28 2T
TRSB	20.18 x 2.82 m	35 tonnes	–/40

62043	MBSO	(ex-units 7327–1127–1753)	Finmere Station, Oxfordshire	York 1965
62364	MBSO	(ex-units 7376–1276–2251–1374)	RVEL, Derby	York 1971
62385	MBSO	(ex-units 7397–1297–2256–1399)	Dartmoor Railway	York 1971
62402	MBSO	(ex-units 7414–1214–1883–1497)	Mid Norfolk Railway	York 1971
62411	MBSO	(ex-units 7423–1223–1888–1498)	Epping Ongar Railway	York 1972
69302	TRSB	(ex-units 7032–1276–2251) "MEGAN"	Abbey View Disabled Day Centre, Neath	York 1963
69304	TRSB	(ex-units 7034–1299–2260)	Northamptonshire Ironstone Railway	York 1963
69306	TRSB	(ex-units 7036–1282–2254)	Spa Valley Railway	York 1963
69310	TRSB	(ex-units 7040–1290–2255)	Dartmoor Railway	York 1963
69316	TRSB	(ex-units 7046–1296–2258)	Waverley Route Heritage Association	York 1963
69318	TRSB	(ex-units 7048–1298–2259)	Mid Norfolk Railway	York 1963
69332	TRSB	(ex-units 7051–2203)	Dartmoor Railway	York 1969
69333	TRSB	(ex-units 7055–1802–2260)	Lavender Line	York 1969
69335	TRSB	(ex-units 7057–2209) "GILLIAN"	Wensleydale Railway	York 1969
69337	TRSB	(ex-units 7058–2210)	St Leonards Railway Engineering	York 1969
69338	TRSB	(ex-units 7054–2206)	Station Restaurant, Gulf Corporation, Bahrain	York 1969
69339	TRSB	(ex-units 7053–2205–1393)	Finmere Station, Oxfordshire	York 1969
70721	TSO	(ex-units 7327–1127–1753)	Finmere Station, Oxfordshire	York 1965
71041	TSO	(ex-units 7373–1273–1819–1306)	Hever Station, Kent	York 1971
71085	TSO	(ex-units 7417–1217–1884)	Morden Wharf, Greenwich, London	York 1970
76048	DTCsoL	(ex-units 7327–1127–1753)	Finmere Station, Oxfordshire	York 1965
76102	DTCsoL	(ex-units 7327–1127–1753)	Finmere Station, Oxfordshire	York 1965
76747	DTCsoL	(ex-units 7397–1297–2256–1399)	Dartmoor Railway	York 1971
76762	DTCsoL	(ex-units 7412–1212–1881)	Barrow Hill Roundhouse	York 1971
76764	DTCsoL	(ex-units 7414–1214–1883–1497)	Mid Norfolk Railway	York 1971
76773	DTCsoL	(ex-units 7423–1223–1888–1498)	Epping Ongar Railway	York 1972
76818	DTCsoL	(ex-units 7397–1297–2256–1399)	Arlington Fleet Services, Eastleigh Works	York 1971
76835	DTCsoL	(ex-units 7414–1214–1883–1497)	Mid Norfolk Railway	York 1971
76844	DTCsoL	(ex-units 7423–1223–1888–1498)	Epping Ongar Railway	York 1972

62402 is named Freshwater and 62411 is named Farringford.

CLASS 423 (4 Vep/4 Vop)   BR

Built: 1967–74 for BR Southern Region.
System: 750 V DC third rail.
Original Formation (4 Vep): DTCsoL–MBSO–TSO–DTCsoL.
Amended Formation (4 Vop): DTSsoL–MBSO–TSO–DTSsoL.
Traction Motors: Four English Electric EE507 of 185 kW.
Maximum Speed: 90 mph.

DTCsoL	20.18 x 2.82 m	35.0 tonnes	18/46 1T	
DTSsoL	20.18 x 2.82 m	35.0 tonnes	−70 1T	
TSO	20.18 x 2.82 m	31.5 tonnes	−/98	
MBSO	20.18 x 2.82 m	48.0 tonnes	−/76	

62236	MBSO	(ex-units 7775–3075–3417)	Clapham Carriage Shed, London	York 1969
62266	MBSO	(ex-units 7805–3105–3463–3905)	Barrow Hill Roundhouse	York 1969
62321	MBSO	(ex-units 7820–3120–3532–3918)	Barrow Hill Roundhouse	York 1970
70797	TSO	(ex-units 7717–3017–3417)	Clapham Carriage Shed, London	Derby 1967
70904	TSO	(ex-units 7753–3053–3463–3905)	Dartmoor Railway	York 1968
70950	TSO	(ex-units 7799–3099–3532–3918)	Barrow Hill Roundhouse	York 1969
76262	DTCsoL	(ex-units 7717–3017–3417)	Clapham Carriage Shed, London	York 1967
76263	DTCsoL	(ex-units 7717–3017–3417)	Clapham Carriage Shed, London	York 1967
76397	DTSsoL	(ex-units 7753–3053–3463–3905)	Dartmoor Railway	York 1968
76398	DTSsoL	(ex-units 7753–3053–3463–3905)	Dartmoor Railway	York 1968
76527	DTSsoL	(ex-units 7799–3099–3532–3918)	Barrow Hill Roundhouse	York 1969
76528	DTSsoL	(ex-units 7799–3099–3532–3918)	Barrow Hill Roundhouse	York 1969
76875	DTCsoL	(ex-units 7861–3161–3545)	National Railway Museum, York (N)	York 1973
76887	DTCsoL	(ex-units 7867–3167–3568)	Woking Miniature Railway	York 1973

CLASS 489 (GLV)   BR

Rebuilt: 1979–84 from Class 414 (2 Hap) as Motor Luggage Vans for the Victoria–Gatwick "Gatwick Express" service. Seats removed.
System: 750 V DC third rail.
Traction Motors: Two English Electric EE507 of 185 kW.
Maximum Speed: 90 mph.

DMLV	20.04 x 2.82 m	45 tonnes	

61269–68500	DMLV (ex-units 6071–9101)	Ecclesbourne Valley Railway	Eastleigh 1959
61277–68503	DMLV (ex-units 6079–9104)	Spa Valley Railway	Eastleigh 1959
61280–68509	DMLV (ex-units 6082–9110)	Barry Rail Centre	Eastleigh 1959
61292–68506	DMLV (ex-units 6094–9107)	Ecclesbourne Valley Railway	Eastleigh 1959

CLASS 491 (4 TC)   BR/METRO-CAMMELL

Built: 1967. Unpowered units designed to work push-pull with Class 430 (4 Rep) tractor units and Class 33/1, 73 and 74 locomotives. Converted from locomotive-hauled coaching stock built 1952–57 (original numbers in brackets).
Original Formation: DTSO–TFK–TBSK–DTSO.
Maximum Speed: 90 mph.

DTSO	20.18 x 2.82 m	32 tonnes	−/64
TFK	20.18 x 2.82 m	33.5 tonnes	42/− 2T
TBSK	20.18 x 2.82 m	35.5 tonnes	−/32 1T

70823 (34970)	TBSK	(ex-unit 412–8012)	London Underground, West Ruislip Depot	MC 1957
70824 (34984)	TBSK	(ex-unit 413–8013)	Midland Railway-Butterley	MC 1957
70826 (34980)	TBSK	(ex-unit 415–8015)	Station Railway Heritage Centre, Sandford	MC 1957
70855 (13018)	TFK	(ex-unit 412–8012)	Midland Railway-Butterley	Swindon 1952
70859 (13040)	TFK	(ex-unit 412–8012)	The Old Station Guest House, Stravithie Station, Fife	Swindon 1952
70860 (13019)	TFK	(ex-unit 417–8017)	Longstowe Station, near Bourn	Swindon 1952
71163 (13097)	TFK	(ex-unit 430–8030)	London Underground, West Ruislip Depot	Swindon 1954
76275 (3929)	DTSO	(ex-unit 404–8004)	St Leonards Railway Engineering	Eastleigh 1955
76277 (4005)	DTSO	(ex-unit 405–8005)	Dartmoor Railway	Swindon 1957
76297 (3938)	DTSO	(ex-unit 415–8015)	London Underground, West Ruislip Depot	Eastleigh 1955
76298 (4004)	DTSO	(ex-unit 415–8015)	Midland Railway-Butterley	Eastleigh 1957
76301 (4375)	DTSO	(ex-unit 417–8017)	Heritage Centre, Bellingham	Swindon 1957
76302 (4382)	DTSO	(ex-unit 417–8017)	Heritage Centre, Bellingham	Swindon 1957
76322 (3936)	DTSO	(ex-unit 427–8027)	Midland Railway-Butterley	Eastleigh 1955
76324 (4009)	DTSO	(ex-unit 428–8028)	London Underground, West Ruislip Depot	Eastleigh 1957

76277 was also numbered DB 977335 for a time when in departmental service.

CLASS 501 BR

Built: 1957 for Euston–Watford and North London lines. Non-gangwayed.
Original Formation: DMBSO–TSO (originally TS)–DTBSO.
System: 630 V DC third rail.
Traction Motors: Four GEC of 135 kW.
Maximum Speed: 60 mph.

DMBSO	18.47 x 2.82 m		47.8 tonnes	–/74
DTBSO	18.47 x 2.82 m		30.5 tonnes	–/74

BR	AD			
61183–DB 977349		DMBSO	Electric Railway Museum, Coventry	Eastleigh 1957
75186	WGP 8809	DTBSO	Electric Railway Museum, Coventry	Eastleigh 1957

CLASS 504 BR

Built: 1959 for Manchester–Bury line. Non-gangwayed.
Original Formation: DMBSO–DTSO.
System: 1200 V DC protected side-contact third rail.
Maximum Speed: 65 mph.
Traction Motors: Four English Electric EE of 90 kW.

DMBSO	20.31 x 2.82 m		50 tonnes	–/84
DTSO	20.31 x 2.82 m		33 tonnes	–/94

65451		DMBSO	East Lancashire Railway	Wolverton 1959
77172		DTSO	East Lancashire Railway	Wolverton 1959

TRAMS GRIMSBY & IMMINGHAM LIGHT RAILWAY

Built: 1925. (* 1927). Single-deck trams built for Gateshead & District Tramways Company.
Sold to British Railways in 1951 for use on Grimsby & Immingham Light Railway.
Motors: 2 x Dick Kerr 31A (* 25A) of 18 kW (25 hp).
Bogies: Brill 39E.
Seats: 48 (* reduced to 44 by BR).

BR	Gateshead			
20 *	5	Crich Tramway Village	Gateshead & District Tramways Co. 1927
26	10	Beamish: The Living Museum of the North	Gateshead & District Tramways Co. 1925

BATTERY EMU BR DERBY/COWLAIRS TWIN UNIT

Built: 1958. Normal formation. BDMBSO–BDTCOL. Gangwayed within unit.
Power: 216 lead-acid cells of 1070 Ah.
Traction Motors: Two 100 kW Siemens nose-suspended motors.
Maximum Speed: 70 mph.

Vacuum brakes.

BDMBSO	18.49 x 2.79 m		37.5 tonnes	–/52
BDTCOL	18.49 x 2.79 m		32.5 tonnes	12/53 1T

79998–DB 975003		BDMBSO	Royal Deeside Railway	Derby/Cowlairs 1958
79999–DB 975004		BDTCOL	Royal Deeside Railway	Derby/Cowlairs 1958

5.10. EUROSTAR POWER CARS

CLASS 373

Built: 1992–93 for the proposed Regional Eurostar services that never materialised. The Regional Eurostars were formed as 7-car half sets, which ran as 14-car trains. Power car 3308, now preserved, never turned a wheel in service and was mainly used for static trials at Temple Mills depot.
Builders: GEC-Alsthom/Brush/ANF/De Dietrich/BN/ACEC.
System: 25 kV AC 50 Hz overhead/3000 V DC overhead.
Continuous Rating: 12 x 240 kW (25 kV AC); 5700 kW (1500 and 3000 V DC).
Maximum Speed: 186 mph.

DM	22.15 x 2.81 m		68.5 tonnes
3308		DM	National Railway Museum, York

▲ Eurostar power car 3308 is now on display at the National Railway Museum, York, where it is seen on 19 December 2015. **Alisdair Anderson**

APPENDIX I. LIST OF LOCATIONS

The following is a list of preservation sites and operating railways in Great Britain where locomotives and multiple units included in this book can be found, together with Ordnance Survey grid references for each place. At certain places locomotives and rolling stock may be dispersed at several locations, in such cases the principal location where locomotives can normally be found is the one given. Enquiries at this location will normally reveal the whereabouts of other locomotives or rolling stock, but this is not guaranteed.

§   denotes site not generally open to the public.

	OS GRID REF
Abbey View Disabled Day Centre, Neath Abbey, Neath, Port Talbot.	SS 734973
Adam Dalgleish Engineering, Lonsdale House, Ross Road, Stockton-on-Tees.§	NZ 457201
Alley's Heavy Haulage, The Slough, Studley, Warwickshire.§	SP 057637
Aln Valley Railway, Lloyds Field, Lionheart Industrial Estate, Alnwick, Northumberland.	NU 200122
Andrew Briddon Locomotives, Darley Dale, Derbyshire.§	SK 273627
Appleby-Frodingham RPS, Tata Steel, Appleby-Frodingham Works, Scunthorpe, Lincs.§	SE 913109
Arlington Fleet Services, Eastleigh Works, Campbell Road, Eastleigh, Hampshire.§	SU 457185
Avon Valley Railway, Bitton Station, Bitton, Gloucestershire.	ST 670705
Barrow Hill Roundhouse, Campbell Drive, Staveley, Chesterfield, Derbyshire.	SK 414755
Barry Rail Centre, Barry Island, Vale of Glamorgan.	ST 118667
Battlefield Railway, Shackerstone Station, Shackerstone, Leicestershire.	SK 379066
Beamish: The Living Museum of the North, Beamish Hall, Beamish, Co Durham.	NZ 217547
Bluebell Railway, Sheffield Park, near Uckfield, East Sussex.	TQ 403238
Bo'ness & Kinneil Railway, Bo'ness Station, Union Street, Bo'ness, Falkirk.	NT 003817
Boden Rail Engineering, Washwood Heath Workshops, Birmingham.§	SP 103892
Bodmin & Wenford Railway, Bodmin General Station, Bodmin, Cornwall.	SX 074664
Bressingham Steam Museum, Bressingham Hall, near Diss, Norfolk.	TM 080806
British Pullman, Stewarts Lane Depot, Battersea, Greater London.§	TQ 288766
Bryn Engineering, c/o Advance Scaffolding, Blackrod Industrial Estate, Scot Lane, Blackrod, near Bolton.§	SD 623089
Buckinghamshire Railway Centre, Quainton Road Station, Aylesbury, Buckinghamshire.	SP 736189
Caledonian Railway, Brechin Station, Brechin, near Montrose, Angus.	NO 603603
Cambrian Railway Trust, Llynclys Station, Llynclys, near Oswestry, Shropshire.	SJ 284239
Cefn Coed Colliery Museum, Old Blaenant Colliery, Cryant, Neath Port Talbot.	SN 786034
Chasewater Light Railway, Chasewater Pleasure Park, Brownhills, Staffordshire.	SK 034070
Chinnor & Princes Risborough Railway, Chinnor Station, Chinnor, Oxfordshire.	SP 756002
Cholsey & Wallingford Railway, St John's Road, Wallingford, Oxfordshire.	SU 600891
Churnet Valley Railway, Cheddleton Station, Cheddleton, Leek, Staffordshire.	SJ 983519
Clapham Carriage Shed, Clapham Junction, London.§	TQ 272755
Class G5 Locomotive Company, Unit 8S, Hackworth Industrial Park, Shildon.§	NZ 223255
Cold Norton Play School, Palepit Farm, Latchingdon Road, Cold Norton, Essex.§	TL 858003
Colne Valley Railway, Castle Hedingham Station, Halstead, Essex.	TL 774362
Crewe Heritage Centre, Crewe, Cheshire.	SJ 708552
Crich Tramway Village, near Matlock, Derbyshire.	SK 345549
Dartmoor Railway, Meldon Quarry, near Okehampton, Devon.	SX 568927
Dartmouth Steam Railway, Queen's Park Station, Paignton, Devon.	SX 889606
Dean Forest Railway, Norchard, near Lydney, Gloucestershire.	SO 629044
Denbigh & Mold Junction Railway, Sodom, near Bodfari, Denbighshire, Wales.§	SJ 103711
Derwent Valley Light Railway, Yorkshire Museum of Farming, Murton, York, N Yorks.	SE 650524
Designer Outlet Village, Kemble Drive, Swindon, Wiltshire.	SU 142849
Didcot Railway Centre (Great Western Society), Didcot, Oxfordshire.	SU 524906
East Anglian Railway Museum, Chappel & Wakes Colne Station, Essex.	TL 898289
East Kent Light Railway, Shepherdswell, Kent.	TR 258483
East Lancashire Railway, Bolton Street Station, Bury, Greater Manchester.	SD 803109
East Somerset Railway, West Cranmore Station, Shepton Mallet, Somerset.	ST 664429
Ecclesbourne Valley Railway, Wirksworth Station, Wirksworth, Derbyshire.	SK 289542
Eden Valley Railway, Warcop Station, Warcop, Cumbria.	NY 753156
Electric Railway Museum, Rowley Road, Baginton, Coventry, Warwickshire.	SP 354751
Embsay & Bolton Abbey Railway, Embsay Station, Embsay, Skipton, North Yorks.	SE 007533
Epping Ongar Railway, Ongar Station, Station Road, Chipping Ongar, Essex.	TL 552035
European Metal Recycling, Trinity Road, Kingsbury, Warwickshire.§	SP 219969
Fawley Hill Railway, Fawley Green, near Henley-on-Thames, Buckinghamshire.§	SU 755861

Finmere Station, near Newton Purcell, Oxfordshire.§	SP 629312
Flour Mill Workshop, Bream, Forest of Dean, Gloucestershire.§	SO 604067
Foxfield Railway, Blythe Bridge, Stoke-on-Trent, Staffordshire.	SJ 976446
Garden Art Plus, 1 Bath Road, Hungerford, Berkshire.	SU 343689
Garw Valley Railway, Pontycymer Locomotive Works, Old Station Yard, Pontycymer, Bridgend.	SS 904914
Glasgow Riverside Museum, Pointhouse Quay, Yorkshill, Glasgow.	NS 557661
Gloucestershire Warwickshire Railway, Toddington Station, Gloucestershire.	SP 049321
Great Central Railway, Loughborough Central Station, Loughborough, Leicestershire.	SK 543194
Gwili Railway, Bronwydd Arms Station, Carmarthen, Carmarthenshire.	SN 417236
Head of Steam, Darlington Railway Museum, North Road Station, Hopetown, Darlington, Co Durham.	NZ 289157
Helston Railway, Prospidnick, near Helston, Cornwall.	SW 645313
Heritage Centre, Woodburn Road, Bellingham, Northumberland.	NY 843833
Hever Station, Hever, Kent.§	TQ 465445
Honeybourne Airfield Industrial Estate, Honeybourne, near Evesham, Worcs.§	SP 115422
Hope Farm (Southern Locomotives), Sellindge, near Ashford, Kent.§	TR 119388
Hydraulic House, West Bank, Sutton Bridge, near Spalding, Lincolnshire.§	TF 479209
Isle of Wight Steam Railway, Haven Street Station, Isle of Wight.	SZ 556898
Keighley & Worth Valley Railway, Haworth, near Keighley, West Yorkshire.	SE 034371
Keith & Dufftown Railway, Dufftown, Moray.	NJ 323414
Kent & East Sussex Railway, Tenterden Town Station, Tenterden, Kent.	TQ 882336
King's Cross Theatre, Good's Way, King's Cross, London.	TQ 302833
Kirklees Light Railway, Clayton West, near Huddersfield, West Yorkshire.	SE 258112
Lakeside & Haverthwaite Railway, Haverthwaite, Cumbria.	SD 349843
Lavender Line, Isfield Station, Station Road, Isfield, East Sussex.	TQ 452171
Leicestershire County Museum store, former Snibston Colliery, Coalville, Leicestershire. §	SK 420144
Lincolnshire Wolds Railway, Ludborough Station, Ludborough, Lincolnshire.	TF 309960
Little Mill Inn, Rowarth, Mellor, Derbyshire.	SK 011890
Llanelli & Mynydd Mawr Railway, Cynheidre, near Llanelli, Carmarthenshire.	SN 495071
Llangollen Railway, Llangollen Station, Llangollen, Denbighshire.	SJ 211423
London & North Western Railway Heritage Company, Crewe, Cheshire.§	SJ 712543
London Transport Depot Museum, Gunnersby Lane, Acton, Greater London.	TQ 194799
London Underground, West Ruislip Depot, Ruislip, London.§	TQ 094862
Longstowe Station, near Bourn, Cambridgeshire.§	TL 315546
Mangapps Railway Museum, Southminster Road, Burnham-on-Crouch, Essex.	TQ 944980
Merseyside Transport Trust, Osprey Place, Guys Industrial Estate North, Burscough, Lancashire.§	SD 428108
Mid Hants Railway, Ropley Station, Ropley, Hampshire.	SU 629324
Mid Norfolk Railway, Dereham Station, East Dereham, Norfolk.	TF 994131
Middleton Railway, Tunstall Road, Hunslet, Leeds, West Yorkshire.	SE 305310
Midland Railway-Butterley, Butterley Station, near Ripley, Derbyshire.	SK 403520
Morden Wharf, Olympian Way, Greenwich, London. §	TQ 389797
Moreton Park Railway, Moreton-on-Lugg, near Hereford, Herefordshire.§	SO 503467
Museum of Canterbury, Stour Street, Canterbury, Kent.	TR 146577
Museum of Liverpool, Pier Head, Liverpool, Merseyside.	SJ 339900
Museum of Liverpool Store, Juniper Street, Bootle, Merseyside.§	SJ 343935
Museum of Science & Industry, Liverpool Road, Castlefield, Greater Manchester.	SJ 831978
National Railway Museum, Leeman Road, York, North Yorkshire.	SE 594519
National Railway Museum, Shildon, Co Durham.	NZ 238256
NELPG, Former Carriage Works, Hopetown, Darlington, Co Durham.§	NZ 288157
Nemesis Rail, Old Wagon Works, Burton-upon-Trent, Staffordshire.§	SK 251245
Nene Valley Railway, Wansford Station, Peterborough, Cambridgeshire.	TL 093979
North Dorset Railway Trust, St Patricks Industrial Estate, Station Road, Shillingstone, Blandford Forum, Dorset.	ST 824117
North Norfolk Railway, Sheringham Station, Norfolk.	TG 156430
North Side Works, Malton Road, Leavening, near Malton, North Yorkshire.§	SE 784637
North Yorkshire Moors Railway, Grosmont Station, North Yorkshire.	NZ 828049
Northampton & Lamport Railway, Pitsford, Northamptonshire.	SP 736666
Northamptonshire Ironstone Railway, Hunsbury Hill, Northampton, Northamptonshire.	SP 735584
Nottingham Transport Heritage Centre, Mereway, Ruddington, Nottinghamshire.	SK 575322
Old Oak Common Depot, Old Oak Common Lane, London.§	TQ 213821
Oswestry Railway Centre, Oswestry Station Yard, Oswestry, Shropshire.	SJ 294297

Peak Rail, Rowsley South Station, near Matlock, Derbyshire.	SK 262642
Plym Valley Railway, Marsh Mills, Plymouth, Devon.	SX 520571
Pontypool & Blaenavon Railway, Furnoe Sidings, Big Pit, Blaenavon, Torfaen.	SO 237093
Quinton Rail Technology Centre, Long Marston, Warwickshire.§	SP 152469
Ribble Steam Railway, off Chain Caul Road, Riversway, Preston, Lancashire.	SD 504295
Riley & Son (Electromec), Premier Locomotive Works, Sefton Street, Heywood, Greater Manchester.§	SE 865103
RMS Locotec, Washwood Heath Workshops, Birmingham.§	SP 103892
Rother Valley Railway, Robertsbridge Station Yard, Robertsbridge, East Sussex.	TQ 734236
Royal Deeside Railway, Milton, Crathes, Banchory, Aberdeenshire.	NO 743962
Rushden Transport Museum, Rectory Road, Rushden, Northamptonshire.	SP 957672
RVEL, RTC Business Park, London Road, Derby, Derbyshire.§	SK 365350
Rye Farm, Ryefield Lane, Wishaw, Sutton Coldfield, Warwickshire.§	SP 180944
Science Museum, Imperial Institute Road, South Kensington, London.	TQ 268793
Science Museum Store, Wroughton, near Swindon, Wiltshire.§	SU 131790
Scolton Manor Museum, Scolton Manor, Haverfordwest, Pembrokeshire.	SM 991222
Severn Valley Railway, Bridgnorth Station, Shropshire.	SO 715926
Somerset & Dorset Railway Trust, Washford Station, Somerset.	ST 044412
Somerset & Dorset Railway Heritage Trust, Midsomer Norton Station, Silver Street, Midsomer Norton, Somerset.	ST 664537
Somerset & Dorset Steam, c/o John Weavers Yard, The Hailey Centre, Holton Road, Holton Heath Trading Park, Poole.§	SY 948905
South Devon Railway, Buckfastleigh, Devon.	SX 747663
Southall Depot, Southall, Greater London.§	TQ 133798
Spa Valley Railway, Tunbridge Wells West Station, Tunbridge Wells, Kent.	TQ 578385
St Leonards Railway Engineering, West Marina Depot, Bridge Way, St Leonards, East Sussex.§	TQ 778086
Stainmore Railway, Kirkby Stephen East Station, Kirkby Stephen, Cumbria.	NY 769075
Station Railway Heritage Centre, Sandford, Somerset.	ST 416595
Steam – Museum of the Great Western Railway, Old No. 20 Shop, Old Swindon Works, Kemble Drive, Swindon, Wiltshire.	SU 143849
Stephenson Railway Museum, Middle Engine Lane, West Chirton, Tyne & Wear.	NZ 323693
Stewarts Lane Depot, Battersea, Greater London.§	TQ 288766
Strathspey Railway, Aviemore, Highland Region.	NH 898131
Summerlee Museum of Scottish Industrial Life, West Canal Street, Coatbridge, North Lanarkshire.	NS 728655
Swanage Railway, Swanage Station, Swanage, Dorset.	SZ 028789
Swindon & Cricklade Railway, Blunsden Road Station, Swindon, Wiltshire.	SU 110897
Tanat Valley Light Railway, Nantmawr, near Llanyblodwel, Shropshire.	SJ 253243
Tanfield Railway, Marley Hill Engine Shed, Sunniside, Tyne & Wear.	NZ 207573
Telford Steam Railway, Bridge Road, Horsehay, Telford, Shropshire.	SJ 675073
The Old Station Guest House, Stravithie Station, Stravithie, near St Andrews, Fife.	NO 533134
Thinktank: Birmingham Science Museum, Millennium Point, Curzon Street, Birmingham.	SP 079873
Thomas Muir (Rosyth), Port of Rosyth, Dunfermline, Scotland.§	NT 100822
Thornton Depot, Strathore Road, Thornton, Fife, Scotland.§	NT 264970
Titley Junction Station, near Kington, Herefordshire.§	SO 329581
Tiverton Museum, St Andrew's Street, Tiverton, Devon.	SS 955124
Tyseley Locomotive Works, Warwick Road, Tyseley, Birmingham.§	SP 105841
UK Rail Leasing, Leicester Depot, Leicestershire.§	SK 597044
Vale of Berkeley Railway, The Engine Shed, Dock Road, Sharpness, Gloucs.	SO 667023
Vale of Rheidol Railway, Aberystwyth, Ceredigion.	SN 587812
Warner Brothers Studio Tour, Leavesden, Hertfordshire.	TL 095005
Waverley Route Heritage Association, Whitrope, near Hawick, Scottish Borders.	NT 527005
Weardale Railway, Wolsingham, Co Durham.	NZ 081370
Wensleydale Railway, Leeming Bar Station, Leeming Bar, North Yorkshire.	SE 286900
West Coast Railway Company, Warton Road, Carnforth, Lancashire.§	SD 496708
West Somerset Railway, Minehead Station, Minehead, Somerset.	SS 975463
Whitwell & Reepham Station, near Alysham, Norfolk.	TG 091217
Willesden Depot (London Overground), Willesden, Greater London.§	SE 200840
Woking Miniature Railway, Barr's Lane, Knaphill, Woking, Surrey.	TQ 966595
Yeovil Railway Centre, Yeovil Junction, near Yeovil, Somerset.	ST 571141

APPENDIX II. ABBREVIATIONS USED

AD	Army Department of the Ministry of Defence	LTE	London Transport Executive
AD	Alexandra Docks & Railway Company	LTSR	London Tilbury & Southend Railway
		MAV	Hungarian Railways
BP	BP (formerly British Petroleum)	MR	Midland Railway
BR	British Railways	MoD	Ministry of Defence
BPGVR	Burry Port & Gwendraeth Valley Railway	MSJ&A	Manchester South Junction & Altrincham Railway
BTH	British Thomson Houston	(N)	Locomotive or multiple unit vehicle that forms part of the National
CARR	Cardiff Railway		Collection.
CR	Caledonian Railway	NBR	North British Railway
DMU	Diesel Multiple Unit	NER	North Eastern Railway
EMU	Electric Multiple Unit	NLR	North London Railway
FR	Furness Railway	NS	Nederlandse Spoorwegen
FS	Ferrovie dello Stato (Italian State Railways)		(Netherlands Railways)
		NSR	North Staffordshire Railway
GCR	Great Central Railway	P&M	Powlesland & Mason
GER	Great Eastern Railway	PKP	Polish Railways
GJR	Grand Junction Railway	PTR	Port Talbot Railway
GNR	Great Northern Railway	S&DJR	Somerset & Dorset Joint Railway
GNSR	Great North of Scotland Railway	SDR	South Devon Railway
GSWR	Glasgow & South Western Railway	SECR	South Eastern & Chatham Railway
GVR	Gwendraeth Valley Railway	SER	South Eastern Railway
GWR	Great Western Railway	SJ	Swedish State Railways
H&B	Hull & Barnsley Railway	SPR	Sandy & Potton Railway
HR	Highland Railway	SR	Southern Railway
L&MR	Liverpool & Manchester Railway	TCDD	Türkiye Cumhuryeti Devlet
L&Y	Lancashire & Yorkshire Railway		Demiryollan (Turkish Railways)
LBSCR	London, Brighton & South Coast Railway	TVR	Taff Vale Railway
		USATC	United States Army Transportation Corps
LCDR	London, Chatham & Dover Railway		
LMS	London Midland & Scottish Railway	W&L	Welshpool & Llanfair Railway
LNER	London & North Eastern Railway	WD	War Department
LNWR	London & North Western Railway	WR	British Railways Western Region
LSWR	London & South Western Railway	WT	Wantage Tramway

APPENDIX III. WEIGHTS & MEASUREMENTS

The following abbreviations are used to denote units of measurement throughout this book.

AC	Alternating current	lbf	Pounds force
DC	Direct current	lbf/sq in.	Pounds force per square inch
hp	Horse power	m	Metres
Hz	Hertz	mm	Millimetres
kN	Kilonewtons	mph	Miles per hour
km/h	Kilometres per hour	rpm	Revolutions per minute
kW	Kilowatts	V	Volts

APPENDIX IV. DEMU & EMU TYPE CODES

Type Codes used by the former BR operating departments to describe the various types of diesel electric and electric multiple unit vehicles are listed here. These have been used in Sections 5.5–5.9.

Brake vehicles contain luggage space and a guard's/conductors compartment.

Second is now known as Standard and before 1956 was referred to as Third.

BDMBSO	Battery Driving Motor Brake Second Open
BDTBS	Battery Driving Trailer Brake Second (non-gangwayed)
BDTBSO	Battery Driving Trailer Brake Second Open
BDTCOL	Battery Driving Trailer Composite Open with Lavatory
BDTCsoL	Battery Driving Trailer Composite semi-open with Lavatory
BDTSO	Battery Driving Trailer Second Open
BDTSOL	Battery Driving Trailer Second Open with Lavatory
DMBS	Driving Motor Brake Second (non-gangwayed)
DMBSK	Driving Motor Brake Second side corridor with Lavatory
DMBSO	Driving Motor Brake Second Open
DMLV	Driving Motor Luggage Van
DMPBSOL	Driving Motor Pullman Brake Second Open with Lavatory
DMRFKO	Driving Motor First Kitchen Open
DMSO	Driving Motor Second Open
DMSOL	Driving Motor Second Open with Lavatory
DTBSO	Driving Trailer Brake Second Open
DTCK	Driving Trailer Composite side corridor
DTCO	Driving Trailer Composite Open
DTCOL	Driving Trailer Composite Open with Lavatory
DTCsoL	Driving Trailer Composite semi-open with Lavatory
DTS	Driving Trailer Second (non-gangwayed)
DTSO	Driving Trailer Second Open
DTSOL	Driving Trailer Second Open with Lavatory
DTSso	Driving Trailer Second semi-open
M	Motor
MBS	Motor Brake Second
MBSK	Motor Brake Second side corridor with Lavatory
MBSO	Motor Brake Second Open
MBSOL	Motor Brake Second Open with Lavatory
MFOL	Motor First Open with Lavatory
MS	Motor Second (non-gangwayed)
MSO	Motor Second Open
MSOL	Motor Second Open with Lavatory
PTFOL	Pantograph Trailer First Open with Lavatory
PTRSBO	Pantograph Trailer Second Buffet Open
TBCK	Trailer Brake Composite side corridor with Lavatory
TBFOL	Trailer Brake First Open with Lavatory
TBSK	Trailer Brake Second side corridor with Lavatory
TBSO	Trailer Brake Second Open
TC	Trailer Composite (non-gangwayed)
TCK	Trailer Composite side corridor with Lavatory
TCO	Trailer Composite Open
TCsoL	Trailer Composite semi-open with Lavatory
TFK	Trailer First side corridor with Lavatory
TFOL	Trailer First Open with Lavatory
TPCK	Trailer Pullman Composite side corridor with Lavatory
TPFKOL	Trailer Pullman First Kitchen open with Lavatory
TPSOL	Trailer Pullman Second open with Lavatory
TRSB	Trailer Second Buffet
TRSBL	Trailer Second Buffet with Lavatory
TRSKB	Trailer Second with Kitchen and Buffet
TRUB	Trailer Unclassified Buffet
TS	Trailer Second (non-gangwayed)
TSK	Trailer Second side corridor with Lavatory

TSO   Trailer Second Open
TSOL   Trailer Second open with Lavatory
TUOL   Trailer Unclassified Open with Lavatory

APPENDIX V. PRIVATE MANUFACTURER CODES

The following codes are used to denote private locomotive manufacturers. These are followed by the works number and build year, eg AW 1360/1937 – built by Armstrong-Whitworth and Company, works number 1360, year 1937. Unless otherwise shown, locations are in England.

AB	Andrew Barclay, Sons & Company, Caledonia Works, Kilmarnock, Scotland.
ABB	ASEA Brown Boveri
AC	AC Cars, Thames Ditton, Surrey.
AE	Avonside Engine Company, Bristol, Avon.
AEC	Associated Equipment Company, Southall, Berkshire.
Alan Keef	Alan Keef Ltd, Ross-on-Wye, Herefordshire.
AW	Armstrong-Whitworth & Company, Newcastle, Tyne & Wear.
BBC	Brown-Boveri et Cie, Switzerland.
BCK	Bury, Curtis & Kennedy, Liverpool, Merseyside.
BE	Brush Electrical Engineering Company, Loughborough, Leics.
BMR	Brecon Mountain Railway Company, Pant, Merthyr Tydfil, Wales.
Boston Lodge	Ffestiniog Railway, Boston Lodge Works, Porthmadog, Wales.
BP	Beyer Peacock and Company, Gorton, Manchester.
BRCW	Birmingham Railway Carriage & Wagon Company, Smethwick, Birmingham.
BREL	British Rail Engineering Ltd (later BREL, then ABB, now Bombardier Transportation).
BTH	British Thomson-Houston Company, Rugby, Warwickshire.
BUT	British United Traction
CE	Clayton Equipment Company, Hatton, Derbyshire.
Cravens	Cravens, Darnall, Sheffield, South Yorkshire.
Darlington Hope Street	A1 Steam Trust, Darlington Hope Street, Darlington, Co Durham.
DC	Drewry Car Company, London.
DK	Dick Kerr & Company, Preston, Lancashire.
Dodman	Alfred Dodman & Company, Highgate Works, Kings Lynn, Norfolk.
EE	English Electric Company, Bradford and Preston.
EP	Electroputere, Craiova, Romania.
FW	Fox, Walker & Company, Atlas Engine Works, Bristol.
Gateshead & District Tramways Co	Sunderland Road Works, Gateshead, Tyne & Wear.
GCR Dukinfield	Great Central Railway Carriage & Wagon Works, Dukinfield, Tameside, Greater Manchester.
GE	George England & Company, Hatcham Ironworks, London.
GRCW	Gloucester Railway Carriage & Wagon Company, Gloucester, Glous.
Hack	Timothy Hackworth, Soho Works, Shildon, Co Durham.
HC	Hudswell-Clarke & Company, Hunslet, Leeds, West Yorkshire.
HE	Hunslet Engine Company, Hunslet, Leeds, West Yorkshire.
HL	R&W Hawthorn, Leslie & Company, Forth Bank Works, Newcastle upon-Tyne.
HLT	Hughes Locomotive & Tramway Engine Works, Loughborough, Leicestershire.
K	Kitson & Company, Airedale Foundry, Hunslet, Leeds, West Yorks.
Kitching	A Kitching, Hope Town Foundry, Darlington, Co Durham.
KS	Kerr Stuart & Company, California Works, Stoke-on-Trent, Staffs.
Leyland	British Leyland Lillyhall Works, Workington, Cumbria.
Llangollen	Llangollen Railway, Llangollen, Clwyd, Wales.
Loco. Ent.	Locomotion Enterprises (1975), Bowes Railway, Springwell, Gateshead, Tyne & Wear.

Manch	Museum of Science & Industry, Liverpool Road, Manchester.
MC	Metropolitan-Cammell Carriage & Wagon Company, Birmingham (Metro-Cammell).
MV	Metropolitan-Vickers, Trafford Park, Manchester.
N	Neilson & Son, Springburn Locomotive Works, Glasgow, Scotland.
NBL	North British Locomotive Company, Glasgow, Scotland.
NR	Neilson Reid & Company, Springburn Works, Glasgow, Scotland.
PR	Park Royal Vehicles, Park Royal, London.
PS	Pressed Steel, Swindon, Wiltshire.
Resco	Resco (Railways), Erith, London.
RH	Ruston & Hornsby, Lincoln.
RS	Robert Stephenson & Company, Newcastle-upon-Tyne, Tyne & Wear.
RSH	Robert Stephenson & Hawthorns, Darlington, Co Durham.
RTC	Railway Technical Centre, Derby, Derbyshire.
S	Sentinel (Shrewsbury), Battlefield, Shrewsbury, Shropshire.
Sara	Sara & Company, Plymouth, Devon.
Science Museum	Science Museum, South Kensington, London
SM	Siemens, London.
SS	Sharp Stewart & Sons, Manchester and then (1888) Glasgow, Scotland.
TKL	Todd, Kitson and Laird, Leeds, West Yorkshire.
VF	Vulcan Foundry, Newton-le-Willows, Lancashire.
VIW	Vulcan Iron Works, Wilkes-Barre, Philadelphia, Pennsylvania, USA.
WB	WG Bagnall, Castle Engine Works, Stafford, Staffordshire.
Wkm	D Wickham & Company, Ware, Hertfordshire.
WMD	Waggon und Maschienenbau GmbH, Donauworth, Germany.
WSR	West Somerset Railway, Minehead, Somerset.
YE	Yorkshire Engine Company, Meadowhall, Sheffield, South Yorkshire.

▲ LMS Class 8P 46233 "DUCHESS OF SUTHERLAND" storms towards Shap at Salterwath with the London Euston–Carlisle "Cumbrian Mountain Express" on 31 January 2015. **Ian Pilkington**